This is a volume of essays that considers the full range of Chekhov's reception and impact on the British stage. Why were his plays slow to find a British audience? What were the early productions and performances in Britain really like? How did Bernard Shaw, the Moscow Art Theatre, or politics influence British Chekhov? These are some of the historical questions addressed. The authors then examine how directors, actors and designers work with Chekhov in Britain today, and analyse the problems of translating Chekhov into English for the stage. The book concludes with a selective chronology of British productions of Chekhov's plays.

CHEKHOV ON THE BRITISH STAGE

CHEKHOV ON THE BRITISH STAGE

EDITED AND TRANSLATED BY
PATRICK MILES

 CAMBRIDGE
UNIVERSITY PRESS

Published by the Press Syndicate of the University of Cambridge
The Pitt Building, Trumpington Street, Cambridge CB2 1RP
40 West 20th Street, New York, NY 10011-4211, USA
10 Stamford Road, Oakleigh, Victoria 3166, Australia

First published 1993

Printed in Great Britain at the University Press, Cambridge

A catalogue record for this book is available from the British Library

Library of Congress cataloguing in publication data

Chekhov on the British stage/edited and translated by Patrick Miles.
p. cm.
ISBN 0 521 38467 2
1. Chekhov, Anton Pavlovich, 1860–1904 – Stage history – Great
Britain. 2. Chekhov, Anton Pavlovich, 1860–1904 – Translations into
English – History and criticism. 3. Theater – Great Britain –
History – 20th century. I. Miles, Patrick.
PG 3458.Z9S833 1993
792.9'5'0941 – dc20 92 26037 CIP

ISBN 0 521 38467 2 hardback

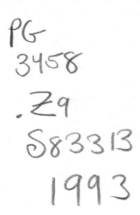

Contents

Illustrations

Contributors

David Allen, *University of Birmingham*
Arnold Aronson, *Columbia University*
Aleksey Bartoshevich, *VNII Iskusstvoznaniya, Moscow*
John Russell Brown, *University of Michigan*
Vera Gottlieb, *University of London*
W. Gareth Jones, *University College of North Wales*
Stephen le Fleming, *University of Durham*
Cynthia Marsh, *University of Nottingham*
Jan McDonald, *University of Glasgow*
Gordon McVay, *University of Bristol*
Patrick Miles, *University of Cambridge*
Jonathan Miller, *Director*
Ariadne Nicolaeff, *Writer-translator*
Anna Obraztsova, *VNII Iskusstvoznaniya, Moscow*
Richard Peace, *University of Bristol*
Valentina Ryapolova, *VNII Iskusstvoznaniya, Moscow*
Robert Tracy, *University of California*
Oleg Yefremov, *Moscow Art Theatre*
Stuart Young, *Queens' College, Cambridge*

Note on style and abbreviations

The standard English version of Chekhov's plays used in this book is that of *The Oxford Chekhov*, translated by Ronald Hingley. The most commonly employed English titles, characters' names and quotations are therefore from this translation, but sometimes the authors have needed to use others. The transliteration system used throughout is also that of *The Oxford Chekhov*. This simplifies certain combinations of Russian vowels and omits hard and soft signs, but an apostrophe has been used in this book to signify a soft sign on the rare occasions when its omission would cause confusion with a different Russian word. English spellings of Russian names that have passed into common usage (e.g. Komisarjevsky) are retained throughout. In quotations from English sources, punctuation (e.g. for play titles) and spelling (e.g. Tchekoff) are kept as they are in the original. All dates are New Style except those of Chekhov's letters, which are always published with their original Old Style dates. The abbreviation used for the Moscow Art Theatre until 1919 inclusive is MKhT; from 1920, when it was made a Soviet 'Academy' theatre, it is referred to as MKhAT. Granville Barker is hyphenated after 1921.

CHAPTER I

Introduction

Patrick Miles

The progress of Chekhov's plays in Britain from the fringe productions of the early twentieth century to a place next to Shakespeare in the late is a remarkable phenomenon, especially in a theatre traditionally so insular. The British profile of Brecht, for example, has been much higher, but his popularity and influence seem to have been more superficial. Actors, audiences, and directors have gradually taken Chekhov to their heart, and his interaction with the British stage has been subtle, all-pervading, and durable. It has amounted to a massive intervention in our theatre.

In this volume of essays theatre scholars, Russianists, directors, and translators examine this phenomenon in terms of both how it came about and how directors, actors, designers, and translators work with Chekhov in Britain today. There is, of course, a connection. Many of the contributors discuss how today's practitioners reject, reshape or re-embody the values of past British Chekhov. Other contributors present differing interpretations of the historical facts themselves. Together, they create a lively dialogue across the book.

In the opening essay, John Russell Brown suggests that it is the British actor who has learnt most from Chekhov – and then applied it to Shakespeare. As a result, he writes, 'Only recently has a Shakespeare play taken over four hours to perform because of what the actors have found to do with the words they speak and what is underneath them and between them.' There are obvious differences between the plays of Shakespeare and Chekhov, but they share a number of features in the portrayal of consciousness and existence that may account for the British acceptance of Chekhov. Nevertheless the root differences in the creative minds of the two dramatists are considerable, and Brown pleads for British productions of Chekhov that will be 'more speculative, more variously enlivened and, finally, more inscrutable'.

I

It has been assumed that the reason Chekhov's plays achieved no popularity in Britain before the First World War was that audiences were not ripe for them, and British theatre-managers were not interested in Russia. Aleksey Bartoshevich disproves the latter using evidence from the archives of the Moscow Art Theatre (MKhT). He shows that sustained attempts were made by Herbert Beerbohm Tree and others to persuade MKhT to come to London, but they were blocked by the war.

Perhaps crucially, then, audiences in the capital made their first acquaintance with Chekhov not in MKhT's productions, but in those of the theatre societies. Jan McDonald analyses these productions and ascribes their failure to the reformist didacticism of the English theatrical avant-garde, the assumption that Chekhov was a supreme naturalist, and the inappropriateness of the Shavian 'demonstration' type of acting to Chekhov. Only George Calderon, she explains, seems to have understood the *form* of the Chekhov play, in his 1909 Glasgow production of *The Seagull*.

Shaw himself greatly admired Chekhov's plays and was instrumental in getting them performed by the Stage Society. Anna Obraztsova explains that Shaw's influential view of Chekhov was not restricted to locating him on the socio-political map of 'Heartbreak House' Europe. He regarded Chekhov as one of the masters of the new genre of tragi-comedy, and Obraztsova traces a dialogue between Chekhov's experimentation with the one-act play and Shaw's own.

One of the central issues in the early reception of Chekhov's plays on the British stage was whether they, and the world they portrayed, were too Russian to be interesting, or even comprehensible, to British audiences. Stephen le Fleming shows that reviewers initially rejected the plays as outlandish. Slowly, however, they and audiences came to admit that the British were as fallible as Chekhov's Russians. The success of J.B. Fagan's 1925 *Cherry Orchard* was due partly to the situation of the mortgaged stately home being regarded as typically English. But Komisarjevsky's 1926 *Three Sisters* took this process much further. From a study of Komisarjevsky's prompt book for this production, Robert Tracy proves that one of the purposes of his extensive textual alterations and redesigning of characters was to give the play a romantic interest, a pace and a shape that would be acceptable to British tastes and expectations. Consequently, although Chekhov's popularity between the two world wars dates from this production, it could be claimed that it was based on an over-naturalization that ignored the 'savage critical core of Chekhov's work', as Graham Greene called it in 1941.

A constant reference point for the British theatre in its work with Chekhov has been MKhT. This is the underlying theme of the next three essays.

Peggy Ashcroft played major roles in key productions of Chekhov both before and after 1945; to some extent her interpretations of these roles exemplify pre-war and post-war British Chekhov. Using interviews, correspondence, and reviews Gordon McVay examines in detail her performances, the productions themselves, and her view of Chekhov. He shows that Peggy Ashcroft was profoundly influenced by MKhT's principles of ensemble-acting and the permanent company. She practised the first in her work with Chekhov, and her life-long quest for the second led her to play a vital part in the formation of the Royal Shakespeare Company.

Although the distinctions may be blurred, there are undoubtedly English, Welsh, Scottish, and Irish styles of Chekhov. In Wales, the national drama movement of the twenties rejected the West End as its model and turned to Komisarjevsky, MKhT and the committed non-professional. This prepared the ground for Chekhov. As Gareth Jones explains, however, the context of the eisteddfod, the university, and the chapel meant that Chekhov took a completely different path on the Welsh stage from the English stage, whilst the problem of a Welsh theatrical language has made Chekhov particularly difficult to translate.

MKhT itself (now called MKhAT) did not bring a Chekhov production to London until 1958. Cynthia Marsh discusses the controversies about Chekhov, Stanislavsky, Naturalism, and cultural transference that this and the visits of 1964 and 1970 sparked off. It was assumed that MKhAT's productions of Chekhov were authentically Russian. After seeing them, many critics questioned whether Chekhov had not been sentimentalized and over-anglicized in Britain. Very few suspected the hand of Communist censorship in the 'robustness' and 'optimism' of the Soviet productions, and Marsh shows that these qualities influenced a series of subsequent British productions.

With the essays by Oleg Yefremov and Jonathan Miller the book moves firmly into the present. These directors seek to overturn their national stereotypes of playing Chekhov. Yefremov describes how he has taken a free approach to the reordering of the action and the redesigning of characters in his Chekhov productions. Yet he does not regard Chekhov as director's theatre. The staging and design of a Chekhov play, he writes, should be born from the 'profoundly two-way' work of the actors and the director: the secret is to create *life* on the stage and only the actor can do this.

Jonathan Miller sees Chekhov's plays as coarser and more comic than the 'genteel approach' to Chekhov in Britain has allowed, and discusses the relevance to Chekhov's plays of recent research into the structure of conversation. If the actors apply to Chekhov's dialogue an understanding of the unwritten rules of listening, turn-taking, interruption, overlap, and other features of ordinary conversation, they can give it a 'glittering sense of social reality'. It may appear more slipshod, but it will possess pace and avoid both the melancholy pausing and the operatic trumpeting of much British Chekhov.

In Vera Gottlieb's view, Chekhov has been trivialized on the British stage by the determination to regard him as a non-political writer. His plays have been persistently detached from their socio-historical context. Only Trevor Griffiths' 1977 version of *The Cherry Orchard*, she feels, has brought out the political significance of a Chekhov play and suggested some responsibility, even culpability, on the part of the characters. This version, and Richard Eyre's production of it, are discussed by David Allen. Drawing widely on interviews, he shows that Griffiths was particularly interested in the revolutionary import of the play, and has been very original in his translation.

One of the most innovative British directors of Chekhov in the last decade has been Mike Alfreds. Stuart Young shows that by building up productions from the 'narrative spine' of Chekhov's plays, and emphasizing the 'Slavic temperament' of their characters, Alfreds has challenged the tradition. His belief in the primacy of the actor has led him to dispense with scenery, evolve his translation in rehearsal, and generate a spontaneous and occasionally grotesque style of per-formance. Even so, Young concludes, Alfreds' methods entail a quite traditional concern with character.

Chekhov's plays are widely thought to have played a major part in the creation of ensemble-acting and director's theatre in Britain this century. Patrick Miles examines why Chekhov's plays should require this kind of acting, and disentangles the Chekhovian ensemble from the Stanislavskian model of a theatre company. The idea of the permanent theatre company is dead in Britain, he claims, and Chekhov can help us achieve 'impermanent' companies that are more viable.

More than any other playwright, Chekhov has created characters intimately bound up with the space and textures that surround them. The design of a Chekhov production is therefore crucial. However, as Arnold Aronson writes, the naturalism of the traditional 'Chekhovian' set can no longer convey the meanings inherent in it at the turn of the century; it has become a self-referent. With numerous photographs, and ranging from Britain to Japan, Aronson describes how, since the 1960s, theatre designers have deconstructed this style and produced sets that 'speak' to their audiences again with the freshness and modernity of the plays themselves.

The last three essays address the subject of translating Chekhov's plays into English. Ariadne Nicolaeff describes her credo as a translator of Chekhov, and explains why in her view it is important for the translator to be immersed in the theatre. As a Chekhov scholar, Richard Peace believes that the translator's first task is one of literary criticism: he must understand the devices, ironies, and poetics of the Chekhov play before he begins his work. A consideration of versions of *The Seagull* shows that often English translators have not been sensitive to these factors. As a Russian theatre historian who speaks English, Valentina Ryapolova is exceptionally qualified to comment on the problems of cultural transference that Chekhov's plays present. She also compares the recent versions and adaptations by British dramatists, such as Trevor Griffiths, with the 'translation proper' of Michael Frayn.

In the course of the book, almost a hundred British productions of Chekhov are discussed from 1909 to 1991. Details of these, the names of the actors in the key roles, and a short bibliography are given in the Appendix.

I am particularly grateful to Dr Gordon McVay for supplying a tape recording of Oleg Yefremov's presentation at the Anglo-Soviet Colloquium 'Chekhov on the British Stage' held in 1987, and to Mr Yefremov, Tatyana Shakh-Azizova, Emma Polotskaya, and Nick Worrall for their work on the text of it published here. I have translated the Russian essays myself, but wish to thank Olga Slobodkina for her draft versions of two of them. Peter Holland has given me invaluable advice and I must acknowledge the unflagging interest of Sarah Stanton of Cambridge University Press and the editorial assistance and patience of my wife.

CHAPTER 2

Chekhov on the British stage: differences

John Russell Brown

Productions of Chekhov's plays in Britain provide yearly proof of this dramatist's wide and lasting influence. But a look behind the playbills will reveal more – that these plays have affected the British sense of what theatre can be. In performance they reinforce a persistent belief that the stage can hold a mirror up to life, and clarify the very forms and pressures of present-day existence.

During the last 350 years, no other dramatist writing in a language that is not English has seemed to speak in Britain with such assurance, or to use means that are so readily understood. Chekhov is more accessible than Molière, Racine, Strindberg, Pirandello, Lope de Vega, Calderón, Schiller, Kleist, Gorky or Bulgakov. Brecht and Ibsen provide many more plays for production, but they are seldom staged with that sense of confidence and possession which usually accompanies revivals of Chekhov's four masterpieces.

Yet in obvious ways great barriers surround these plays: language difficulties, of course; different folk and intellectual traditions; different social values and social behaviour; divergent histories; and little familiar access from one nation to another. The Russian language is not spoken by many in Britain, and for centuries few theatre people have travelled to Moscow, Leningrad or the varying countryside that Chekhov knew and loved. But for all this, following the first London productions of Chekhov's plays – whether 'Comedy', 'Scenes from Country Life', or 'Drama' – the difficulties which belong to works originating in so remote a 'world' have either been overcome and forgotten, or else forgotten and ignored. These plays have been appropriated by a theatre and a public which knew comparatively little about the stage or the audience for which they were written.

I

Few British theatre directors have come to prominence in recent years without working on Chekhov's plays; and each of them seems to have had a powerful and individual compulsion to do so. In 1978, Peter Hall knew that he had to turn to Chekhov. After directing Harold Pinter's *No Man's Land* – set in a single room overlooking a park, with memories of the past heavy in each character's mind, while the present proves to be inscrutable and resistant – Hall chose to direct *The Cherry Orchard* and started rehearsals sure of his intentions.[1] Its characters seemed to him to be forever separate, absorbed in their own unsatisfied concerns, possessed of no certain territory. Yet the production also had that sense of ensemble and finesse which was notable in Hall's productions of Mozart's operas undertaken during the same years. These isolated and unappeased individuals were locked, as if by destiny, in unavoidable impasse.

Jonathan Miller, a director who can animate the interface of characters in argument with brilliant and unexpected wit, who is able to free his actors to find new life in the words they speak, was also drawn to Chekhov. His *Seagull* (1974) at Greenwich was played in repertoire with *Hamlet* and Ibsen's *Ghosts*, which he also directed, so that mothers and sons, and absent fathers, were defined in part by contrast to those in their companion plays. This Chekhov production was not sumptuous or lyrical in setting, or delicately real in portraying lived experience, as others have been, and it had little sense of continuous social or political life; but the director's pleasure in what had happened between characters in rehearsal, and his encouragement of his actors to explore differences of intention and meaning, seemed to have sharpened the intelligence of all his cast. This Chekhov had unusual edge and spirit, and a sense of quest; its characters engaged with each other, using words with accuracy and relish.

Lindsay Anderson arrived at Chekhov after directing a number of politically responsible films, which could be meticulously realistic or else fantastic and surreal, and after staging a series of plays by David Storey at the Royal Court Theatre which were grounded in shared social and professional activity – *The Contractor*, *The Changing Room*, *Life-Class*. He brought to the Russian texts a sense of corporate and continuous life, and of ingrained habits and unspoken objectives. According to one commentator, his *Seagull* of 1975 was 'despite a good ensemble ... surprisingly heavy';[2] but other critics found the production to be strong, responsible, and enlightening.

Mike Alfreds, founder and Artistic Director of the small touring company Shared Experience, had developed a style of acting that was active and demonstrative. He specialized in lively narrative productions using literary texts and employing a few actors in multiple roles, such as *The Arabian Nights* and *Bleak House*. He had also staged a free-moving *commedia dell'arte* production of *The Merchant of Venice*. His actors could move across an empty stage at any speed and interact like percussionists, without embarrassment at the unlikeliness of such an overflow of energy in life off stage. When Alfreds turned to Chekhov, the plays became explosive at times; he emphasized the dynamics of their action, the clashes of the characters' temperaments and intentions, the discordance of their activities. Unlikely physical reactions were encouraged from the actors, who seemed to perform with improvised spontaneity. Very quickly he achieved a series of productions (1981–6).

The *Cherry Orchard* of the now-expatriate Peter Brook reached Brooklyn, in 1987, after many cast-changes and several years of reconsideration. Here the characters were quietly and slowly involved with their own selves; they seemed to choose what they said and did as if, as people, they were all very special actors but not necessarily very talented ones. The play seemed pampered, and the consciousness of the characters both profound and ordinary, in a theatrical manner. The show was all of a piece: it was a slow pageant about life as theatre, existence as a serious-minded performance which had been meticulously crafted.

Michael Blakemore, Michael Bogdanov, Richard Eyre, John Gielgud, Peter Gill, Trevor Nunn, Laurence Olivier, Philip Prowse, Toby Robertson – each of these British directors has found his own way of working with Chekhov's texts and in doing so they have all attracted gifted casts for their productions. But the story is different for British actors: rather than making distinct contributions to the way Chekhov is performed and perceived, actors have developed, refined, and deepened their talents by appearing in Chekhov's plays. The actors seem to fit into their characters unostentatiously, almost easily.

Gielgud, Guinness, Laughton, Olivier, Redgrave, Richardson, Scofield; Peggy Ashcroft, Judi Dench, Edith Evans, Vanessa Redgrave, Flora Robson, Athene Seyler, Sybil Thorndike, Dorothy Tutin;

Albert Finney, Michael Gambon, Ian McKellen, Jonathan Pryce, Ronald Pickup, and so on: the roll-call of actors in Chekhov is a short-list of the most accomplished in Britain during the last half-century. In 1984 Ian McKellen would claim that 'Anton Chekhov is every British actor's second-favourite playwright' – even though at that time his own appreciation was 'as a theatre-goer rather than an actor'.[3] Part of the attraction, beyond individual roles gratifying to the best of actors, has been the opportunity to develop a very British sense of team-work. Ian McKellen continued:

We recognize of Chekhov, what we don't yet, in our hearts, accept of Shakespeare, that only when every part – each lazy valet, each stoical nanny, each gypsy violinist – has been perfectly cast, costumed and acted, can the whole play be fully realized. Actors climb up Chekhov like a mountain, roped together, sharing the glory if they ever make it to the summit.[4]

II

Unquestionably Shakespeare has been the most influential single force in shaping a distinctly British theatre, and a brief list of differences between his plays and those of Chekhov, or between the worlds and theatres that give rise to them, would seem to argue against any easy assimilation of the Russian dramatist by British theatre. Certainly Shakespeare's plays which are focussed strongly on a single hero – Richard II and Richard III, Henry V, Hamlet, Lear, Shylock, Rosalind, Falstaff, Prospero – require different casting, rehearsal, and direction from Chekhov's, which depend upon eight or nine characters of almost equal weight, exposure, and significance. When Shakespeare does hold the focus on a pair of characters – the Macbeths, Antony and Cleopatra, Benedick and Beatrice, Othello and Iago – both hold equal attention for only a few scenes. When his plays depend upon six or more characters, these are not members of a single family or small social circle as in Chekhov, but they come from very separate worlds, such as the rival parties of the history plays or the social divides of *A Midsummer Night's Dream*, *Twelfth Night*, *The Winter's Tale*, *Cymbeline*.

   In choice of action, setting, and dialogue, the two authors could scarcely have worked more differently: prose opposed to verse; the present time and place, rather than historical action or foreign and fantastic settings. In structure, perhaps, the plays are still more obviously different: for Chekhov, a few acts of continuous business, shaped by such simple activities as arrivals and departures, meals, parties, artistic enterprise, courtship, family disputes, estate management, and housekeeping; while in Shakespeare's plays, action is displayed in twenty to forty separate scenes and presents a great variety of incident, commonly involving matters of life and death, or of power and politics, and not infrequently leading to acts of violence, treachery, suffering, and fortitude. When more intimate affairs are involved in Shakespeare, some unusual pressures such as illegality, personal danger or ignorance of one another's identity or sex are commonly supplied to complicate matters and heighten dramatic tension. Crisis, destruction, courage, and deception are found in Chekhov's plays, but the development of these elements is slow and viewed only intermittently; naked presentation is reserved for rare moments.

Yet Chekhov and Shakespeare are close in one very fundamental way, in that they share both vision and technique in the presentation of individual consciousness and existence. This draws the two dramatists together and, with them, British and Russian theatres. Firstly their characters function in mind and body with similar subtlety and strength; and they seem to be in search of a similar inward peace. Their identities are imminent, and not defined by words or constantly apparent. What they are to others is not what they feel themselves to be, and self-consciousness is never expressed easily or completely. The persons in these plays know themselves and each other with only occasional and partial clarity; often what happens to them defines their existence, as if in despite of their conscious minds. What they say of themselves is conditioned by each changing context, and carries a burden of past and present deceptions. They can neither say what they are, nor know what they may be; yet, by the end of the play, a reckoning has been made, through all the varying impressions of words and actions, and, in some ways, in contrast to them. And the smallest character in the plays of both dramatists seems to have been created with the same pragmatic and responsible understanding.

In this respect it may be argued that a knowledge of Chekhov has changed our view of Shakespeare's plays, rather more than the other way round. Only recently has a Shakespeare play taken over four hours to perform because of what the actors have found to do with the words they speak and what is underneath them and between them. Previously performances have been lengthy to accommodate elaborate scene-changes, large ceremonies employing many super-numeraries, or the ornate and impressive delivery of the text by leading actors. But now time is often taken to share the actors' aware-ness of their characters' personal dilemmas and aspirations, and of previously hidden or unregarded movements of unspoken thoughts. Stanislavsky's notion of a 'subtext', developed at the Moscow Art Theatre when Chekhov's plays were its greatest achievement, has given to every actor the intellectual means to discover conflicting intentions and half-conscious awarenesses existing within the words of Shakespeare's text, revealing the mazy and sensitive consciousness with which the dramatist has endowed his principal characters. An actor is now more able to sense the complex individual being whom he or she is invited to apprehend and assimilate into performance. The temptation has arisen to labour for the public's full appreciation of this subtlety, rather than assume that rehearsals have given the actors the ability to dazzle and shine; to create the wonder of character – as the dramatist has done – with almost insensible touches. Chekhov's plays, which depend on the inner reality of their characters to sustain both form and meaning, have encouraged British actors to find a similar inner reality for their characters in Shakespeare. Whether his plays are performed very slowly or with energy and speed, the text and the imitation of life upon the stage have become even more marvellous in consequence.

Over a number of years, critics and dramaturgs have been catching up with what actors and directors have discovered in rehearsals.[5] It is now understood more widely that Shakespeare's characters encounter each other as fully imagined beings whose speeches hide as well as reveal, so that a few simple words or a silent gesture can suggest deep-seated thoughts and feelings. Because they know that Andrey, in *The Three Sisters*, expresses a complicated sense of his predicament by saying simply 'My wife is my wife', or Chebutykin by singing to himself, while Tuzenbakh actually acknowledges that 'trifles, such silly little things, sometimes become so important suddenly, for no apparent reason', and because of countless other examples, actors and critics have come to recognize the importance of similar means – 'silly little things' – provided at crucial moments in Shakespeare's plays, in conjunction with his more usual mode of sustained poetic and rhetorical dialogue.

Some of these moments have long been recognized in the theatre. Shylock's exit from the Trial Scene of *The Merchant of Venice*, with no verbal means of expressing the depth of his pain, frustration or perseverance, has often provided the strong but silent conclusion for a major performance of the role: as this single man moves through the assembled company, emotions and thoughts have been sub-textual for many years before Stanislavsky employed the term. But increasingly, during the last fifty years, many more opportunities of this kind have been discovered and used. *The Merchant of Venice* has been performed so that it ends with a silent Antonio, alone on the stage, or moving to join the lovers unwillingly, or with forced good humour, after all words have been spoken. More subtly, the few simple words spoken by Jessica (in other company than Lorenzo's and Launcelot's) have served as points of focus to offset the good spirits of the comedy, and sometimes as a reproach to Portia who, in all other ways, seems fully in command of the play's conclusion.

Some unpretentious phrases have proved capable of expressing the heart of Shakespeare's drama, with as much effect as the golden verse which first attracts the attention of actors, directors, and critics. When Hamlet has seen his father's Ghost and has drawn Horatio and his fellow witnesses into his confidence, he concludes the scene with dynamic and explicit words:

> So, gentlemen,
> With all my love I do commend me to you,
> And what so poor a man as Hamlet is
> May do t'express his love and friending to you,
> God willing, shall not lack. Let us go in together,
> And still your fingers on your lips, I pray.
> The time is out of joint. O cursed spite
> That ever I was born to set it right!   (*Hamlet*, 1.5.190 ff.)

But after the clinching and conclusive couplet follows an incomplete verse-line: 'Nay, come, let's go together.' It was this apparently artless remark which lodged in the memory of Donald Sinden when, as a young actor, he played the Ghost in a touring company led by John Gielgud. He listened nightly to his older colleague, who had acted in some of the earliest British productions of Chekhov, including Michel Saint-Denis' renowned *Three Sisters* a few years previously in 1938:

I wish I could describe how many facets Gielgud gave to that simple line. ('Please go with me.' 'I don't want to let you out of my sight.' 'It would look better if we arrived together.' 'Let us leave this awesome place.' 'Don't leave me.') I learned from that one line what infinite possibilities are open to an actor.[6]

Another quality which Chekhov and Shakespeare share, and which makes British actors feel instinctively at home in the Russian plays, is an open-handedness: neither playwright insists upon one way, or one level, of interpretation. Gielgud as Hamlet, disciplined actor though he has always been, could vary the implications of that concluding line from night to night, according to how the scene had developed, changing his Hamlet subtly for each new audience. In Chekhov's plays he had already (in 1925) experienced this freedom: every night he had been the sole judge of the precise manner – the speed, tidiness, confusion, desperation, regret – with which Treplev spends the last two minutes he has on stage tearing up his manuscripts without saying a word. In his last Chekhovian role, as Gayev, he was to decide what happens as he says, at the conclusion of Act I of *The Cherry Orchard*: 'Coming, coming! Go to bed! In off the cushion! I pot the white!' Such 'silly little things' invite an actor to conclude a performance as seems right to him or her, and so to suggest reactions deeper and more subtle than many words would define.

Perhaps it was a consequence of this shared sense of the inner life of the persons of a drama that neither Shakespeare nor Chekhov was confined by prescriptive ideas of what was suitable for 'Tragedy' or 'Comedy'. They do not present their characters in a sequence of distinctly different modes within a single play, in the manner of more primitive dramas or the dialectical theatre of Bertolt Brecht; rather a freedom from stylistic restraint was theirs from moment to moment. Both dramatists use a play's action to lead their characters through a gamut of reactions towards a culminating 'moment of truth' which sums up and revalues earlier impressions; and, in doing this, they both refuse to exclude any kind of response which the characters can encompass. So Shakespeare's 'comic' characters – Bottom, Benedick, Beatrice, Rosalind, Falstaff – are more than that word implies; they all draw forth our laughter at the very edge of defeat or pain, and then stop that laughter. And so do Kulygin, Vershinin, Andrey, and Chebutykin. None of these are 'comic characters' in any conventional or limiting sense of those words. Even Natasha is possibly capable of awakening laughter, more certainly of becoming ridiculous, as she rises more and more to a position of power.

Similarly, Shakespeare's 'tragic' heroes have an irreducible element of the grotesque or absurd in their make-up, often developing into madness or, on one occasion, into 'valiant fury'. As she kills herself to satisfy 'immortal longings' – or so she says – Cleopatra thinks of a 'poor venomous fool', as if able, in one part of her mind, to share the laughter of the clown who had brought her the means to die; and she seems to take light-hearted pleasure in the thought that great Caesar is 'an ass unpolicied'. Chekhov's three sisters do not often play or fantasize light-heartedly, but Olga is able to recognize how 'cheerfully and jauntily that band is playing ... so cheerfully and joyfully'. The concluding words 'If only we knew, if only we knew ...' might, just possibly, reflect upon the cheerful innocence with which baby Bobik sits up now in his pram and surveys the scene, representative of another generation which may wish to 'know': if Olga has seen him, so that the audience is encouraged to perceive this contrast, her words might almost raise laughter at the dramatist's contrivance. The shooting incident in Act 3 of *Uncle Vanya* – 'Missed again!' – is one of the clearest examples of Chekhov's refusal of ordinary categories of tragedy and comedy, and ordinary notions of theatrical decorum.

Perhaps Shakespeare and Chekhov are most obviously alike in their refusal to provide clear answers to the largest problems which are raised by the action of their plays. Should Othello and Desdemona have married? Will Fortinbras be a good ruler of Denmark, and was Hamlet's revenge a noble act that frees all faults? Henry V is shown winning the French crown, but the Chorus is at hand to tell the audience that in his son's reign that realm was lost and England had to bleed for it: so was God to be praised for a great and good victory as the king had declared? Shakespeare left such questions posed but not answered. His comedies show how diverse are the couples which are found 'coming to the ark' (*As You Like It*, V.4.36), but few unions are allowed to be tested by time. The 'happy' conclusions of the comedies are seldom effected without the intervention of some strange or even magic circumstance for which the participants can scarcely be held responsible. While many wise words are spoken in the plays, it needs great ingenuity to pluck from them any confident answers to basic questions about human conduct. And so with Chekhov: he was sometimes pressed to pronounce judgement on society and on the characters in his plays, but, like Shakespeare, he did not 'abide' such questions, remaining 'free'. We do not know Shakespeare's response to those who read political or moral certainties in his works, but we do have some of Chekhov's; for example:

You are right to demand that an author take conscious stock of what he is doing, but you are confusing two concepts: answering the questions and formulating them correctly. Only the latter is required of an author ... It is the duty of the court to formulate the questions correctly, but it is up to each member of the jury to answer them according to his own preference.[7]

III

The assimilation of Chekhov into British theatre, so unlikely in view of its insular resistance to other foreign-language dramatists, may well have proved so easy, pleasurable, and influential in practice because of deep-seated similarities between Shakespeare and Chekhov. Yet the rush to participate has its dangers. The outward differences of language, structure, setting, dialogue, theme, and so forth, are bound to be seen and respected, but, if Chekhov is to contribute fully and grow to his true stature in Britain, other hidden differences – the roots of the tree – must also be sought out, respected, and used when producing the plays.

Where these two dramatists are most alike their *root* differences will be most significant, because here both are most original and sensitive. In the presentation of the individual persons of their dramas, they seem to have reached the same kind of understanding, and developed similar techniques, but by following totally different paths. For Shakespeare the idea of men and women as actors occurs again and again:

> All the world's a stage,
> And all the men and women merely players ...
> *(As You Like It*, II.7.139ff.)

> What would he do
> Had he the motive and the cue for passion
> That I have? He would drown the stage with tears ...
> *(Hamlet*, II.2.544ff.)

> Life's but a walking shadow, a poor player
> That struts and frets his hour upon the stage
> And then is heard no more ... *(Macbeth*, V.4.24ff.)

> When we are born, we cry that we are come
> To this great stage of fools. *(Lear*, IV.6.179–80)

> You have put me now to such a part which never
> I shall discharge to th'life. *(Coriolanus*, III.3.105–6)

The analogue of the stage haunts this writer's view of persons in action and interaction, in thought, speech, and appearance; and he has given this consciousness to his principal characters. He had been an actor himself and become a 'motley to the view' (Sonnet cx), and so the men and women in his plays know both cowardice and 'pitiful ambition' as they seek, instinctively, for a 'truth' in performance. (Yet 'The players cannot keep counsel; they'll tell all': *Hamlet*, III.2.134–5.) By these means they are also shown seeking satisfaction, delight, peace, freedom, all the possible rewards of acting, as Hamlet details them when the players' arrival is announced in Elsinore:

He that plays the king shall be welcome – his majesty shall have tribute of me – , the adventurous knight shall use his foil and target, the lover shall not sigh gratis, the humorous man shall end his part in peace, the clown shall make those laugh whose lungs are tickle o'the'sere, and the lady shall say her mind freely ... (*Hamlet*, II.2.314–19)

Shakespeare's characters have a theatrical uncertainty and a theatrical energy or ambition; together these qualities are at the very basis of his art.

But Chekhov was different. He was a doctor, not an actor: he knew that each day new illness would need attention; he had a sense that this work was never-ending, that his knowledge and ability to respond to obvious need were always inadequate, and that his own health was as precarious as that of his patients. He learnt to observe objectively and in great detail. But he not only practised medicine; as a student he had chosen for his thesis-topic no less a subject than 'A history of medicine in Russia'. In Chekhov's mind, it seems, the world never shrank to the dimensions of a stage, as in a theatre; but each individual person and each moment were part of a much wider reality and a slow process of change. He distrusted simple solutions, not least that 'bookish, learned psychology' which purported to explain what motivated human beings: 'Knowing [such a psychology] is just about the same as not knowing it, since it is more a fiction than a science, a kind of alchemy, and it is high time for it to be filed away in the archives.'[8] As a doctor and as an observer of human behaviour, Chekhov seems to have maintained a careful scepticism. To the British translator and dramatist Michael Frayn, the plays show that he had – quite unlike Shakespeare – an objective quality of mind, as if 'appearing to inhabit his characters, yet standing outside them, being cool about them ... People tend to think his characters are warm and lovable. But that's not really how he sees them himself. He is quite distant towards them.'[9]

Chekhov could call himself lazy, but the energy of his mind is remarkable and the variety of its concerns. Scepticism or 'coolness' did not lead to inaction. He was prepared to plan, finance, build, and supervize new country schools, to organize famine relief, to conduct hundreds of interviews for a census in a remote convict settlement, and to reorganize and run his own estate. His first published writings of 1880 were humorous articles and short stories, but he was to write hundreds of them, and continued to develop their range and refine his techniques until, in 1889, he abandoned a projected novel. His earlier plays were either rejected or ill-received, but he persisted; and so he reworked and developed much of the material of *The Wood Demon* for *Uncle Vanya*, completed some eight years later. Clearly his career as an experimental writer and then as a dramatist, struggling with misunderstanding and inadequate productions, and with appalling ill-health, is in great contrast to Shakespeare's regular output of one or two plays each season for a single company over a period of some twenty years. Moreover Shakespeare was also a poet and not a writer of short prose-fiction: words were forever over-reaching themselves in his mind, leading his imagination onward and becoming 'wanton' (*Twelfth Night*, III.1.14–24). Whereas it is appropriate to speak of the 'quick forge' of Shakespeare's creative mind (*Henry V*, IV.8, Chorus, 23), Chekhov's seems to have had a different temper: more watchful, more practical and persistent; and, in some ways, lighter too.

Perhaps Chekhov was self-aware in a different way from Shakespeare. Gorky's reminiscence of a visit to the older dramatist's house at Kuchuk-Koy gives a vivid impression of his host's 'animation' as he talked about school teachers and the need to provide very practically for their intellectual and personal well-being, but he also tells of Chekhov's sudden unease and smile. He judged that it was characteristic of him to speak 'so earnestly, with such warmth and sincerity, and then suddenly to laugh at himself and his speech'.[10]

The briefest and most selective consideration of how Chekhov's mind was formed, and of how it worked, shows that it was not at all like Shakespeare's. While recognizing the intimate kinship between the works of the two dramatists and the ease with which Chekhov has become assimilated into British theatre, the differences between

them in the nature of their creative minds should also be sought
out and taken into account. In the process of making Chekhov's
plays their own, directors, designers, and actors need to take time
to become aware of the roots of his imagination.

Chekhov's own letters and short stories are the principal sources
for this study, and then memoirs, letters, and other writings by his
close friends and associates. Beyond that, enquiry will need to discover
a great deal about Russia, the land and its resources, its climate,
society, economy, history, culture, theatres. Chekhov's curiosity
fed upon many kinds of observation, so that to follow where his
mind leads is to become involved in a fine and complex web of lived
experience – some threads old and others very new, some strong
and some weak, some firmly in place and others insecure.

Returning from such an enquiry to the plays themselves, the
question will arise as to whether a production in which the characters
seem trapped is a suitable response to the text, or one which is lively
and argumentative, or dynamic and explosive. Is it helpful if the
characters appear to be acting a role? Is an 'ensemble', in which
every actor knows each other, the best kind of company to stage
the plays? All these approaches have proved rewarding – Chekhov's
popularity in Britain proves this – but perhaps there is more to
discover within the texts by respecting the less obvious differences from
the plays on which our tastes have been formed. Might a production
be created which was, in some way, more speculative, more variously
enlivened and, finally, more inscrutable? While reinterpreting the
plays for the present time and place, how closely can directors be
attuned to Chekhov's imaginative processes? How far can audiences
share the view of the world which was in his mind's eye?

Notes

1 See *Peter Hall's Diaries*, ed. John Goodwin (London: Hamish Hamilton,
   1983), pp. 331–7.
2 Patrick Miles, *Chekhov on the British Stage, 1909–1987* (Cambridge: Sam
   and Sam, 1987), p. 39.
3 'Wild flowers, wild bees, wild honey', *Drama*, 1984, April, p. 5.
4 *Ibid.*
5 See, for example, Una Ellis-Fermor, 'The revelation of unspoken thought
   in drama', *The Frontiers of Drama* (London: Methuen, 1945), pp. 96–126,
   and *Shakespeare the Dramatist* (London: Methuen, 1961), especially pp. 21–52;
   John Russell Brown, 'Shakespeare's subtext, I & II', *Tulane Drama*

Review, 8:1 and 2 (1963), pp. 72–94 and 85–102; E. A. J. Honigmann, *Shakespeare: Seven Tragedies* (London: Methuen, 1976), especially ch. 2, 'Impressions of character', and ch. 6, 'Secret motives in *Othello*', and Michael Goldman, *Acting and Action in Shakespearean Tragedy* (Princeton: Princeton University Press, 1985).

6 Donald Sinden, *A Touch of the Memoirs* (London: Hodder and Stoughton, 1982), p. 61.

7 *Letters of Anton Chekhov*, trans. M. H. Heim (New York, London, etc.: Harper and Row, 1973), p. 171.

8 *Ibid.*, p. 143.

9 'Under the sisters' skin' (an interview), *The Guardian*, 23 March 1987.

10 *The Note-Books of Anton Tchekhov, together with Reminiscences of Tchekhov by Maxim Gorky*, trans. S. S. Koteliansky and Leonard Woolf (London: Hogarth Press, 1921), pp. 91–3.

CHAPTER 3

The 'inevitability' of Chekhov: Anglo-Russian theatrical contacts in the 1910s

Aleksey Bartoshevich

English-language productions of Chekhov's plays were not warmly received in the British theatre before 1914, and theatre historians have commonly argued that it was the experience of the Great War that facilitated their appreciation and popularity in the 1920s.[1] An examination of some little-known facts and documents concerning Anglo-Russian theatrical contacts before the war, however, suggests that the situation may have been more complicated.

On the evening of 21 January 1914 the Moscow Art Theatre (MKhT) was performing *Three Sisters*. The production was in its thirteenth year. As always, Vershinin was played by Stanislavsky. He was in fact seriously ill and running a temperature of almost 104°F. An understudy was at hand to take his place, and Stanislavsky was advised to go home. Nevertheless, he managed not only to get through the performance but, as usual, to receive visitors during the intervals. One of these visitors was H. G. Wells. He wanted to express to Stanislavsky his admiration for the production, but he also had a more concrete purpose. As the correspondent of *Nov* accompanying Wells told his readers, Wells 'tried his utmost to persuade the directors of the Moscow Art Theatre to come to London, if possible with plays by Chekhov, and said they were sure to be a success as people in England were now extremely interested in Russian theatre'.[2]

The interest of the British in Russian art and literature, and Russia generally, during the 1910s, was indeed great.[3] As is well known, it was part of a larger process of change that occurred in English culture in the first few decades of the twentieth century. People were beginning to look upon English culture as an organic part of European culture, whereas the Victorians had traditionally regarded it as standing in 'splendid isolation'. Of course, before the First World War these changes had only just begun. Nevertheless, there is plenty of evidence that the new ideas about English culture existed not only in the minds of Bloomsbury. The exhibitions of the French Post-Impressionists held in London between 1910 and 1912 provoked tremendous debate. The works of Russian Post-Impressionists such as Roerich and Petrov-Vodkin also appeared in the galleries. Max Reinhardt toured productions to Britain in 1911, and in 1912 directed a production of *Oedipus Rex* at Covent Garden with John Martin-Harvey in the title role. The novels of Tolstoy and Dostoyevsky, and Chekhov's prose, were becoming more and more widely read. In 1913 Chaliapin sang *Boris Godunov* in London. Finally, between 1910 and 1913 English audiences discovered Russian ballet: first Anna Pavlova danced in London with a small company from the Russian Imperial Ballet, then Diaghilev's company came with Karsavina and Nijinsky. On 26 June 1911 Diaghilev's Russian Ballet danced at the coronation gala before the new king and queen. The part played by Russian ballet in the formation of an English school of choreography is, of course, well known, but its influence extended far beyond the dance: one of the first books on the Russian Ballet, for instance, was written by Ellen Terry,[4] and London critics discerned the influence of Bakst and Nijinsky on Granville Barker's productions of Shakespeare.[5] As Samuel Hynes has shown, it was in these years that the term 'Russianness' became part of the English critical vocabulary.[6]

I have briefly rehearsed these facts because I think it is important to remember that this was the cultural context in which the first translations of Chekhov's plays, by George Calderon (*The Seagull*), Arthur A. Sykes (*The Bear*), Constance Garnett (*The Cherry Orchard*) and R.S. Townsend (*Uncle Vanya*) appeared and were staged. It is also the context in which we should view the facts concerning Anglo-Russian theatrical contacts to which I wish to refer.

The central event in the history of these contacts is Gordon Craig's 1912 production of *Hamlet* at the Moscow Arts, which has been described in great detail elsewhere.[7] The documents and facts I am concerned with are less well known and much less important. However, they begin to look meaningful when related to the broader cultural developments discussed above. As was to be expected, they nearly all concern MKhT, which was at its best in these years and rapidly becoming world-famous – primarily as the theatre of Chekhov. It is also highly relevant that two of the staunchest supporters of MKhT in England after Craig were the committed 'Chekhovians' Maurice Baring and George Calderon.[8]

For the fact is that it was in this period that the idea took shape in England of inviting MKhT to London. A proposal was put to MKhT by the English impresario A. Brough; negotiations began in 1908, but they stalled. In 1911, however, the idea was revived, and Michael Lykiardopoulos, secretary to the directors of MKhT and interpreter to Craig whilst he was at MKhT, travelled to London to conduct talks with, strange as it may sound, Sir Herbert Beerbohm Tree.

Tree's enthusiasm for MKhT can be judged from the traditional end-of-season speech that he delivered to the audience of His Majesty's Theatre in July 1911. Basically it was devoted to the Moscow Art Theatre. According to Lykiardopoulos, in his characteristic, elevated style Tree spoke of MKhT as a 'truly national theatre in Russia, where art is warmed by the fervour of its actors and watered by the tears of its people'.[9] And Tree expressed the earnest desire that London itself should see the art of the Moscow Art Theatre.

At about the same date, after a prolonged absence and six months before *Hamlet* opened in Moscow, Gordon Craig arrived back in England. Stanislavsky wrote to him: 'We sincerely wish you as much recognition and success in your native land as you have won for yourself abroad.'[10] A dinner was held in Craig's honour on 16 July 1911, which was attended by many literary and theatrical celebrities. Lykiardopoulos was also invited, and was asked to talk about Craig's work at MKhT.

In the accounts that he sent Stanislavsky and Nemirovich-Danchenko separately, Lykiardopoulos described in detail the business negotiations concerning future MKhT tours to London, and the speeches that were made at the dinner. 'Yesterday's celebration of Craig', he wrote, 'was actually more a celebration of the Art Theatre'.[11] Presumably he had some grounds for saying this. The speakers must have paid tribute to the Russian theatre for inviting Craig to stage a production, when he had not found a single English theatre he could work in since 1903. However, the secretary to the directors of MKhT was also being somewhat over-patriotic and telling them what he thought they wanted to hear. The letters he wrote them were identical except at one point. According to his letter to Stanislavsky, people shouted 'Hurrah' after he mentioned Stanislavsky in his speech; according to his letter to Nemirovich-Danchenko, it was after he mentioned Nemirovich-Danchenko! The point is, though, that the reputation of MKhT in these English theatrical circles was obviously extremely high.

So Tree set about organizing a visit by MKhT to London. It was not his fault that once again it did not materialize. On 24 October 1911, at a meeting of the company, Stanislavsky came out against the idea of Paris and London tours in the 1911–12 season, saying that 'we have no repertoire for a foreign tour'.[12] The repertoire at that moment was, without exaggeration, at its most brilliant: in addition to plays by Chekhov and Gorky, it contained *The Brothers Karamazov*, and the theatre was rehearsing Craig's *Hamlet*. However, as this demonstrates, Stanislavsky was a perfectionist and hyper-selfcritical.

For his part, Tree was no less obstinate. In January 1913 he went to Moscow to see Craig's *Hamlet* and resume discussions about a tour. Although famed as an exponent of traditional 'archaeological naturalism' and in Tatyana Bachelis' words a 'belated Victorian',[13] Tree appreciated the revolutionary originality of what Craig was doing. In his book *Thoughts and After-Thoughts* Tree praises Craig's direction of *Hamlet* even though the reader senses how far removed Craig's art was from the author's own theatrical tastes.[14] In the 1910s Tree was bound to feel that his own system of theatrical values was aesthetically exhausted. This may explain why he took a lively interest in new departures in the theatre such as Craig's experiments (Tree had invited him to work in his theatre in 1908) or MKhT, whom he tried to persuade to come to England with all his customary energy. 'Mr Tree', a Russian newspaper reported, 'is insisting on the MKhT company undertaking a tour to London and has offered to put his own theatre at their disposal'.[15]

The actor-manager of His Majesty's Theatre had first become interested in MKhT in 1908 after hearing about its production of Maeterlinck's *L'Oiseau Bleu*. On 26 October 1908, less than a fortnight after the play opened, Stanislavsky received a letter from the Russian ambassador in London, Count A. K. Benckendorff, who wrote: 'Mr Tree, whose eminent position in this country's artistic and theatrical world is doubtless familiar to you, is sending his representative Mr Stanley Bell to Moscow to acquaint himself with and study the new play by Maeterlinck in your production. The success of your productions is well known in London and of extreme interest to Tree.'[16] Bell's stay coincided with Craig's first visit to Moscow, and they went to MKhT together to see Ibsen's *A Public Enemy* (with Stanislavsky as Stockmann) and *L'Oiseau Bleu* itself.

The interest of the English theatre in MKhT's production of *L'Oiseau Bleu* did not end there. Tree probably passed on details of the production to Herbert Trench, the director of the Haymarket Theatre, who wrote to Stanislavsky in May 1909 offering to present it at his theatre. Unfortunately, Stanislavsky could not accept Trench's terms. However, Trench had also asked him if he might send a representative to Moscow to make copies of the sets, costumes, and staging of *L'Oiseau Bleu*, and to this Stanislavsky agreed. As photographs show, the production of *The Blue Bird* directed by Trench that opened at the Haymarket on 8 December 1909 was an exact copy of MKhT's. It enjoyed a successful run (276 performances), although Craig expressed himself scathingly to Stanislavsky about its artistic merits.

There was nothing unusual about Trench's procedure – exact copies of other companies' productions were very much in vogue at the turn of the century. Both inside and outside Russia productions were mounted that advertised themselves as 'in the *mise-en-scène* of the Moscow Art Theatre'. It was rare for these copies to be made with the assistance of members of MKhT. An exception was the replica of *L'Oiseau Bleu* presented by L. Sulerzhitsky and Ye. Vakhtangov at the Théâtre Réjane in Paris in 1911.

Finally, fresh from the opening of his production of *A Midsummer Night's Dream* at the Savoy Theatre, in February 1914 Harley Granville Barker arrived in Moscow. Barker had several long meetings with Stanislavsky, in the course of which it was agreed that two of Barker's pupils would be invited to work at MKhT. The productions Barker saw at MKhT were *The Cherry Orchard*, Turgenev's *A Provincial Lady*, and *The Brothers Karamazov*. He was hoping to recreate the latter in London. Whilst in Moscow he commissioned copies of the models and sketches of the sets, props, and costumes, and invited Luzhsky, a MKhT director, to stage the crowd scenes. On 16 February 1914 a newspaper reported: 'yesterday the directors of the Art Theatre gave the English director the complete text of the stage adaptation and *mise-en-scène* of *The Brothers Karamazov*'.[17] All of these plans were frustrated by the outbreak of war six months later.

The history of Anglo-Russian theatrical contacts in the first decade of this century, then, is largely that of unfulfilled hopes and unrealized plans. Yet the mere existence of these plans is revealing. It indicates that the English theatre had a genuine, indeed passionate, interest in what was happening on the Russian stage; that there was definitely a theatrical component to the 'Russian theme' in the complex pattern of pre-1914 English culture. The crucial fact remains, however, that

London saw no MKhT productions in the original. It did not experience MKhT at the height of its powers.

Presumably the interest of the English in Russian theatre entered into Lidiya Yavorskaya's calculations when she appeared with a Russian company in London in 1909. On the other hand, she may simply have been invited by Tree, as the performances the company gave in Russian of *La Dame aux Camélias*, Ostrovsky's *Vasilisa Melentyeva*, and *Hedda Gabler*, were presented at His Majesty's Theatre by the Afternoon Theatre Society with which Tree was associated. They amounted to seven matinées between 30 November and 9 December 1909. 'On the whole', one critic wrote, the celebrated actress-manager 'produced a very favourable impression'.[18] Following this, however, Yavorskaya (or Yavorska as she was often known in England) threw herself into improving her stage English and making friends in the English theatre. She played opposite Lady Beerbohm Tree in Strindberg's *The Stronger*, worked with the young playwright John Pollock, who was a friend of Shaw and later became her third husband, and had considerable success in 1911 as Nora in *A Doll's House*. She never acted in England with a Russian company or in Russian again; although two of her longest-running English productions were Gorky's *The Lower Depths* (1911) and Pollock's adaptation of *Anna Karenina* (1914).

Opinions of Yavorskaya's acting were as divided in England as they had always been in Russia.[19] Although undoubtedly talented and intelligent, she tended to regard acting as a contest to establish her personal domination of the play, the director, and the other actors. She was not remotely the person to represent Russian dramatic art in London alongside Chaliapin in opera and Nijinsky in ballet. It is, in fact, one of the ironies of theatrical history that the English public's acquaintance with the Russian stage began not with Chekhov in a Moscow Arts production, but with the actress who was the prototype of the *cabotine* Arkadina in *The Seagull*.

Where the introduction of Chekhov's plays to Britain in MKhT performance is concerned, then, it was a 'no-win' situation of a type that theatre historians are very familiar with. A whole range of cultural factors in the 1910s seemed to indicate that Chekhov would be received in Britain by this route, in which case he would probably have appeared on the commercial English stage much earlier and his reputation have grown much faster. However, at every point something happened to prevent it, culminating with the war.

The time for Chekhov on the English-language stage came in the twenties, and not solely as a result of the arrival of Komisarjevsky. In Russia itself in the 1910s Komisarjevsky had been drawn to monumental, philosophical, and poetical drama (he had staged *Faust*, for instance, and *The Tempest*). Chekhov was generally alien to him. Paradoxically, however, Komisarjevsky happened to be in England at the time when English culture was ripe for Chekhov, indeed craving for him, and it seemed natural to invite a Russian director to stage him. In any case, a quite surprising amount of interest in Russian culture and the Russian theatre had been carried over from before the war in which Russia and Britain had been allies. Not only did two dozen English-speaking theatre people present Tolstoy's *The First Distiller* and Chekhov's *Swan Song* and *The Wedding* at the Russian Exhibition in London in May 1917, and eighty participate in the committee that organized the Exhibition's Dramatic Section, including Lady Cunard, Aylmer Maude, Nigel Playfair, Ellen Terry, and Lady Tree; many of these people attached to Russian culture survived the war to play an active part in the English Chekhov productions that followed it. There was in fact great *continuity* in the English theatrical background to Chekhov productions from the 1910s to the 1920s. It was not the theatre people who turned to Chekhov as a consequence of the war, it was the audience – the post-war intelligentsia of the lost generation who sought spiritual comfort in Chekhov, much as Russians had at the turn of the century.

By contrast, in the Russia of the 1920s Chekhov was leaving the stage. To the people of the revolutionary years his plays seemed too intimate, too refined, too far from the social struggle. Mayakovsky mocked the theatre in which 'Auntie Manyas and Uncle Vanyas sit around whining on sofas'.[20] Even Stanislavsky said at this time that it was impossible for people to regard as tragic the story of how 'an officer goes away and his lady friend is left behind' (*Three Sisters*). In 1925 Ilya Erenburg attended a performance of Komisarjevsky's *Three Sisters* at Barnes and was astonished that 'when the very right and proper English engineer I was sitting next to saw and heard the three sisters intoning "To Moscow, to Moscow!" he neither batted an eyelid nor yawned, but responded to their groans with sighs of sympathy'.[21]

Erenburg was not to know that ten or twelve years later Soviet audiences would rediscover Chekhov and 'respond with sighs of sympathy' to the sisters' tears in the MKhAT production of 1940, which opened a fresh chapter in the Russian theatrical history of

Chekhov's plays. There would be nothing sentimental about this sympathy; it would derive from a sober knowledge of history, from courage, and from faith in the future. Our audiences, too, would feel that Chekhov spoke to *them*. Eighteen years later, with new actors, this production by Nemirovich-Danchenko would be seen on MKhAT's first visit to London.

Notes

1 See, for example, Robert Tracy, 'The flight of a seagull: Chekhov on the English stage' (Ph.D. Thesis, Harvard University, 1959), p. 99, and Patrick Miles, *Chekhov on the British Stage 1909–1987* (Cambridge: Sam and Sam, 1987), p. 7.
2 *Nov*, 23 January 1914.
3 See L. H. Honigwachs, 'The Edwardian discovery of Russia 1900–1917' (Ph.D. Thesis, Columbia University, 1977).
4 Ellen Terry, *The Russian Ballet* (London: Sidgwick and Jackson, 1913).
5 See A. B. Bartoshevich, *Shekspir na angliyskoy stsene; konets XIX-pervaya polovina XX v. (Shakespeare on the English stage, from the end of the nineteenth to the mid-twentieth century)* (Moscow: Nauka, 1985), pp. 148–9.
6 Samuel Hynes, *The Edwardian Turn of Mind* (Princeton, NJ.: Princeton University Press, 1968), p. 345.
7 See Laurence Senelick, *Gordon Craig's Moscow Hamlet: a Reconstruction* (Westport, Conn.: Greenwood Press, 1982) and T. I. Bachelis, *Shekspir i Kreg (Shakespeare and Craig)* (Moscow: Nauka, 1983).
8 See Baring's account of MKhT performances that he attended in 1905, in Maurice Baring, *The Puppet Show of Memory* (London: William Heinemann, 1922), pp. 265–8. According to Calderon's wife, in 1914 MKhT was even going to stage one of Calderon's plays, *The Red Cloth*, 'when the War came' (Calderon archives).
9 Letter from M. Lykiardopoulos to K. S. Stanislavsky 17 July 1911. Stanislavsky Archive, MKhAT Museum, no. 12940.
10 Copy of letter from K. S. Stanislavsky to G. Craig, Stanislavsky Archive, MKhAT Museum, no. 1636.
11 Letter from M. Lykiardopoulos to K. S. Stanislavsky, *ibid*.
12 I. Vinogradskaya, *Zhizn i tvorchestvo K. S. Stanislavskogo. Letopis. Tom vtoroy, 1906–1915 (Stanislavsky's life and art, a chronicle. Vol. 2, 1906–1915)* (Moscow: VTO, 1971), p. 306.
13 Bachelis, *Shakespeare and Craig*, p. 52.
14 Herbert Beerbohm Tree, *Thoughts and After-Thoughts* (London: Cassell and Company, 1913), p. 155.
15 *Russkiye vedomosti*, 19 January 1913.
16 Letter from A. K. Benckendorff to K. S. Stanislavsky, Stanislavsky Archive, MKhAT Museum.

17　*Nov*, 16 February 1914.
18　*Athenaeum*, 11 December 1909, p. 741.
19　See Edward Morgan, 'Lydia Yavorska', *Theatrephile*, 3:9, (1990), pp. 3–7, and A. Ya. Altshuller, 'Tip vo vsyakom sluchaye lyubopytny (An interesting type at least)', in *Chekhoviana; stati, publikatsii, esse (Chekhoviana; Articles, publications and essays)*, ed. V. Ya. Lakshin (Moscow: Nauka, 1990), pp. 140–51.
20　Vladimir Mayakovsky, *Polnoye sobraniye sochineny (Complete collected works)*, II (Moscow: Khudozhestvennaya literatura, 1956), p. 248.
21　Ilya Erenburg, *Sobraniye sochineny v devyati tomakh (Collected works in nine volumes)*, VII (Moscow: Khudozhestvennaya literatura, 1966), pp. 456–7.

CHAPTER 4

Chekhov, naturalism and the drama of dissent: productions of Chekhov's plays in Britain before 1914[1]

Jan McDonald

There were five British productions of plays by Chekhov before the First World War. The first was *The Seagull*, translated by George Calderon, presented by the Glasgow Repertory Theatre in November 1909. Less important was the production of *The Bear* translated by Arthur A. Sykes and performed as part of a double-bill at the Kingsway in May 1911. The Stage Society presented Constance Garnett's translation of *The Cherry Orchard* at the Aldwych in the same month. The Adelphi Play Society repeated Calderon's version of *The Seagull* at the Little Theatre in March 1912, and the Stage Society, again at the Aldwych, mounted Mrs R. S. Townsend's translation of *Uncle Vanya* in May 1914.

Despite the fact that pioneer societies had previously performed major Russian plays such as Gorky's *The Lower Depths* (1903) and Tolstoy's *The Power of Darkness* (1904), the first performance of a Chekhov play in London was not until 1911. As early as 1905, Shaw suggested in a letter to Laurence Irving that he might translate a play by Chekhov for the Society, but nothing had come of the idea.[2] Still it was at Shaw's instigation that the Stage Society did turn its attention to *The Cherry Orchard*, the production of which he described to Constance Garnett as the most important in England since that of *A Doll's House*. Others who had pioneered the plays of Ibsen and the avant-garde continental dramatists in the 1890s, were markedly unenthusiastic about Chekhov's plays. William Archer confessed himself unable to see any merit in them at all.

This lack of interest may have been the result of a quite understandable mellowing of the pioneers themselves. The Stage Society can be credited along with its predecessor, the Independent Theatre Society (ITS), with the beginning of the movement which produced the triumphs of the Barker period at the Court. This flourishing

school of dramatists, and the expanding repertory movement, was,
according to some, becoming a fashionable intellectual coterie who
gained social prestige by attending 'difficult' plays on Sunday evenings.
J. T. Grein in the *Sunday Times* (4 June 1911) attacked the Stage Society
audiences of *The Cherry Orchard* as being 'not students of the drama,
who respect efforts even when they do not understand them but ...
they look upon these productions as a mere antidote to the dullness
of an English Sunday'. John Palmer wrote in *The Future of the Theatre*:

> The Incorporated Stage Society ... seating more dramatic authors, critics
> and actors to the cubic inch than any other institution in Europe, has
> during the last few years had two splendid opportunities of exhibiting the
> true critical worth of an expert assembly. It has had an opportunity of
> welcoming the first plays in English of August Strindberg and of Anton
> Tchekoff. The reception of these plays by this Society ... showed quite
> conclusively that here were the lineal descendants of the experts who turned
> down Ibsen in the nineties.[3]

Another reason for the comparative lack of interest in Chekhov's
work in Britain is found in the fact that historically the avant-garde
movement in the drama in England had always been closely linked
to a political or social reform movement. The Fabians had constituted
a fairly significant part of the audience for the old ITS, for the Stage
Society and for the early productions of Ibsen, which were mistakenly
seen as a propaganda vehicle for unconventional but enlightened
views about women, marriage, and society. The Actresses' Franchise
League and the Reform Party of the Actors' Association that established
a minimum weekly wage for actors in London, found leaders in the
Court company, whose policy was to prefer new plays which had 'a
critical dissenting attitude towards contemporary codes of morality'.[4]

Shaw's idea of the stage as a platform was strongly rooted in the
dramatic reformers, and so they found the plays of Chekhov baffling
and lacking in the strong sense of purpose that they considered a
dramatic work should offer. As Maurice Baring forecast in 1908,
the lack of a 'text' or a 'message' was likely to make it difficult for
a British audience to accept Chekhov's work. 'In ... Britain, France
and Germany, dramatists were all actuated by some definite purpose
– the stage was a kind of pulpit ... The English public has especially
delighted in the last fifteen years in a sermon on the stage with a
dash of impropriety in it.'[5]

The reformist creed was essentially optimistic. Equal opportunities for men and women of all classes in education, housing,

and employment would make a better society and a better world. The view of the Russian intellectual at the turn of the century, disillusioned by the failure of the impetus to reform in his own country in the 1870s, was much less sanguine. His struggle was for something less tangible than votes for women or slum clearance. George Calderon, one of the most sensitive British interpreters of Chekhov, sums up this attitude: 'While our Western playwrights, confined within the boundary of the attainable, wage a heavy-handed polemic with social institutions and conventions, the Russians are at grips with the deepest craving of their inward nature.'[6]

The mood reflected in Chekhov's plays resembles more that of Britain after the Great War than before it. In 1920, J. Middleton Murry was able to write: 'Today we feel how intimately Tchekov belongs to us.'[7] D. S. Mirsky went further in 1927: 'To the stripped and outcast mankind of today, Chekhov is the arch-seducer.'[8] The twenties saw a spate of productions of the plays.

In the first decade of the century, however, the political, social, and moral outlook of the British audience was not receptive to Chekhov. Egan Mew in his review of *Uncle Vanya* for *The Academy* (23 May 1914) held that the play belonged 'to a world apart from ours, to a state of mind as foreign to that of Western Europe as it is possible to find'. The only way in which the London audience could interpret his work was as supreme photographic naturalism. The plays were seen as presenting detailed and accurate pictures of Russian life. The *Westminster Gazette* (30 May 1911) called *The Cherry Orchard* 'a slice of life comedy, but the life was very foreign and the slice was rather big'. The impressionistic side of his work was apparently lost on them. In addition, English audiences had little idea of what life in Russia was actually like, and there was also a strong feeling that the actors who were trying to recreate it were equally ignorant, so that results were unsatisfactory.

J. T. Grein in his review of *The Cherry Orchard* in the *Sunday Times* (28 May 1911) saw the play's interest and value as lying in its portrayal of Russian social history, illuminating 'Russian life of fifty years ago and showing the circumstances in which the liberating laws set up by Nicholas II were necessary'. He went on to excuse the actors some of their errors, since 'it is nobody's fault that you cannot make Muscovites of Englishmen'.

A few enlightened critics, such as Desmond MacCarthy, opposed this misconception. In his review of *Uncle Vanya* (1914), he wrote:

'We have no right to label this atmosphere "Russian" and regard it with complacent curiosity. Have you not felt the fog in your throat on English lawns in English country houses?'[9] Ashley Dukes, in an article entitled, 'Russia in England', objected to the explaining away of 'this important contribution to drama as something "typically Russian" as though *Hamlet* were "typically English". To give local or national significance only to a thing of universal beauty like the tragi-comic *Cherry Orchard* showed a complete lack of perception.'[10]

But these were the exceptions, and the commonly held view that Chekhov's main aim in his work was to present as accurate as possible a picture of Russian upper-middle-class society greatly influenced both the reception of his plays by critics and by audiences, and the approach the actors and directors had towards them.

A sizeable number of the actors who first performed Chekhov's plays in Britain had had some previous experience of appearing in the 'new drama', either in earlier Stage Society productions, with Barker at the Court or the Savoy, or in one of the repertory theatres. Their experience, therefore, would be gleaned from playing in the works of Shaw, Galsworthy, Barker, and their followers, as well as in plays by distinguished European dramatists, notably the Naturalists, Brieux and Hauptmann. There is no doubt that their approach to Chekhov's plays was coloured by their experience of such a repertoire. George Calderon felt that the same passion for a 'message' that had blinded the theatrical pioneers to the merits of Chekhovian drama also rendered the actors ill-equipped to cope with what he called the 'centrifugal method' of Chekhov's work: 'The "centrifugal" Drama requires above all things "centripetal acting", acting designed to restore the unity of impression'.[11] British actors were used to plays that were 'toughly made', with a strong central theme so they could 'indulge their natural propensity to make their parts stand out'.

In other words the pre-Brechtian 'demonstration' type of acting that was desirable for the plays of Shaw, for example, was eminently unsuitable for Chekhov. But if there was Shaw, there was also Barker, whose plays *The Marrying of Ann Leete* and *Waste* had been performed by the Stage Society in 1902 and 1907. *The Voysey Inheritance* had been successfully performed at the Court in 1905 and *The Madras House* at the Duke of York's during Frohman's repertory season in 1910.

Although there is a strain of social comment present in his work, it is not primarily as a propagandist that Barker succeeds, and there are marked similarities between his dramatic technique and that of

Chekhov. Desmond MacCarthy, in his review of the 1929 production of *The Three Sisters*, was reminded by the play of Barker's method of writing dialogue: 'Tchekov solved, far better than his contemporaries, the problem of naturalistic dialogue, of preserving the triviality and broken rhythms of ordinary talk and still making every word significant of character. Granville Barker has made the most competent and successful attempt (in English) to write drama this way.' [12] Certainly the brilliant opening moments of *Ann Leete* and the delicate handling of the grotesque dress show in *The Madras House* have strong Chekhovian echoes.

P. P. Howe finds similarities not only in their handling of dialogue, but also in the way in which each dramatist builds up mood or atmosphere. Barker, like Chekhov, does not stop at the creation of individual characters but goes on to create the corporate character of a group: 'This recognition of the needs of the play's momentary mood as the primary arbiter in a play's construction is the discovery of Tchekoff and of Mr Granville Barker.' [13]

One can draw the conclusion, therefore, that the methods of Chekhov in the delineation of character, the use of elliptical dialogue with great depths of subtext, and the masterly creation of mood or atmosphere on stage, were not wholly strange to actors who had previously worked with the Stage Society at the Court or with one of the repertory companies. The acting in the plays of Barker had been widely praised. One reason for their success may have been that Barker directed all his own plays with a group of actors he knew well, and who had worked together before. Here one finds a clue as to why the Glasgow *Seagull* was more successful artistically than the London productions by the Societies. In the first place, Glasgow Repertory Theatre had a regular company who had worked together before the Chekhov production, and, secondly, the play was directed by the translator, George Calderon, whose knowledge of the language and of the techniques and methods of production of the plays in Russia must have been of inestimable value to the actors. He was also a practising dramatist and his play *The Fountain* had been mounted by the Stage Society in March 1909.

Performance by the Societies had many practical drawbacks. Both the Stage Society's *Cherry Orchard* and the Adelphi Play Society's *Seagull* were criticized for lack of rehearsals, the same fault that had been held responsible for the failure of the first performance of *The Seagull* in St Petersburg. In productions by the Societies there were immense problems of assembling a cast, each member of which would have varying professional commitments, making it difficult to rehearse together regularly. There were problems of finding a place to meet, very few rehearsals taking place on the stage of the theatre in which the play was to be performed. Finances for setting and properties were limited, and time for technical rehearsals almost non-existent. These conditions were scarcely ideal for any play, but for those of Chekhov, in which so much depends on the creation of an ensemble among the actors aided by a texture of visual and aural effects, the limitations were even more serious.

The Glasgow Repertory Theatre, working under much better conditions than the Societies, came closest to the Moscow Art Theatre's ideal of ensemble, as expressed by Nemirovich-Danchenko: 'The deepest force of spiritual communion on the stage united the group which participated in his [Chekhov's] plays ... The group was welded even more compactly, and its members infected one another with the Chekhovian sense of life.'[14]

Of Glasgow's production of *The Seagull*, the critic of the *Glasgow Herald* (3 November 1909) wrote: 'The impression of overwhelming humanity owed much to the fine all-round acting last night for the ensemble was so perfect that it would almost seem invidious to select individual names.' Actors of minor parts were praised for 'subduing themselves to the prevailing tone'. Lest *The Herald* be considered too partisan, *The Stage* (4 November 1909) can be cited as a corroborating witness: 'To catch and give expression to Tchekhov's intentions is no easy matter, and it says much for the company that they presented so good an ensemble.'

The Adelphi production of *The Seagull* in 1912 was harshly criticized on this point. The critic of the *Saturday Review* (13 April 1912) admits that the play depends on 'the cumulative effect of a method which concerns itself rather with groups than with individuals composing them', but the leading players failed to realize that the individual part was 'important only in correlation with the rest' and so they upset the balance and rhythm of the play. 'General unity of effect', wrote E. F. S. of the *Westminster Gazette* (2 April 1912) 'was out of the question'. The *ad hoc* company with insufficient rehearsal time and continuous casting difficulties was scarcely equipped to achieve the successful communion between actors that the play demanded.

It seems to have been difficult to find suitable people to undertake the challenging leading roles, and, once found, prior commitments in the commercial theatre often caused them to leave the Societies' productions at very short notice. Leon Quartermaine, for example, withdrew from the Stage Society's *Uncle Vanya* just prior to the performance, the title role being taken by the producer, Guy Rathbone.

Chekhov's fascinating but feckless women were to prove a problem for both the established ladies of the theatre and the talented novices who sought acting opportunities with the Societies. In *The Cherry Orchard*, the part of Madame Ranevsky was given to an inexperienced actress, Katherine Pole, described by the *Pall Mall Gazette* (30 May 1911) as 'a pretty young lady with a refined personality, and within its limits, an effective little gift for acting' – a patronizing dismissal with which other critics concurred. Chekhov had stressed in his letters to Olga Knipper that Ranevsky was a mature woman, describing her as 'the old mother', 'an elderly lady', 'the old lady'. While the Stage Society would not then have had the benefit of access to Chekhov's letters, it is fairly clear from the text of the play that Ranevsky is hardly 'a pretty young lady', and it is no wonder that Katherine Pole was 'a little overweighted' (*Westminster Gazette*, 30 May 1911). Calderon, in discussing *The Cherry Orchard*, said the leading parts demanded 'players of imposing personality',[15] and Grein in his review in the *Sunday Times* (4 June 1911), wrote that 'a magnetic woman, a *grande dame*, should have been chosen for the part' of Madame Ranevsky. But the Societies had to cast from actors who were free, and, perhaps more important, who were willing to work at difficult roles with only two performances and their expenses as a reward.

But the answer was not always to be found in the established actress, either British or Russian. In the Adelphi Play Society's production of *The Seagull*, Gertrude Kingston played Arkadina, and the forty-year-old Russian, Lydia Yavorskaya,[16] took the part of Nina. Both had shown commitment to the 'new drama'. Gertrude Kingston had played for the Independent Theatre Society, for the Stage Society, and at the Court, and managed her own establishment at the Little Theatre; Yavorska had played many Ibsen parts in Russia, and also premièred Shaw's *Candida* there. *The Era* (6 April 1912) maintained that she had played the part of Nina in Russia, and the *Saturday Review* (13 April 1912) went further and credited her with being 'Tchekoff's original heroine'. In fact Chekhov had refused her permission to stage the play in her theatre in St Petersburg, but she had some connection with the work. The first reading of the play by Chekhov to his friends had taken place in her blue drawing-room in 1895, but she, like the others present, appears to have found the work baffling and embarrassing. Later, when the Moscow Art Theatre productions had made Chekhov's work highly regarded, she sought parts from him, but he carefully prevented her from performing in any of his plays, rightly feeling that the showy melodramatic acting style for which she was noted was ill-suited to his plays. Chekhov's brief affair with the lady led to his recommending her to Suvorin as a member of his company, but even as he did so, he commented on her 'tendency to pose' and on the fact that she had been 'ruined by her training'.[17]

Acting in English, a language which she had not fully mastered, was clearly a handicap, but the London critics were also quick to fasten on the very faults in her acting that Chekhov himself had found objectionable. She 'over-acted consistently' (*Pall Mall Gazette*, 1 April 1912), and she 'made a difficult task worse by awkward gesture and ruinous pronunciation' (*The Academy*, 13 April 1912).

Gertrude Kingston fared rather better with the press. She seemed to understand the part, and gave the audience the benefit of 'a really fine piece of acting' (*The Academy*, 13 April 1912) but the problem was that she failed to fit in with the rest of the cast. 'Neither Miss Kingston, nor the Princess Bariatinsky [*i.e.* Lydia Yavorskaya] seemed to realize that her individual part was important only in correlation with the rest. It is not possible to be angry with Miss Kingston for the whole tradition of British acting which she so admirably adorns, was against her in this particular venture' (*Saturday Review*, 13 April 1912).

This last comment is rather unfair. As can be seen from the productions at the Court and the Savoy, and indeed from the Glasgow *Seagull*, it was perfectly possible for British actors to achieve the spirit of communion among characters that a Chekhov play demands. But in order to do this it was necessary to have assembled a group of actors who could work together for a fairly extended period under a director of the calibre of Shaw, Barker, or Calderon. Maurice Elvey's direction of the Adelphi *Seagull* was said to be non-existent.

The success or otherwise of Chekhov's plays in Britain seems to have been very closely related to the calibre of the men who directed them. What was needed was someone who understood fully the originality in form and content of the plays, and who could convey the meaning to the actors. It is strange, considering that many of the actors who appeared in these early productions were used to dealing with the 'difficult' plays of the 'new drama', apparently with considerable success, that so many critics comment on the fact that the actors did not seem to understand what was demanded of them in Chekhov. This is in direct contrast to comments on the early Ibsen performances, when, however much the plays were attacked, the intelligence of the playing was almost invariably praised. But, as Ashley Dukes pointed out in 'Russia in England', 'Direction plays a greater part with Tchekov than with Ibsen', and the actors, however good they were individually, needed help to achieve the correct overall effect, and convey the meaning of this to the audience.

Maurice Baring supports this view: 'In London, I saw *The Cherry Orchard* and another play of his done, where the company had not even realized the meaning of the action.' He cites as an example the total lack of comprehension on the part of the actors of a piece of Chekhovian business, Konstantin's tearing the bandage from his head in the course of the quarrel with his mother in Act 3 of *The Seagull*:

The company had, I suppose, read the stage direction, which says: 'Man removes bandage', but the words of the scene were spoken without any emotion or emphasis. At one moment, the man quietly removed his bandage and dropped it on the floor, as though it were in the way, or as if he were throwing down a cigarette which he had done with. In Moscow, in the Art Theatre, every effect was made to tell.[18]

This lack of comprehension of the actors goes hand-in-hand with the view that the plays were relevant only in Russia, and showed 'a slice of Russian society'. The fallacy of seeing Chekhov as the apotheosis of the Naturalist movement misled the actors as well as the critics. A director who understood both form and content was necessary.

James Agate held the view that the embryonic state of the art of production was one of the reasons why the works of Chekhov had not met with more success in Britain. Chekhov's plays were a severe test for the producer particularly on account of the need to create and sustain atmosphere, a skill which early producers had to learn by experience.

The man who came closest to achieving the correct atmosphere through unity of interpretation and orchestration of the actors was George Calderon. He fully realized that 'A play by Tchekhof is a reverie, not a concatenation of events.'[19] The most important thing for the actors to convey to the audience was not necessarily the action, but how the action illuminated individuals. 'The players have to show, by difference of tone and gesture, when they are speaking

to the action, which concerns them as individuals and when they
are speaking to the atmosphere, which concerns them as the group.'
He cites as an example of a transfer from group mood to individual
reaction the opening of the second act of *The Seagull*. 'The conversation
and behaviour of the personages have nothing to do with the action
of the piece, but are directed to convey the atmosphere of tedium
and heat ... the passive group emotion becomes suddenly active
on the entrance of Shamraev. A burst of anger breaks out, from
each according to his interest or disposition.'[20]

This is precisely the state that John Gielgud describes in recalling
his realization of the demands of a Chekhovian part made on the
actors. 'One seems to become part of the life of a group of people
as well as an individual stage character.'[21] It is also the point that
Baring, who was familiar with the Moscow productions, made about the
plays: 'In them the clash of events is subservient to the human figure;
and the human figure to the atmosphere in which it is plunged.'[22]

But the achievement of this swing between individual reaction
and group emotion, Calderon felt, was hard for the British actor
who tended, he said, to fall into 'cataleptic silence', as soon as another
actor spoke. 'His [Chekhov's] disjunctive manner is defeated of its
purpose unless the whole company keeps continuously alive.'[23] What
Calderon seems to be aiming for is the 'through-line' or 'superobjective' of character and the 'communion' between actors so
important in the Stanislavsky system. The 'through-line of action',
Calderon went on, should not only be maintained when a character
was on stage, but when he was off stage as well:

With Tchekhof the call of the business to be done behind the scenes is
almost more insistent than the call of what is to be enacted by the footlights; the stage is not so much a point or a focus as a passage over which
his personages drift or scurry, a chance meeting place where we hear only
fragments of their talk and see less important moments of their action ...
The student in the last act of 'The Cherry Orchard' does not come on stage
to say good-bye to Lopakhin, but only to find his goloshes for departure;
the farewell scene is an accident.[24]

This idea is reminiscent of the Moscow Art Theatre actors being
asked to act out scenes immediately prior to those which actually
took place on stage.

Calderon's other great contribution was to lift the plays of Chekhov
out of the 'naturalistic' category in which they had been firmly placed
by most critics. He sees the dramatist's work rather as a progression

from the fairly crude symbolism of *The Seagull* – the seagull itself he calls 'a symbol of the artless kind that can be stored in the property room' – to the sophistication of the later work which shows 'the events of the drama as being emblems and generalizations about life at large'.[25] Calderon understood better than his contemporaries the true form of a Chekhov play, and the same might be said of him, as Komisarjevsky said of Stanislavsky in explaining the success of the latter's work on the Chekhov plays, that he 'found the emotional movement of the "Sea Gull" only because he understood the form in which the play was written'.[26]

That 'form', Stanislavsky learned, was not the photographic naturalism of the Meininger, that had so far distinguished the Moscow Art Theatre productions. As Chekhov is reputed to have said to the naturalistic producer, 'A real nose stuck through a portrait instead of a painted one is natural enough but does not constitute art.' The message that here was a new form, not a kind of super-naturalism with inexplicable lapses into artificial soliloquies from time to time, came slowly to English audiences, critics, and actors. Calderon's appreciation of the fact that the plays were more than 'a marvel of accurate observation' was one of the reasons that made his production of *The Seagull* for the Glasgow Repertory Theatre successful. Walter Elliot, then writing theatre reviews for *Glasgow University Magazine* (10 November 1909), understood from seeing the production that the play was 'full of more than Ibsenite symbolism', and the critic of the *Glasgow Herald* (3 November 1909) remarks on its 'odd and elusive symbolism'. Reviewers of other productions dismiss any non-naturalistic touches as lapses by the dramatist. The use of the monologue in *The Cherry Orchard* was picked on by the critic of the *Pall Mall Gazette* (30 May 1911): 'Characters talked to the audience again and again in that bad old-fashioned way which we hoped never to see at a Stage Society performance.' Calderon, on the other hand, believed that a Chekhov play was largely composed of soliloquies. The actors appear to be talking to each other. In fact, they sit side by side and think aloud. The sympathetic reception of *The Seagull* in Glasgow may have been partly the result of the public lecture given by Calderon on the play a few days before the performance. He was advertised as repeating his talk prior to the London production, but did not in fact do so. Calderon's interpretation appears to have followed the possibly mistaken Moscow Art Theatre production line. 'Disillusion' was the keynote and the main theme, and Chekhov might well have denounced Calderon as another 'crybaby'.

Other directors of Chekhov receive either faint praise – at least Guy Rathbone's *Uncle Vanya* was competent – or harsh criticism. Kenelm Foss' *Cherry Orchard* was apparently 'taken too slowly' (*The Star*, 30 May 1911) and 'dragged' (*Westminster Gazette*, 30 May 1911). This may not have been so much a question of pace as failure on the part of the actors to fill the pauses with meaningful and thoughtful action. Also 'the players at times seemed conscious themselves of the play's peculiar structure' (*The Star*, 30 May 1911). Clearly the creation of atmosphere and the understanding of their parts by the characters were lacking in this venture. 'The spectators ... didn't know who anybody on the stage was or what anybody on the stage was there for' (*The Nation*, 22 June 1911). Those who were not baffled were, according to Calderon, misled by the production. 'On the whole after the Stage Society performance, the general opinion was that the owners of the Cherry Orchard were meant to be delightful people and Lopakhin a brute.'[27] This was the result of the players' misreading of their parts. Calderon felt that it was silly to ask where the audience's sympathies should lie in a Chekhov play for there are no villains or heroes, and the author was scrupulously fair in sharing out virtues and vices equally among his characters. Once again an old-fashioned view of drama as conflict seems to have blinded the performers and the director to the true form of the play. There was no normal dramatic progression as they understood it, and one critic (*The Era*, 3 June 1911) was misguided enough to call Yepikhodov 'the raisonneur'. The production of *The Seagull* by Maurice Elvey was universally attacked. *The Stage* (4 April 1912) found 'the handling of the play loose and indecisive' and the *Saturday Review* (13 April 1912) felt that 'the play didn't seem to have been produced at all'. It is important to stress that the directors, Foss and Elvey, were quite competent men of the theatre who had previously worked with the avant-garde societies and with Granville Barker.

The question left unanswered, of course, is why Barker, the man whose plays most closely resembled those of Chekhov, who had created a new type of ensemble company at the Court, and who had independently devised methods of eliciting the full creative potential from his actors that closely resembled those of Stanislavsky, did not turn his hand to Chekhov's plays. 'Mr Granville Barker, I implore you, put this play in your repertory', wrote Desmond MacCarthy[28] after the Stage Society's *Uncle Vanya* in 1914, but by then war was imminent. Perhaps Barker came to realize his omission later. In a letter to William Archer in 1923, he wrote: 'it was when I saw the Moscow people interpreting Chekhov that I fully realized what I had been struggling towards and that I saw how much actors could add to a play'.[29]

The creative process of collaboration among actors and between them and the dramatist was, Barker felt, one of the most important lessons he learned from his talk with Stanislavsky in Moscow in 1914. He compared, by implication, the quality of the Moscow Art Theatre's *Cherry Orchard* and the London production, when he wrote: 'to read the play afterward was like reading the libretto of an opera – missing the music'. The differences were not in 'brilliance of execution, but absolutely in the meaning extracted from the play and in the observable addition of dramatic values'. It seems from the evidence that the main drawback to the successful production of Chekhov's plays in Britain prior to the Great War was that, with the exception of Calderon, there was no director sufficiently at ease with the material to recreate the dramatist's vision on stage.

In fact, the plays were misunderstood by audiences, critics, and actors. Out of tune with the current mood of political and social reform, failing to fit into either a totally naturalistic or a propagandist concept of drama, they made demands that, with few exceptions, the British theatre was at that time unable to meet. Possibly, had it not been for the war, the development of Chekhovian production, like other theatrical and social phenomena, could have continued uninterrupted and could have achieved the artistic standards that the plays deserved before the late twenties, when Gielgud felt himself justified in claiming that 'English actors certainly seem to have a special gift for playing Chekhov.'[30]

Notes

1 This paper was first published in *Theatre Notebook*, 34:1, (1980). I am grateful to the editors for permission to reprint.

2 Letter from Shaw to Laurence Irving (25 October 1905). *Bernard Shaw. Collected Letters 1898–1910*, ed. Dan H. Laurence (London: Max Reinhardt, 1972), p. 569.

3 John Palmer, *The Future of the Theatre* (London: G. Bell and Sons, 1913), p. 90.

4 Desmond MacCarthy, *The Court Theatre* (London: A. H. Bullen, 1907), p. 13.

5 Maurice Baring, 'The plays of Tchekov', *The New Quarterly*, 1908, October, p.408.
6 George Calderon, 'The Russian stage', *The Quarterly Review*, 1912, July, p.31.
7 J. Middleton Murry, *Aspects of Literature* (London: W. Collins Sons and Co., 1920), p.84.
8 D.S. Mirsky, 'Chekhov and the English', *Monthly Criterion*, 1927, 6, p.302.
9 Desmond MacCarthy, *Drama* (London: Putnam, 1940), p.125.
10 Ashley Dukes, 'Russia in England', *Theatre Arts Monthly*, 1936, September, p.224.
11 George Calderon, *Two Plays by Tchekhof* (London: Grant Richards, 1912), p.10.
12 MacCarthy, *Drama*, p.49.
13 P.P. Howe, *Dramatic Portraits* (London: Martin Secker, 1913), p.196.
14 Vladimir Nemirovich-Danchenko, *My Life in the Russian Theatre*, trans. John Cournos (London: Geoffrey Bles, 1937), p.202.
15 Calderon, *Two Plays by Tchekhof*, p.16.
16 This actress' name in Russian is Yavorskaya, but she was always known in the West as Yavorska.
17 *Letters of Anton Chekhov*, trans. M. H. Heim and Simon Karlinsky (London: Bodley Head, 1973), p.265.
18 Maurice Baring, *The Puppet Show of Memory* (London: Heinemann, 1922), p.266.
19 Calderon, 'The Russian stage', p.28.
20 Calderon, *Two Plays by Tchekhof*, p.10.
21 John Gielgud, *Stage Directions* (London: Heinemann, 1963), p.92.
22 Baring, *The Puppet Show of Memory*, p.266.
23 Calderon, *Two Plays by Tchekhof*, p.10.
24 George Calderon, 'The fourth wall', *The Manchester Playgoer*, 1911.
25 Calderon, *Two Plays by Tchekhof*, pp.20−1.
26 Theodore Komisarjevsky, *Myself and the Theatre* (London: Heinemann, 1929), p.138.
27 Calderon, *Two Plays by Tchekhof*, pp.16−17.
28 MacCarthy, *Drama*, p.130.
29 *Granville Barker and his Correspondents*, ed. Eric Salmon (Detroit: Wayne State University Press, 1986), p.102.
30 Gielgud, *Stage Directions*, p.92.

CHAPTER 5

Bernard Shaw's dialogue with Chekhov

Anna Obraztsova

HEARTBREAK HOUSES

Shaw wrote *Heartbreak House* during the First World War and sub-titled it 'A Fantasia in the Russian Manner on English Themes'. In his Preface he says: 'Heartbreak House is not merely the name of the play which follows this preface. It is cultured, leisured Europe before the war.'[1] Then he adds: 'A Russian playwright, Tchekov, had produced four fascinating dramatic studies of Heartbreak House, of which three, The Cherry Orchard, Uncle Vanya, and The Seagull, had been performed in England.'[2]

What Shaw does not mention here is his own part in getting these plays staged in Britain. He professed himself a 'fervent admirer' of Chekhov's plays,[3] wrote to the Russia-enthusiast Laurence Irving as early as 1905 asking if he 'had any of them translated for the Stage Society',[4] and was the driving force behind the Stage Society's 1911 production of *The Cherry Orchard* in Constance Garnett's translation. More than this, however, Shaw influenced the whole interpretation of Chekhov's plays in Britain before and after the war.

As comedy-writer, satirist, and paradoxer, Shaw had his own original, if subjective, view of Chekhov. Through *Heartbreak House*, his Preface to it, and other utterances, he offered theatres a kind of programme for interpreting Chekhov's plays. Whether one agrees with this programme or not, it is worth knowing what it was.

First, Shaw could see the relevance of Chekhov for the European stage and how his plays might become part of the permanent repertoire of the British theatre. He saw a resemblance between the Russian 'cherry orchards' and the English 'gardens' and 'estates' of the post-Victorian period which by the turn of the century were already beginning to crumble:

Tchekov's plays, being less lucrative than swings and roundabouts, got no further in England, where theatres are only ordinary commercial affairs, than a couple of performances by the Stage Society. We stared and said,

43

'How Russian!' They did not strike me in that way. Just as Ibsen's intensely Norwegian plays exactly fitted every middle and professional class suburb in Europe, these intensely Russian plays fitted all the country houses in Europe in which the pleasures of music, art, literature, and the theatre had supplanted hunting, shooting, fishing, eating, and drinking. The same nice people, the same utter futility.[5]

Shaw was one of the first to see Chekhov in a European context like this. In doing so, he was disagreeing with Chekhov himself, who had been extremely doubtful that his characters would be comprehensible or interesting to anyone outside Russia.

Second, neither at the beginning of the twentieth century nor subsequently did Shaw associate Chekhov merely with the cultural achievements of the nineteenth century. He had lived almost half of his own life in the nineteenth century and was apt to name Wagner, Ibsen, and Tolstoy as its artistic giants. He accused it of 'strange confidence' and spoke of how 'one fierce hand after another – Marx's, Zola's, Ibsen's, Strindberg's, Turgenief's, Tolstoy's – stripped its masks off and revealed it as, on the whole, perhaps the most villainous page of recorded human history'.[6] Shaw did not include Chekhov in their ranks; he placed him squarely in the twentieth century, and saw in his plays the theatre of the future.

Nevertheless, Shaw confidently associated Chekhov's plays with the Russian tradition. This is the third aspect of his view of Chekhov's dramatic art. Although he considered Chekhov 'A star of the first magnitude in the Pleiad of great European dramatists who were contemporaries of Ibsen', he pointedly added: 'alongside Tolstoy and Turgenev'.[7] He probably did not know that Tolstoy rejected Chekhov's plays or that Chekhov was rather sceptical about Tolstoy's and the productions of them by the Moscow Arts. What was important to Shaw was the two Russian writers' attitude to the social and historical phenomenon that he called Heartbreak House, and the innovations they had made in the realm of theatrical genre.

Shaw was convinced that in *The Fruits of Enlightenment* Tolstoy had also depicted Heartbreak House, and shown it 'in his most ferociously contemptuous manner':

Tolstoy did not waste any sympathy on it: it was to him the house in which Europe was stifling its soul; and he knew that our utter enervation and futilization in that overheated drawing-room atmosphere was delivering the world over to the control of ignorant and soulless cunning and energy, with the frightful consequences which have now [1919] overtaken it. Tolstoy was no pessimist: he was not disposed to leave the house standing if he could bring it down about the ears of its pretty and amiable voluptuaries ... He treated the case of the inmates as one of opium poisoning, to be dealt with by seizing the patients roughly and exercising them violently until they were broad awake.[8]

However, Shaw concluded that Chekhov was more of a fatalist than Tolstoy, as Chekhov had 'no faith in these charming people extricating themselves. They would, he thought, be sold up and sent adrift by the bailiffs; therefore he had no scruple in exploiting and even flattering their charm.'[9]

In comparing Tolstoy and Chekhov, Shaw touched on a fundamental feature of European drama, namely its refusal to divide characters into positive and negative. Chekhov had expressed this as 'depicting neither villains nor angels'. He wrote to his brother apropos of *Ivanov*:

Playwrights today cram their plays with angels, rogues and buffoons; but you try and find these elements anywhere in Russia! All right, you may find them, but not in the extreme forms that these playwrights want ... I was trying to be original: I didn't bring on a single villain or a single angel (although I couldn't resist a few buffoons), I didn't arraign anyone, and I didn't defend anyone.[10]

Shaw differed from Chekhov in many things, but on this point he was in total agreement. In *The Quintessence of Ibsenism* he too rejected the conflict in contemporary drama between 'clear right and wrong', explaining that 'the villain is as conscientious as the hero, if not more so: in fact, the question which makes the play interesting (when it *is* interesting) is which is the villain and which the hero. Or, to put it another way, there are no villains and no heroes.'[11]

The new, modern theatrical genre that Tolstoy and Chekhov were aiming at was in Shaw's view tragicomedy, that is to say a play that was essentially a comedy but into which the tragedy of life boldly intruded.[12] This was the fourth aspect of the artistic programme that Shaw offered theatres staging Chekhov. He particularly stressed the comedic nature of Chekhov's drama. In doing so he was arguing against the attempts to portray Chekhov as the bard of 'twilight Russia' and 'hopelessness' that were widespread at the turn of the century in both Russian and English criticism.

The fact that it was Shaw who insisted Chekhov's plays were comedies, and that their tragedy existed *within* the comedy, should not be surprising. For all their differences, Shaw and Chekhov were the two European dramatists of the turn of the century with the most highly developed sense of comedy. Some of their playwright contemporaries lacked it altogether, in others it was barely developed. Shaw the satirist, however, is unthinkable without his one-act farces and extravaganzas, and Chekhov's full-length plays grew out of the vaudevilles and one-act 'jokes' that he wrote in his early years.

VAUDEVILLE OR FARCE?

The one-act plays of Shaw and Chekhov are one of the points of contact between the theatres of these two writers; an important topic in the dialogue that was bound to exist between them as two of the greatest innovators in modern European drama.

Almost all of Chekhov's one-act plays were written in a relatively short period in the late 1880s and early 1890s, which is why critics tend to regard them as a run-up to his late full-length plays. This is quite different from Shaw, who turned to the one-act play at moments all through his life.[13] Chekhov often wrote to his friends that he wanted to write a vaudeville or had already written one, and this has led most critics to talk of him as a 'vaudevillist' when discussing him as a one-act playwright. His own sub-titles for his one-act plays are extremely varied: *Smoking is Bad For You* is a 'play-monologue', *The Wedding* simply 'a play', and *On the High Road* and *Swan Song* 'dramatic studies'. Even the works pre-eminently regarded as vaudevilles – *The Bear*, *The Proposal*, and *The Anniversary* – are sub-titled by Chekhov 'jokes' (*shutki*).

Shaw was even fussier in defining the genres of his one-act plays. They include 'A fictitious paragraph of history' (*The Man of Destiny*), 'A brief tragedy for barns and booths' (*Passion, Poison and Petrifaction; or, the Fatal Gazogene*), 'A tragedietta' (*The Glimpse of Reality*), 'An interlude' (*The Dark Lady of the Sonnets*), 'A piece of utter nonsense' (*The Music-Cure*), 'A true-to-life farce' (*Augustus Does His Bit*), 'A revolutionary romancelet' (*Annajanska, the Bolshevik Empress*), 'A medieval war story' (*The Six of Calais*), and so forth.

However varied Chekhov's and Shaw's descriptions of the genre of their one-act plays may be, these plays have something in common: they are experiments conducted primarily in the genre of comedy with the object of discovering new techniques and forms of comedy and reaffirming its innovatory, aesthetic, and ideological power.

This marks out Chekhov and Shaw from other exponents of the New Drama. For Shaw and Chekhov to achieve what they did in their full-length plays, they had to go back to the traditions of comedy – Shaw to English and Irish farce, Chekhov to the Russian and partly French vaudeville.

It is difficult to agree with Vera Gottlieb's description of *The Bear*, *The Proposal*, *A Tragic Role*, *The Anniversary*, and *The Night Before the Trial* as 'farce-vaudevilles'.[14] Vaudeville and farce are not the same thing, especially Russian vaudeville and English farce. They have different ancestries, and set out to do different things with different techniques. In order to create new dramatic genres, both Shaw and Chekhov had to rethink the old (sometimes ancient) genres, modify them, transform them, and occasionally consciously parody them. This led them to pay particular attention to the farce and vaudeville respectively.

By the time Shaw came to write his one-act plays, the English farce had noticeably 'settled down'. It had begun to forget its boisterous, distant past on the market-place and was content with love-intrigues and the affirmation of respectable bourgeois values. This kind of farce easily found its way on to the stage of many London theatres, made itself at home there, and became a firm favourite of the commercial theatre. Shaw decided to do battle with the commercial theatre by using the same plots and subjects as his contemporaries, but reverting to the glorious traditions of the farce.

Whereas in *How He Lied to Her Husband* (1904) the farcical essence of the work is somewhat veiled, in *Passion, Poison and Petrifaction* (1905) it bursts forth shamelessly, challengingly, almost aggressively. Why, then, was it sub-titled 'A brief tragedy for barns and booths'? Perhaps because Shaw understood that in art as in life opposite poles attract. Thus, in response to a request from the actors Irene Vanbrugh and Cyril Maude to write a spoof melodrama for the annual summer theatre festival in Regent's Park for 1905, he produced not so much a pseudo-melodrama as a pseudo-farce, or a new type of farce that overturned the canons of late nineteenth-century English farce; an ironical farce, harnessing both tragic and comic moments, pouring the one into the other.

Here the absurd rushes out of Shaw's beloved paradoxes and rages about on the surface, engulfing everything – the situations, the way characters interact, and their speech. Reading the play you have the impression that it was written half a century later:

THE LADY. How much did the clock strike, Phyllis?
PHYLLIS. Sixteen, my lady.
THE LADY. That means eleven o'clock, does it not?
PHYLLIS. Eleven at night, my lady. In the morning it means half-past two;
   so if you hear it strike sixteen during your slumbers, do not rise.[15]

This is a quite different absurd, however, from that of European
drama of the 1950s and 60s. It is not the absurd of total meaninglessness
and despair, but an absurd that contains the salve of laughter –
laughter capable of healing life itself. It is an absurd drawn from the
very depths of popular culture, from a time when the show genuinely
did unite stage and audience (if there was a stage). Shaw's absurd
here is an expression of that 'aboriginal need for an occasional carnival'
of which he wrote.[16]

Shaw may have taken a lot from the traditions of the English
and Irish farce, but he also enabled the genre to develop further.
He laid the foundations for the twentieth-century political farce.
Particularly interesting in this respect is *Augustus Does His Bit*, written
in 1916.

The play is frankly democratic. At the end, when the recruiting
officer Lord August Highcastle berates the heroine for wasting the
time of 'the hardworked officials who are doing their bit for their
country whilst our gallant fellows are perishing in the trenches',
she rounds on him with: 'Oh, the gallant fellows are not all in the
trenches, Augustus. Some of them have come home for a few days'
hard-earned leave; and I am sure you won't grudge them a little
fun at your expense.'[17] In effect this is a direct appeal to the audience,
in the hope that some of the 'gallant fellows' will be there. The
dramatist promises them fun and is as good as his word.

The first sub-title of this play is 'Official dramatic tract on war
saving and cognate topics', after which comes the description of its
genre as 'A true-to-life farce'. In other words it is a farce drawn
from life, free from the theatrical clichés that accreted round the
farce in the nineteenth century, and it cleverly uses all the techniques
of the age-old popular shows to air the most acute, most up-to-the-
minute political issues and concerns. It involves substituted letters,
disguises, constant references to punch-ups, and in the end the
characters come to blows (Lord Augustus throws the clerk downstairs
and the latter returns 'with his head bandaged, carrying a poker').[18]
Above all, the play creates from its characters new, daring, and
witty farce-'masks', yet leaves theatres free to play it in two entirely

different ways. They can either perform it as off-beat knock-about comedy, or as an outwardly straight play whose irony, satire, and biting paradoxes are concealed behind plausible-sounding behaviour and motivation. It is a short step from Shaw's political farces to Brecht's satirical political pamphlets such as the full-length *Resistible Rise of Arturo Ui*.

As I have said, Shaw wrote one-act plays all through his life. They were not just trial-runs or sketches of future subjects and characters. They constituted a quite independent genre, a rich ground for experimentation that enabled him to influence readers and audiences almost at a moment's notice. In his preface to *Trifles and Tomfooleries* he apologizes for these 'tomfooleries pure and simple' and their 'irresponsible laughter', but feels the need to cite Mozart and Beethoven as artists who 'threw off' a few 'bagatelles' and 'bravura pieces' between longer works.[19]

According to Boris Zingerman, Chekhov's vaudevilles 'provide the key to his dialectics, and thereby to his drama generally'.[20] They are viewed mainly in terms of what he wrote for the theatre afterwards. Let us alter the perspective slightly and look at them not in terms of the future, but in terms of the period immediately preceding them, i.e. from the point of view of the Russian vaudeville in the second half of the nineteenth century.

Chekhov not only broke the basic rule of the vaudeville that the action should be interspersed with couplets and that dialogue, singing, and dancing should be woven into an organic whole. He also rejected the simplification of the characters, which was *de rigueur* but had often been done with some elegance and finesse. It is sometimes thought that, like nineteenth-century Russian literature generally, the Russian vaudeville 'came out of Gogol's *Overcoat*'. But the different genres of literature and dramatic art developed in their own ways. The 'little man' often occupied a central place in Russian vaudevilles because by and large the Russian vaudeville was closer to the Russian one-act plays of Gogol and Turgenev than to its French namesake. This 'little man' differed radically, however, from the classic 'little men' of Russian literature. He was more mawkish and tearful. Whereas the heroes of Pushkin's, Gogol's, Turgenev's, and Dostoyevsky's prose can profoundly shake one and evoke searing compassion, the most the vaudeville characters were meant to evoke was sentiment and pity. The vaudeville, and particularly the Russian vaudeville, differs from the farce in not having a stock of stage masks that are repeated in different permutations from play to play. Nevertheless, there is undoubtedly a tendency towards stage types, quasi-masks, or figures vaguely reminiscent of masks. In pre-Chekhov vaudevilles good and evil often confront each other, vice is punished, and virtue triumphs. Where good and evil are separated like this, you inevitably get heroes without a blemish to their character and villains painted only in black. Lensky's celebrated *Lev Gurych Sinichkin* (1839) is a typical example of Russian vaudeville art, the epitome of its charms and limitations.

The characters of Chekhov's vaudeville jokes are ordinary living people. Nothing human is alien to them. Good and bad, the angelic and the diabolical, are mixed up in them. The unique combination that results can create uncontrollable laughter one moment and slight sadness the next, which in its turn may deepen into something more serious. This quality of Chekhov's one-act plays was immediately noticed. As Nemirovich-Danchenko put it: 'The beauty of these "jokes" lay not only in their hilarious situations but in the fact that their characters were real people, rather than vaudeville types, and they spoke in a language replete with humour and their own quirks.'[21]

What, then, did the vaudeville give Chekhov, and what did Chekhov give the vaudeville?

The answer to the first question must be: a very great deal, however much Chekhov the playwright resisted it, however much he argued with this tried and tested genre beloved of actors and audiences alike. Above all he took from the vaudeville its hilarity, its clear, bright laughter. What Chekhov's one-act plays share with the traditions of the Russian vaudeville (and the vaudeville generally) is their conception of humour. They are simply very, very funny. The stream of laughter that they produce is not malicious or scathing, but sympathetic, even in a way purifying. The performers do not need to emphasize or exaggerate anything, strain for effect, or play for laughs. The audience seems to laugh as a matter of course, and not so much at the characters themselves as the situations that these characters dictate and then become prisoners of. It laughs at the absurdities of human existence and the proliferation of outrageous, unforeseen events. Each of these events seems to pop like a champagne cork and 'pure humour fizzes from every line'.[22]

In addition, as a playwright Chekhov inherited from the best examples of the vaudeville its popular appeal, its 'democratism'. These qualities are just as intrinsic to this genre, in its higher manifestations, as they are to the farce when it is flourishing. Something miraculous and unforeseen happened to Chekhov's vaudevilles: everyone everywhere wanted to perform them, from professional theatres to amateurs, from the very highest echelons of society to the lowest – not, of course, that this meant they were always performed well.

As for what Chekhov did for the vaudeville, he killed it. The genre has not launched off anywhere new in the Russian theatre since. However, this is not all Chekhov's fault. The vaudeville has been encroached upon from many sides. Farce and its various modifications have proved closer in spirit to the twentieth century. The farce has squeezed the vaudeville from one side, and the new musical–theatrical genres advanced upon it from another. As soon as the vaudeville allowed itself slightly more freedom, for instance a modicum of coarseness, it was accused of ceasing to be vaudeville and turning into farce.

In fact the two genres have always had certain things in common. They both require a talent for improvisation, they both lean towards the anecdote, and they both give scope for clowning and buffoonery. As the famous Russian theatre director Diky put it, the origins of the vaudeville lie in 'uproarious jokes: popular humour: the juicy language of the people'.[23] This may appear to contradict what I said earlier about Chekhov's plays not being 'farce-vaudevilles' because farce and vaudeville are different things. My point is, however, that although the two genres came closer to each other in the nineteenth and twentieth centuries, and indeed overlapped, they never actually fused; nor can they.

The most difficult thing for the British stage, as for British readers of Chekhov's prose, has been to apprehend Chekhov's 'shot-silk "laughter-through-tears" effect'.[24] This is as true of his one-act plays as it is of his full-length plays.

A 'Grotesque' of Galsworthy's, written during the First World War (1917) and set in 1947, contains the following dialogue between the Angel Aethereal and his earthly guide:

'Laughter', said the Angel Aethereal, applying his wineglass to his nose, 'has ever distinguished mankind from all other animals with the exception of the dog. And the power of laughing at nothing distinguishes man even from that quadruped.'

'I would go further, sir,' returned his dragoman, 'and say that the power of laughing at that which should make him sick distinguishes the Englishman from all other varieties of man except the negro. Kindly observe!'[25]

In the 1880s both Chekhov and Shaw were preparing themselves to laugh at many things that made mankind sick. Through the 1890s they were both absorbed in this painful but necessary task. For Shaw there were many new topics still to come – in the first instance, two world wars. But both the Russian and the English writer needed the traditions of the vaudeville and the farce to give fresh edge to their comic writing, and to consolidate their artistic positions.

Notes

1 *Prefaces by Bernard Shaw* (London: Constable, 1934), p. 376.
2 *Ibid.*
3 Nigel Playfair, *Hammersmith Hoy: A Book of Minor Revelations* (London: Faber and Faber), 1930, p. 260.
4 *Bernard Shaw, Collected Letters 1898–1910*, ed. Dan H. Laurence (London: Max Reinhardt, 1972), pp. 568–9.
5 *Prefaces*, p. 376.
6 *Three Plays by Brieux*, with a Preface by Bernard Shaw (London: A. C. Fifield, 1911), p. x.
7 *Literatura i iskusstvo*, 15 July 1944.
8 *Prefaces*, p. 376.
9 *Ibid.*
10 A. P. Chekhov, *Polnoye sobraniye sochineny i pisem v tridtsati tomakh (Complete collected works and letters in 30 vols.)*, II *(Pisma) (Letters)* (Moscow: Nauka, 1975), pp. 137–8.
11 Bernard Shaw, *The Quintessence of Ibsenism: Now Completed to the Death of Ibsen* (New York: Brentano's, 1928), p. 221.
12 See Bernard Shaw, 'Tolstoy: tragedian or comedian?', *London Mercury*, 1921, no. 4 (May), pp. 31–4.
13 For a discussion of possible links between *The Cherry Orchard* and Shaw's last one-act play, *Why She Would Not* (1950), see E. A. Polotskaya, 'Spor Ranevskoy s Lopakhinym i poslednyaya pyesa Shou' ('Ranevskaya's argument with Lopakhin, and Shaw's last play'), in *Chekhovskiye chteniya v Yalte: Chekhov v Yalte (Chekhov symposium in Yalta: Chekhov in Yalta)*, eds V. I. Kuleshov *et al.* (Moscow: Min. Kultury SSSR, 1983), pp. 72–8.
14 Vera Gottlieb, *Chekhov and the Vaudeville: A Study of Chekhov's One-Act Plays* (Cambridge: CUP, 1982), pp. 46–109.
15 *The Complete Plays of Bernard Shaw* (London: Constable, 1931), p. 1114.
16 'Mr Irving takes paregoric', *The Saturday Review*, 11 May 1895.
17 *Complete Plays*, p. 848.
18 *Ibid.*, p. 847.
19 Bernard Shaw, *Translations and Tomfooleries* (London: Constable, 1932), p. 81.

20 B. I. Zingerman, *Teatr Chekhova i yego mirovoye znacheniye (Chekhov's theatre and its world significance)* (Moscow: Nauka, 1988), p. 200.
21 *Chekhov v vospominaniyakh sovremennikov (Chekhov in his contemporaries' memoirs)*, eds. N. L. Brodsky *et al.* (Moscow: GIKhL, 1952), p. 356.
22 *Novoye Vremya*, 2 May 1903.
23 Aleksey Diky, 'Zabyty zhanr' ('The forgotten genre'), in *Stati. Perepiska. Vospominaniya (Articles, correspondence and memoirs)* (Moscow: Iskusstvo, 1967), p. 195.
24 J. B. Priestley, *Anton Chekhov* (London: International Textbook Company, 1970), pp. 70–2.
25 'Grotesques', in *The Works of John Galsworthy. Abracadabra and other Satires* (London: William Heinemann Ltd., 1924), p. 177.

CHAPTER 6

Coping with the outlandish: the English response to Chekhov's plays *1911 – 1926*

Stephen le Fleming

Chekhov's assimilation into the English theatre is a cultural phenomenon difficult to overestimate: it is no exaggeration to talk of a process
of enlightenment. It was a painful process – one of accepting ideas
of theatre and of life that verged on the outrageous.

Reading what the English wrote about Chekhov in reviews of
his stories and plays, in literary criticism about him specifically
and about the short story and drama generally, we find ourselves
following a gradual evolution in awareness: the emergence of the
English in the twentieth century as an enlightened public is epitomized
in their response to Chekhov. He was for many intellectuals a focal
point of discussion, the catalyst for their reassessment of personal values
and attitudes to life. Chekhov came to be seen as the personification
of a civilized outlook.

Even if only part of this outline is valid it is still worth examining
the process of Chekhov's adoption in England; it will show us how
long it took for Chekhov to become 'anglicized' and it will illustrate
how a development in the theatre teaches us to look differently at
life and people in the real world. It will also show the progression
from reviewing to criticism – from relatively spontaneous uninformed
comment on a performance, to knowledgeable and informative
consideration of the writer.

To preserve some continuity in following the relationship between
the English and Chekhov the playwright we shall concentrate on
the theatre reviews in *The Times*, which were written by people
who knew the paper's responsibilities as a record and as an influence
on the success of a production and its cast. Their reviews were unsigned,
but at least some were presumably written by their chief drama
critics – Arthur Walkley up to 1926 and Charles Morgan from
1926 to 1939. We shall refer to these and intermittently to others.
They constitute a chorus of voices who, though not necessarily in

unison, were in the same key; reviewers and critics who were aspiring to comparable cultural levels.

It was 1911 before the Stage Society produced *The Cherry Orchard*. Although this was not the first production of a Chekhov play in Britain, it provides a convenient starting point of total incomprehension in the relationship between the English and Chekhov's full-length plays. This is evident in *The Times'* anonymous review. We are reminded by the reviewer of Dr Johnson's friend who considered foreigners fools simply because they weren't English; but, says the reviewer,

even so, it is highly improbable that they [the Russians] are such fools as they seem in the English version of Tchehov's comedy. The fact is, when actors are set to present alien types which they have never seen and which they can only imagine from the necessarily imperfect indications of a translation, they are bound to produce grotesques.[1]

The reviewer went on to bewail the inevitable loss of balance in translating a work of art which could well be harmonious in the original and which was seen by people who knew the life depicted in it. However, 'Mrs Edward Garnett's *Cherry Orchard* cannot but strike the English as something queer, outlandish, even silly.'[2]

Translation, inevitably, and the actors' unfamiliarity with 'types' whom the reviewer assumes to be 'alien', were to blame for the play's failure; true, there was a note of irony about English insularity, but in the end *The Times* brought its sights to bear on the play itself, sparing the cast: 'genuine comedy and scenes of pure pathos are mixed with knock-about farce. The players did their best; it was not their fault that the entertainment was not entertaining.'[3]

Other explanations for this failure included the audience's understandable ignorance about Russia and about Chekhov's aims as a dramatist, as well as their less understandable reluctance to learn. *The Daily Telegraph's* anonymous reviewer sympathized, perhaps not without irony: 'to be plunged, without any preparation whatsoever, into an atmosphere, a social life, a set of characters so different from those which we habitually meet, was, and must be, a shock to a well-regulated and conventional English mind'.[4]

A few days later the editor of the weekly *The Nation* took up Chekhov's cause in a stiff rejoinder to *The Times'* reviewer, whom he names as Mr Walkley, for his opinion that 'there is something inherently un-English in setting upon the stage what he calls "queer, outlandish, even silly" types of human beings'.[5] It was equally misleading of Walkley to dismiss the play's construction merely as:

a mixture of 'pure pathos' and 'genuine' comedy and 'knock-about farce': it is a weeping comedy ... It does vary between harsh and delicate effects; indeed its subject is so balanced in actual life, for a cause or a social class that falls by its own folly is by turns pathetic, merely unwise, and wildly ridiculous. Tchekov's irony is at its root a sad and profound sentiment.[6]

Yet the play was true to life itself which allows for comedy, farce, and tragedy as well as the 'riotous play of unknown forces over it all'.[7] So, unwittingly, *The Times* provoked the first critical defence of Chekhov in the English press: Chekhov's innovatory mixture of genres was recognized as true to life.

For Arnold Bennett, writing in the monthly *The New Age*, the play was historically true in presenting an average picture of Russian society, but the play's originality was artistic, rather than historical in any exalted sense:

in naturalism the play is assuredly an advance on any other play that I have seen in England. Its naturalism is positively daring. The author never hesitates to make his personages as ridiculous as in life they would be ... He has carried an artistic convention much nearer to reality and achieved another step in the revolution of the drama.[8]

Bennett qualifies his praise at the end, admitting that he does not think it a great play, although intensely original and interesting, and he finds the ending rather too theatrical.

Despite several attempts and some success on the part of reviewers to discover and articulate Chekhov's significance as an original playwright, it has to be said that this first London *Cherry Orchard* was considered at the time and subsequently a flop. It was not comparable to the fiasco of *The Seagull*'s première in St Petersburg in 1896, simply because the audience walked out rather than express their disappointment in the extrovert way that Miss Levkeyeva's fans did.

Already prominent in English reviews after the 1911 *Cherry Orchard* is one of the critical contradictions which will be so characteristic of Chekhov's reception: on the one hand his characters and background are seen as 'grotesques' and 'something queer, outlandish, even silly'; on the other, as historically typical and 'positively daring' in their naturalism. For some, at least, Chekhov's Russianness was still an enigma: that is to say, the characters were seen as incomprehensible in their exotic, feckless, and melancholic behaviour, and this was seen as alien and therefore 'Russian'. The English were presumed to be free from such futile inertia. As *The Times Literary Supplement* put it, reviewing George Calderon's translations of *The Seagull* and *The Cherry Orchard* published early in 1912: 'Will he attain to love and admiration in England? We believe not ... It is quite possible that impatience with the flabby people whom Tchekhof shows us yearning vaguely, talking glibly, suffering helplessly, may blind the public in general to the beauty of his work.'[9] The thank-goodness-we're-not-like-that syndrome slides uncomfortably close to jingoism in these pre-First World War comments on Chekhov's characters. The originality of Chekhov for an English audience lay at least partly in his demand that they recognize precisely that they were like that – an admission not easy for the builders of empire.

By the time Chekhov was next performed in England (*The Seagull*, Little Theatre in London, 31 March 1912), reviewers, though not perhaps cast, had assimilated Calderon's now famous introduction to his translations. Even *The Times* saw that subtlety of acting and coherence among the ensemble were required to convey the full meaning of the play, which the reviewer still implied was specifically Russian: 'he is concerned to show us a family, a social class, a nation'.[10] *The Daily Telegraph*'s reviewer, while acknowledging that 'like all fine art, it needs a very capable and enlightened interpretation', went on to make one of the first suggestions that Chekhov's concerns are with the characters and not specifically with Russian reality. Like earlier Russian critics, however, he was puzzled by their antics:

it is difficult to say what particular object Tchekhof had in view in writing the play. The story is distinctly subordinate to the characters; it is in the personages of the drama that both Tchekhof and ourselves find most interest ... Tchekhof does not allow himself to pass judgements on any of them. He tries to put them before us as he sees them; but whether they are good or bad, noble or mean, right or wrong, he will not or cannot tell us.[11]

Already some of the main ideas which would provide the key to opening Chekhov's mysteries had come into circulation. The importance of ensemble playing was recognized by several reviewers. In *The Saturday Review*, for instance, the novelist John Palmer wrote of this as a literary fact: 'as soon as we realize that the players, all and several, are hero of the piece, the play falls naturally into perfect form'.[12] Palmer also explained Chekhov's failure on the London stage by the absence in his plays of the kind of message which contemporary playgoers had come to expect: 'Tchekoff, not being a social missionary, will never become a watchword with reformers and social prophets.'[13]

Calderon's perceptive introduction had pointed, amongst other things, to one more quality of Chekhov's plays which the English still found difficult to accommodate within their notions of drama, namely the absence of clear motivation: 'the differentia of Tchekhoff is that the extraordinary moments which explode in pistol-shots are never the result of sudden causes, but are brought about by the cumulative tragedy of daily life; not ordinary daily life, but the life of men tragically situated, like Treplef, or Ivanof, or Uncle Vanya'.[14] *The Academy*'s anonymous reviewer, for one, found poor motivation of the characters a weakness in the play itself; a good play should begin with postulates from which the subsequent actions would follow: 'but this logical development is the essence of characterisation, which is the greatest of difficulties that the dramatist has to face; and it was in this very problem that Tchekof failed to convince'.[15] The reviewer fell back, albeit apologetically, on the strangeness of Russia for the English, 'a strangeness that is the outcome of the wide difference between the whole framework and basis of thought and emotion in Russia and England. The personal and social assumptions are drawn from quite different depths of human nature.'[16] Strangeness was still the keynote of *The Times*' review of *Uncle Vanya* which the Stage Society produced at the Aldwych Theatre, London, on 10 May 1914. However, strangeness now meant *artistic originality* rather than Russianness, and the disjointed dialogue was found recognizable rather than alien:

A very strange play it is, utterly opposed to all our English notions of playmaking, a play with unity of mood but without unity of action, a play of will-less people, futile people, drifters, just pottering on with their disappointed lives ... It is a world of talkers without listeners. This may be, for all we know, distinctively Russian, or distinctively Tchehovian, but it is also undeniably human.[17]

The first Chekhov play to be produced after the First World War was once again *The Seagull*. It opened on 1 June 1919 at the Theatre Royal, Haymarket, and *The Times* next day was, as usual, perturbed – this time by another Russian quality: 'these Russians of Chekhov's do strike one as a remarkably odd lot. They are like grown-up children, entirely without self-control, flaring up into sudden "tempers", and as abruptly cooling down again, all talking at once and no-one listening ... The play is really a picture, sombre, ironical, masterly of the solitariness of human lives in a crowd.'[18]

This seems to be the starting point for what was probably the most durable and pervasive misconception to affect Chekhov's plays in England – the assumption that characters who do not listen to one another are failing to communicate. The assertion that characters who know each other well and may be closely related could be isolated and lonely in each other's company, as opposed to being merely bored or unwilling to make concessions to each other's point of view, infected producers of Chekhov in England with a virus of despondency for the next 30 to 40 years. Far from helping to understand the Russians, this tells us something about the English: either they wanted plays which corresponded to their own mood after the First World War and on into the Depression, or they recognized a familiar trait in the characters' difficulties in sustaining dialogue, and thought they could ascribe this to 'these Russians'.

However, Chekhov was now confirmed as a modern dramatist whom any theatre or producer aspiring to be serious should consider attempting. On 7 March 1920 *The Three Sisters* opened at the Royal Court, whereupon *The Times* belaboured its general sense of despondency, for which it came up with the term 'spiritual dry-rot'; but in the end it decided that

strange to say it is not a depressing tale. It is pitiful. One gets an affection for these people, as for poor listless children; not a dislike, as for doleful and self-pitying adults. And the most impatient spectator could not fail to be lured into enjoyment of Tchekhov's magical selection of minute and significant touches and his masterly manner of arranging them, like separate notes and chords, into music with a dying fall of haunting beauty.[19]

'Atmosphere' was a point stressed in reviews of subsequent productions of Chekhov's plays. When *Uncle Vanya* was revived by the Stage Society at the Royal Court on 27 November 1921 under Komisarjevsky's direction, *The Times* noted that Chekhov's plays

are not deliriously gay. But they have a strange, morbid, hectic beauty ... They express, in terms of the theatre, the futility of existence, the 'cussedness' of things, frustrated lives, depression of spirit. But they express these things beautifully and, therefore, are not depressing ... The atmosphere – and if ever there was a play of 'atmosphere', this is – remains uncontaminatedly Russian, or rather, Chekovian. And it remains *one* atmosphere, an all-important point. For here it is the atmosphere that constitutes the unity of the play, its preservative from the mere haphazard incoherence which English disciples mistake for Chekovism.[20]

There was now a hiatus. Perhaps people were expecting Chekhov to sink without trace, and when J. B. Fagan's production of *The Cherry Orchard* ran for a week in May 1925 to shrinking houses at the Lyric Theatre, Hammersmith, in West London, these expectations still seemed reasonable. But the reviews had been good. *The Times* found the performance at the opening night intelligent, comparing it to the 'puzzle and fiasco' of the 1911 production; once having grasped the notion of atmosphere as something which had to be allowed past one's emotional defences, the English found Chekhov (and Russians generally) more comprehensible:

it must not be supposed that the play addresses itself to the intellect. It is a play of atmosphere, of mood, of those vague feelings which we English are reluctant to express and hesitate to acknowledge even to ourselves. The general atmosphere, the resultant impression of the whole, is one of the futility of life. We may say to comfort ourselves, 'Oh, but we are not so futile as these Russians'; yet it seems we have enough in common with them to feel the effect of Tchehov's picture.[21]

The reviewer went on to summarize the characters in recognizably English terms: Gayev, for example, 'can only talk, be rhetorically vapid and "flop" all over the place'.[22] Yet there was an intriguingly un-English quality about the absence of conflict, of action, and of a moral which now made this play viable in England. Francis Birrell in *The Nation and Athenaeum* found the play in some ways reminiscent of English comedy, but 'the whole play [is] held together by a single female character so violently un-English, so exaggeratedly Russian, that it must defeat almost any Englishwoman who tries to play it. The feckless, irresponsible, passionate Mme Ranevsky.'[23]

It was difficult to tell whether it was the Englishness or the Russianness of the play which appealed, though what these were depended on point of view. From the English point of view, while Englishness meant normality, Russianness was something illogical and unknowable, the product of a vast impenetrable land. Yet once Chekhov's acceptability on the English stage had registered, he permeated the English consciousness to the point where even his settings seemed familiar.

Ashley Dukes saw the situation of the mortgaged manor house as typically English and in the odd characters who inhabited it 'a picture of true humanity, which is better than local colour'.[24] This amounted to a claim on Chekhov for his Englishness and a denial of his Russianness: the house and orchard could be in Wiltshire, while the characters, though idiosyncratic, are universal.

After the 1925 *Cherry Orchard* English reviewers and audiences had to recognize that Chekhov had been attempting something quite new in the theatre. The reviewers recorded the process of recognition step by step, building up awareness in the public at large of the criteria appropriate to Chekhov's drama, groping for the outlines of individual performances, and providing some of the preliminaries for serious criticism which would establish Chekhov's place in world literature with authority.

The distinction between reviewing, which records the impressions of an intelligent member of the audience, and criticism, which analyses and makes informed comment, is exemplified by J.B. Priestley's review of an edition of Chekhov's letters published in 1925. He quotes Chekhov's advice to 'write with more phlegm, coolly' – in other words, that no writer should let his feelings show in his writing – and linked this to the apparent indifference towards one another of the characters in Chekhov's plays:

a play has no narrator, to show phlegm at more emotional moments, but it has a number of characters brought together. Suppose one character is feeling something very deeply, wistfully touching on some secret dream, then if the other personage or personages display inattention or indifference, busy with their own thoughts and affairs, the same effect will be produced in the minds of the audience. If no one will show any interest, will be touched, then they, the audience, will show interest, will be touched. And that explains, of course, what may have puzzled so many people who saw the recent production of *The Cherry Orchard*, it explains why its characters seem so independent, so indifferent and inattentive to one another.[25]

Priestley with his writer's experience argues an original insight which, if not startlingly profound, is more perceptive than the reviewer's usual generalized observations, and does contribute to our understanding of Chekhov's plays. Reviewing at this level aspires to criticism; Priestley can analyse a fellow writer's style without scholarly knowledge of Russian literature. Indeed, professional writers, or people who would become professional writers, were prominent among Chekhov's favourable reviewers in England – Arnold Bennett in 1911, Frank

Swinnerton and Virginia Woolf in 1920, and, presumably, Charles Morgan in at least some of *The Times'* anonymous pieces.

Even *The Times'* reviewer, however, was not expected to subject his readers to solid critical assessments of plays and their authors. He began his notice on the Little Theatre's production of *The Seagull*, which opened on 19 October 1925, with the exclamation 'What an evening of strange sensations!' and explained his bewilderment at the exultation he felt, despite the prevailing sense of futility, by his having gained 'not a new, but a deeper vision of life, and entry into the more recondite secrets of the human heart'.[26] The reviewer took this lyrical approach even further in his comments on Komisarjevsky's *Three Sisters*, matching his own style to the play's content: 'Irina, from the other window, looks out upon life with a gaiety upon which her years have cast as yet but the edge of the shadow that is fallen upon her sisters.'[27] The reviewer sees each of the characters standing at a different stage in their journey of disillusionment through life: 'when the play is done, still their journey is not ended. We have watched them march a few miles in the deepening shadow. That is all. But in spirit and in mind we have marched with them.'[28]

By now there was no suggestion of anything alien or outlandish in Chekhov. There was no talk of emptiness or meaninglessness, since the play's poetic meaning had been clearly evoked: there was no moral, no lesson of any kind, simply a hymn to life. Chekhov's name was not mentioned anywhere in the review, his authorship by now being assumed to be sufficiently well known to readers of *The Times*.

The Chekhov play, familiar, assimilated, anglicized, was now in danger of becoming a set piece in which the audience concerned itself with points in the actors' performances rather than with the 'poet'. Reviewing *The Cherry Orchard* at the Barnes Theatre on 28 September 1926, *The Times* noted that such a response 'means missing more in Tchekov's case than in most others, for he was preeminently not a writer of parts for actors but of plays that depend for their effect upon a slow and delicate gathering together of minor impressions into a perfected whole'.[29]

Reviewers, it would seem, and at least some of the audience, had learnt to appreciate Chekhov. When Chekhov arrived on the English stage reviewers and audiences expected, as in Russia in the 1890s, a social message from their drama. The new, unstilted drama of Ibsen, and even more so of Shaw, addressed itself to 'serious' issues; confronted with Chekhov, reviewers in England, as in Russia, were frustrated: if there were any conclusions to be drawn from Chekhov's plays about relations between master and servant, merchant and landowner, or the problem of alcohol addiction among teachers' wives, they tended to contradict what was expected of a progressive, socially committed writer.

Reviewers looked for some holds on the amorphous enormity of Russian life, but found a thoroughly *English* absence of drama. The gradual recognition by English theatregoers that Chekhov's plays do have something to tell us about civilization was reflected, and is recorded, in the reviewers' tentative, bewildered, curious, and eventually confident and patronizing responses, which denoted Chekhov's arrival as a classic of the English stage.

Notes

1 *The Times*, 30 May 1911.
2 *Ibid.*
3 *Ibid.*
4 *The Daily Telegraph*, 30 May 1911.
5 H. W. M.[assingham], 'A Russian comedy of manners', *The Nation*, 3 June 1911, p. 359.
6 *Ibid.*, p. 360.
7 *Ibid.*
8 Jacob Tonson (Arnold Bennett), 'Books and persons', *The New Age*, 9:6, 8 June 1911, p. 132.
9 'Anton Tchekhof', *Times Literary Supplement*, 1 February 1912, p. 45.
10 *The Times*, 1 April 1912.
11 *The Daily Telegraph*, 1 April 1912.
12 John Palmer, 'Tchekoff in London', *The Saturday Review*, 13 April 1912, p. 454.
13 *Ibid.*
14 *Tchekhoff. Two plays. The Seagull. The Cherry Orchard*, translated with an introduction and notes by George Calderon (London: Grant-Richards, 1912), p. 18.
15 'The Adelphi Play Society', *The Academy*, 13 April 1912, p. 471.
16 *Ibid.*
17 *The Times*, 12 May 1914.
18 *The Times*, 3 June 1919.
19 *The Times*, 9 March 1920.
20 *The Times*, 29 November 1921.
21 *The Times*, 26 May 1925.
22 *Ibid.*

23 Francis Birrell, 'Chekhov arrives at Hammersmith', *The Nation and Athenaeum*, 30 May 1925, pp. 267–8.
24 Ashley Dukes, 'The stage of the day', *Illustrated Sporting and Dramatic News*, 6 June 1925, p. 632.
25 J. B. Priestley, 'Chekhov as critic', *The Saturday Review*, 17 October 1925, p. 446.
26 *The Times*, 20 October 1925.
27 *The Times*, 17 February 1926.
28 *Ibid.*
29 *The Times*, 29 September 1926.

CHAPTER 7

Komisarjevsky's 1926 'Three Sisters'

Robert Tracy

British recognition of Chekhov as a major playwright dates from the London performances of his plays which Theodore Komisarjevsky directed in the nineteen-twenties, and especially from his 1926 *Three Sisters* at the Barnes Theatre. Although there were various literary and even social reasons for Chekhov's success with British audiences in the twenties and thirties, after he had failed to please them before the First World War, Komisarjevsky deserves much of the credit for the change. But he also deserves some blame. His productions adapted Chekhov's plays to make them acceptable to British tastes and expectations, as Komisarjevsky understood them. His audiences saw a selectively anglicized Chekhov, who would not startle them by being exotically Russian or by sympathetically anticipating the October Revolution.

What exactly did Komisarjevsky *do* to *Three Sisters* to make Chekhov succeed with British audiences? What did he alter, what did he delete, and what did he add?

Let us begin with his alterations, especially those affecting the portrayals of characters throughout the play. Komisarjevsky's most striking change was to transform Baron Tuzenbakh (John Gielgud) from an earnest, drab young officer to 'a neurotic Adonis who might well have fascinated Irina',[1] removing or altering references to him as ugly or plain. Chekhov's 'It's true he's not handsome' became 'It's true he's not *clever*.'[2] Gielgud has speculated about this change:

he cut all references to the Baron being an ugly man – which is Tchechov's reason why Irina cannot love him – and made me play the part in a juvenile make-up, with a smart uniform and side-whiskers, looking as handsome as possible. I have never been able to discover why he did this – but I have a suspicion that he felt that a juvenile love-interest was essential in any play that was to appeal to an English audience. He persisted in casting the part in this way in every subsequent revival ... and it was extraordinary to me that not one of the critics, who went into ecstasies over the beauty of the production, noticed this very marked divergence from the express stage-directions and dialogue of the author.[3]

The result was to make Tuzenbakh precisely the handsome, romantic lover Irina presumably hopes for, and suggest that she is perversely incapable of recognizing this. Her perfectly understandable reasons for not loving him, and for seeing her eventual acceptance of him as an abandonment of her dreams of romance, are removed, to make her appear frivolous and incapable of love. Making Tuzenbakh desirable skews Irina's muted reaction to his death, which seems cold.

Komisarjevsky also made Vershinin more romantic, diminishing his 'comedy side'[4] as a garrulous bore – though when Komisarjevsky revived the play in 1929, *The Times* reviewer noted the 'neatly laid stress on the self-winding mechanism behind Vershinin's oft-repeated speech'.[5] The romantic treatment of Vershinin made his affair with Masha seem exciting and glamorous, for Ivor Brown a 'glowing at the heart of the play', Masha and Vershinin 'nobly kindled by the flame'.[6] Even Solyony was apparently romantic rather than, as Chekhov wrote the part, at once sinister and pathetic. By making the men more attractive, Komisarjevsky turned Masha and Irina into romantic heroines, adding a false numinosity to their relationships. One reviewer saw Masha as a failed Gounod heroine, and another compared her to Camille.[7]

Komisarjevsky deliberately altered the play's period, making it more remote in time and so more picturesque. His prompt-book and programmes specify the time as between May 1870 (Act 1) and August 1872 (Act 4). Act 2 takes place in January 1871, Act 3 in October 1871. Chekhov does not specify a time, but clearly meant the action to be contemporary; that is, about 1900. Constantin Nabokoff noted the anachronism of Fedotik's Kodak, and described the women's costumes as those of the 1840s;[8] Gielgud suggests that this was to make those costumes more becoming. A comparatively recent but outmoded style can look dowdy, as the dress of 1900 might look to a 1926 audience; a remoter style can seem charming. Gielgud describes the sisters as wearing 'the bustles and chignons of the eighties, which looked very attractive and certainly heightened their picturesque appearance'.[9] This may reflect Komisarjevsky's theories about the sentimental needs of British audiences. But he may also

1   John Gielgud as Tuzenbakh and Beatrix Thomson as Irina in *Three Sisters*,
Barnes 1926

have worked to prevent any effort to relate the play to recent events
in Russia. By moving the action back 30 years, and cutting many
of Irina's and Tuzenbakh's speeches about their need to work, he
made it unlikely that the play would be seen as anticipating the
Revolution in any way.[10]

Komisarjevsky also altered the settings. In Chekhov's text, Act I
takes place in the Prozorov drawing-room, a spacious dignified room
with columns. The dining-room is visible beyond, the table laid for

2   Ion Swinley (Vershinin), Margaret Swallow (Masha), Mary Sheridan (Olga),
and Beatrix Thomson (Irina), in Act 1 of *Three Sisters*, Barnes 1926

a festive luncheon. Act 4 is set outside the house, in a garden, with
a view of the trees Natasha wants to cut down, and of the distant
river beside which Tuzenbakh will die. We are outside at last, with
an initial sense that Irina at least is to escape into a wider world.

Komisarjevsky used the same set for Acts 1 and 4, a kind of compromise set combining indoors and outdoors. Downstage was a
broad veranda from left to right across the whole stage. The drawing-
room was upstage, with the dining-room beyond. The two areas
were separated – and yet interrelated – by a broad entrance and
a series of large French windows. 'He arranged the first and last acts
on a sort of terrace', Gielgud recalls:

Through big open windows, stretching right across the stage, one could see the room within – the dining-table (to seat thirteen) angled off-stage into the wings. In front, a clothes-line on one side and the shadow of a tree on the other (a branch tied with a piece of string to the front of a strong lamp in the wings was responsible for this effect) gave the feeling of outdoors.[11]

Komisarjevsky used the upstage room more or less as Chekhov's stage directions suggest, using the dining-room as a place where – until all go to lunch – characters can withdraw from the group and yet remain visible and audible. But he also had to use it for certain important actions – Vershinin's arrival, the presentation of the silver samovar, the luncheon itself – which were consequently played at some distance from the audience, though clearly visible through the broad windows and door.

The veranda helped to establish the springtime atmosphere of Act 1 as well as the autumnal mood of 4. It offered the actors plenty of space for movement on the Barnes' tiny stage, and Komisarjevsky kept them moving, making them seem more energetically British, and perhaps more nervous, more highly strung. At times he also forced them to converse while far apart. The play opened with Olga seated Centre Right behind a window, Masha on a bench Down Left, reading, Irina Up Right at the dining-table, which she is helping to set. Her bustle with knives and forks is not the pensive brooding Chekhov suggests. In the text, Irina's lack of movement comments ironically on her rhapsody about hard work a few moments later and Olga's tart comment about her habit of lying in bed. Here she is busy and helpful. Her eagerness to work is endorsed rather than undercut.

Komisarjevsky's use of the same set for 4 was probably dictated by his budget.[12] It represents an effort to save the most important elements of Chekhov's two different settings. If so, this mixture of salvaging and discarding can be seen as a kind of metaphor for the production, and for Komisarjevsky's approach to Chekhov.

In Act 4 this re-used set weakened two very important statements that Chekhov made by requiring an outdoor setting: Natasha has inexorably taken over the house, room by room, throughout the play, so that the sisters have been excluded, an exclusion Komisarjevsky underlined by removing some of the drawing-room furniture in Act 2, to re-appear in the sisters' crowded attic room in 3. He reminded us of Natasha and her children in 4 by stretching a clothes-line with children's clothing Down Left. 'The birch trees on one side of the house are for apostrophising', James Agate wrote; 'on the other side hangs out the clothing of Natasha's babies'.[13] But the trees and vistas Chekhov indicated for 4 show for the first time a larger world, and so imply the possibility of escape, to make the closure of that possibility more poignant. With the sisters already outside for part of Act 1, this visual emphasis on their expulsion is muted. We need them securely inside at the start. Restricting everyone to Downstage in 4 must have seemed crowded; one critic complained that it 'necessitated "business" which spoils the tension of the scene'.[14]

When we turn to Komisarjevsky's deletions, our sense that the play has been simplified, romanticized, sentimentalized, and anglicized is reinforced. He retained Natasha's comic bad French in Act 2, but made her less human, more vindictive in 4 by cutting it. Kulygin has his pedantic Latin tags in Act 1, but Komisarjevsky removed them in 4, and the pointless school-boy anecdotes that go with them, perhaps fearing that the audience would not take Kulygin seriously enough in his brave little scene with the false beard.

Komisarjevsky eliminated Fedotik's appearance in Act 3, dancing and laughing hysterically about losing everything in the fire, a well-observed scene of behaviour under stress. Komisarjevsky may have considered it un-British, too frenzied. He also cut Tuzenbakh's moving request for coffee before he leaves for the duel, perhaps because it did not seem clearly connected to the mood at the play's end. He removed the re-entrance of Kulygin and Vershinin at the end of Act 2, and their disappointment at not finding a party. More seriously, he deleted Tuzenbakh's early comment that Vershinin's wife is peculiar, and all Vershinin's remarks about her strange behaviour, which partially explain his readiness to have an affair. Komisarjevsky even cut Natasha's walk across the stage with a candle near the end of Act 3, and Masha's hostile 'She walks about as though it were she had set fire to the town', a scene Chekhov compared to Lady Macbeth's sleep-walking, and wanted to be 'terrifying'.[15]

As the end of the play approaches, Komisarjevsky's cuts became more drastic, in an effort to speed the action and avoid any sense of a dying fall. Just after Kulygin's false beard scene, and Natasha's last sweeping progress across the stage, Chebutykin returns from the duel. As he enters we hear the band off, playing John Philip Sousa's rousing march, 'Under the Double Eagle'. Chebutykin delivers his bad news, and Olga crosses to embrace Irina. After

Masha's brief speech – briefer in Komisarjevsky's version – Irina loses about half of her final speech, with most of the references to work deleted. Olga's long speech is essentially intact, but Komisarjevsky lets her say, 'If we only knew' once, not four times. His notes suggest that he thought of dropping the phrase entirely. He cuts her last speech, twice repeating the phrase, and instead ends thus:

> IRINA ~~(lays her head on OLGA's bosom)~~. A time will come when everyone will know ~~what all this is for~~ (Pause) why there is all this misery, why are we suffering ... ~~there will be no mysteries and, meanwhile, we have got to live ... we have got to work, only to work~~! Tomorrow I shall go alone; I shall teach in the school, and ~~I will~~ give all my life to those ~~to whom it may be of use~~. Perhaps need it ~~Now it's autumn; soon winter will come and cover us with snow, and I will work, I will work~~.
>
> OLGA (embraces both her sisters). Listen to The music. It sounds ~~is~~ so gay, so confident, ~~and~~ one longs for life! ~~O my God~~! Time will pass, and we shall go away for ever, ~~and~~ we shall be forgotten, our faces will be forgotten, our voices, and how many there were of us; but our sufferings will pass into joy for those who will live after us, ~~happiness and~~ peace will be established upon earth,
FADE and ~~they~~ happy people will remember kindly and bless ~~those~~
MUSIC ~~who have lived before~~ them who have suffered ... ~~Oh~~, dear sisters,
FLICKER our life is not ended yet. We shall live! The music is so gay, so joyful, and it seems as though a little more and we shall know what we are living for, why we are suffering ... If we only knew – ~~if we only knew!~~
> ~~(The music grows more and more subdued; KULIGIN, cheerful and smiling, brings the hat and cape; ANDREY pushes the perambulator in which BOBIK is sitting.)~~
> ~~TCHEBUTYKIN (humming softly). 'Tarara boom-dee-ay!' (Reads his paper.) It doesn't matter, it doesn't matter.~~
> ~~OLGA If we only knew, if we only knew!~~
> (The music sounds more and more distant)
> DOCTOR (humming softly while reading his paper)
> 'Ta-ra-ra-boom-dee-ay!
BAND I was then young and gay ...'
OFF (Continues the tune, whistling it softly)
> KULIGIN, beaming, brings Mary's hat from the house while the CURTAIN COMES DOWN SLOWLY.

Komisarjevsky drastically cut or completely eliminated the 'philosophical' speeches of Vershinin and Tuzenbakh, presumably to make these characters not seem boring, and so make them more probable as romantic lovers. In Act I, recalling the sisters' mother leads to

Vershinin's first long speech, about how people in the future will regard us. Komisarjevsky shortened it by half:

> VERSHININ Yes. They will forget us. (Violin starts) ~~Such is our~~ ~~fate, there is no help for it.~~ It can't be helped! VERSHININ crosses to Right Centre). What seems to us serious, significant, very important, will one day be forgotten or ~~will~~ seem unimportant
> VIOLIN (a pause sits bench Right). ~~And it's curious that we can't possibly~~
> PLAYING ~~tell what exactly will be considered great and important, and~~ ~~what will seem paltry and ridiculous. Did not the discoveries of~~ ~~Copernicus or Columbus, let us say, seem useless and ridiculous~~ ~~at first, while the nonsensical writings of some wiseacre seemed~~ ~~true?~~ And it may be that our present life, which we accept so readily, will in time seem queer, uncomfortable, ~~not sensible,~~ ~~not clean enough,~~ stupid, perhaps even sinful . . .
> TUZENBACH (Moves from Left Centre behind window to Centre Stage between OLGA and MASHA; at this point, OLGA, TUZENBACH,
> VIOLIN MASHA, and IRINA stand in a row extending Right-Left, from
> PLAYING Up Centre to Down Left; SOLYONY is apart, Up Left; VERSHININ and CHEBUTYKIN are seated on bench Down Right, VERSHININ to CHEBUTYKIN's left). Who knows? Perhaps our age will be called a great one and remembered with respect. ~~Now we have~~
> VIOLIN ~~no torture chamber, no executions, no invasions, but at the same~~
> PLAYING ~~time how much unhappiness there is!~~

Vershinin's next long speech, about the seminal role of a few educated people, is heavily cut, as is his Act 2 speech about his reading and his hope that his descendants will be happy, and his last 'philosophical' speech in 4.

Komisarjevsky usually cut or altered specific Russian references. When Ferapont tells Andrey that two thousand people were frozen to death (Act 4), they freeze 'in Norway, or Iceland', not, as Chekhov wrote, in Petersburg or Moscow. He has heard this from the porter 'at the Midland bank'. Komisarjevsky dropped Chebutykin's 'Balzac was married at Berdichev' (Act 2), the *cheremsha/chekhartma* dispute, and even the word *Russian* when Vershinin praises 'the splendid healthy Russian climate' (Act 2). Whenever possible, characters' names are replaced by Colonel, Doctor, Baron, while patronymics and affectionate diminutives – Olya, Andryusha – disappear.

What did Komisarjevsky add to make his production original, and adapt it to his ideas of British taste? First of all, he added a good deal of stage business, to make the characters appear energetic, even sprightly. He kept his actors almost constantly in motion, often having one deliver a line, cross the stage, then re-cross. In Act I, for example, Solyony is seated Up Right when Vershinin begins to reminisce about Moscow. As Vershinin talks about the gloomy bridge, Solyony rises, comes Down Right, and stops behind a window. There he delivers his enigmatic 'if the station had been near it would not have been so far, and if it is far, it's because it is not near'. Then he crosses to Up Left and sits alone at the luncheon table during the 'philosophical' speeches of Vershinin and Tuzenbakh. He rises to deliver his 'Chook, chook, chook' remark, then returns to his earlier position Up Right. This is a lot of movement, using most of the playing area, to deliver two brief and separated lines. But it does emphasize Solyony's restlessness and his outsider role, his inability to be part of a group.

Masha responds to Vershinin's second 'philosophical' speech, here quite brief, with movement. At his last line, 'And you complain that you know too much', she rises from her bench Down Right, crosses to Up Centre, puts her hat on the piano, and sits on the piano-stool. 'Vershinin gazes after her and steps up slightly' closer to her. She rises and moves to a chair Up Right Centre; Vershinin takes her place on the stool.

When Kulygin enters in Act I, he comes in Down Right, crosses to Centre to greet Irina and present his book, then turns and shakes hands with Solyony (Up Right), Tuzenbakh (Down Right), kisses Masha (Up Centre), then shakes hands with Vershinin at Right Centre. As Kulygin gives Irina the book, Tuzenbakh moves from behind the window Down Right onto the veranda to sit in front of the same window, and Vershinin is moving from Up Left to Right Centre.

Komisarjevsky apparently stressed movement to combat the notion that Chekhov's characters were passive, lethargic. Even in later acts, with the mood growing ever more subdued, the characters continue strong and constant movements. In Act 4, Chebutykin, fairly static earlier, is unexpectedly active, perhaps to make him more sympathetic by suggesting he is uneasy about the duel.

One or two details of stage business are worth noting. At the end of Act I, Natasha dashes from the table after being teased. Andrey follows her Down Right and they embrace, an action made more emphatic when Fedotik snaps a picture of them embracing. In Act 2, Natasha's refusal to admit the mummers is important. Komisarjevsky did bring them on stage for a moment, among them Solyony disguised as a bear. After they leave he slips back, frightening Irina, who is alone; he removes his bear mask for his threatening avowal of love for her. The costume accentuates his uncanny and intimidating role throughout the play.

One of Komisarjevsky's critics complained about his 'obsession of strange lighting for the sake of pictorial effect when it obscures the drama'.[16] Here he was able to suggest a sunny spring day in Act 1, a snowy evening in 2, the glow of the burning town in 3, autumn in 4. He was also able to achieve subtler effects. At the end of 3 we are in the attic room which Olga and Irina share, sleeping behind screens. Irina is close to tears at the news that the brigade will leave. Both sisters are behind their screens, invisible to the audience:

> IRINA Then we shall be alone. <u>Pause.</u> ~~Olya!~~ Olga!
> OLGA Well?
> IRINA My dear, my darling, I <u>consent</u> ~~respect the baron, I think highly of him, he is a fine man~~ – I will marry <u>the baron</u> ~~him, I consent,~~ only let us go to Moscow! ~~I entreat you, do let us go! There's nothing in the world better than Moscow! Let us go, Olya! Let us go!~~
> OLGA <u>Darling! Do let us go! (Sobs).</u>
> CURTAIN <u>moderately slow.</u>

'The younger sister's flood of passion is not yet stilled', James Agate wrote, 'and as you listen to the last of its ebb you see the giant shadows of these two figures of grief thrown by the candle upon the upper wall and ceiling'.[17] The hugely projected embracing shadows are at once a striking visual correlative for the closeness of their relationship, and for the real shadows that are about to engulf them.

Komisarjevsky's final innovation was to bring Protopopov (here Petrov) on stage. In the text he is a powerful unseen presence, Natasha's lover, perhaps the father of her second child, Andrey's employer, and eventually, as mortgage holder, the owner of the house. But Komisarjevsky cast the role and brought him on with Natasha in Act 4, just after Kulygin describes the quarrelsome encounter between Solyony and Tuzenbakh: '<u>NATASHA and PETROV enter Up Right and sit at table Up Right. KULIGIN up to them, shakes hands with PETROV</u>'. Petrov stays there while Natasha plays 'The Maiden's Prayer', and Irina draws our attention to his presence ('he has come again to-day'); later Andrey complains about the noise and laughter from Natasha and Petrov inside the house, which the audience could hear.

THE BABY IN THE CASE.

Mr. Douglas Burbidge (Andrey Prozorov). "You must take my word for it that there's an infant inside this."

3   Cartoon of Andrey (Douglas Burbidge) in Act 4 of *Three Sisters*, Barnes 1926

One further aspect of Komisarjevsky's *Three Sisters* remains to be mentioned, namely his effort to avoid the gloom and funereal pace of earlier Chekhov productions. He did not strive for comic effect, but lightened the play by speeding it up. Here he conformed to Chekhov's own wishes: the playwright often complained about the slow pace of Stanislavsky's productions.[18]

Komisarjevsky may have been a little too eager to universalize, to simplify, to romanticize, to sentimentalize. Nevertheless, his work at the Barnes with *Three Sisters* and Chekhov's other plays made it possible for them to be accepted and eventually cherished by British playgoers, and prepared the way for their admission into the theatrical canon.

Notes

1 *Spectator*, 27 February 1926.
2 Komisarjevsky's prompt book for the production. The prompt book is a black leatherette notebook with lined pages, into which the printed text of Constance Garnett's translation is pasted. It is part of the Komisarjevsky Collection in the Theatre Collection, Houghton Library, Harvard University, and is quoted by permission of the Harvard Theatre Collection. In the present article underlined words or passages are Komisarjevsky's additions to, or alterations of, the Garnett text. Words or passages he deleted are shown thus: ~~what all this is for.~~
3 John Gielgud, *Early Stages* (New York: Macmillan, 1939), p.107. 'To suit the public's taste, life on the English stage had to be shown through a mist of loveliness' (Theodore Komisarjevsky, *Myself and the Theatre* (New York: Dutton, 1930), p.67). 'He is bitter and cynical about the English stage and the English public', Gielgud noted (p.104). In an interview (Northfield, Minnesota, November 1958), Gielgud suggested to me that Komisarjevsky's wandering life allowed him to use in one city tricks he had observed in another: Stanislavsky's devices in London, Meyerhold's in Paris, Jouvet's in New York. This damaged his artistic integrity. As he relied more and more on such tricks, he came to despise audiences for being impressed by what he knew was not original.
4 Gielgud, *Early Stages*, p.108.
5 Victor Emeljanow, ed., *Chekhov: the Critical Heritage* (London: Routledge and Kegan Paul, 1981), p.361.
6 *Ibid.*, p.302.
7 *Ibid.*, p.300.
8 *Ibid.*, p.311.
9 Gielgud, *Early Stages*, p.107.
10 Komisarjevsky may have recalled Basil Macdonald Hastings' comments on *The Cherry Orchard* in the *Daily Express* (26 May 1925): 'Lenin achieved something after all. He wiped out of existence all of the characters in Tchehov's plays ... thanks to the Soviet, a great deal of absurd material must perish.' J.B. Fagan, who produced *The Cherry Orchard*, placed Hastings' notice on the posters beside James Agate's favourable review, urging people to see the play and decide which critic was right.
11 Gielgud, *Early Stages*, p.106.
12 *Ibid.*
13 James Agate, *The Contemporary Theatre, 1926* (London: Chapman and Hall, 1927), p.58.
14 Emeljanow, *The Critical Heritage*, p.362.

15 M.N. Stroyeva, 'Rezhissura K.S. Stanislavskogo v chekhovskikh spektaklyakh MKhT ('Chayka', 'Dyadya Vanya,' 'Tri sestry' 1898–1901)' ('K.S. Stanislavsky as director of Chekhov at the Moscow Art Theatre (*The Seagull, Uncle Vanya, Three Sisters,* 1898–1901)'), in *K.S. Stanislavsky, Teatralnoye nasledstvo: materialy, pisma, issledovaniya (K.S. Stanislavsky, Theatrical heritage: materials, letters, research)* (Moscow: Izdatelstvo AN SSSR, 1955), I, p. 659.

16 Emeljanow, *The Critical Heritage,* p. 299.

17 Agate, *The Contemporary Theatre,* p. 57. See also Gielgud, *Early Stages,* pp. 106–7.

18 E.g., Chekhov to Olga Knipper 29 March 1904, on the MKhT *Cherry Orchard*: 'Stanislavsky in Act 4 acts disgustingly, so that it drags painfully ... He makes the act, which ought to last twenty minutes maximum, run for forty.'

CHAPTER 8

Peggy Ashcroft and Chekhov

Gordon McVay

My whole life has been spent seeking to be part of a permanent company. A permanent company has always been my ideal ...

Peggy Ashcroft, 1971[1]

Chekhov's work is totally based on ensemble, completely orchestrated ...

Peggy Ashcroft, 1960[2]

Peggy Ashcroft's Chekhovian début, in Komisarjevsky's 1936 production of *The Seagull*, crowned a triumphant decade for herself as an actress, for Chekhov as a dramatist accepted in Britain, and for Komisarjevsky as his outstanding interpreter.

Ashcroft (1907–1991) had witnessed the British discovery of Chekhov. As a first-year student at Elsie Fogerty's drama school, she avidly read Stanislavsky's *My Life in Art* (1924), with its account of the birth of the Moscow Arts Theatre and the historic Chekhov productions of 1898–1904. Stanislavsky's book 'quickly became Peggy's Bible' – it 'demanded of the actor dedication, concentration, imagination and a systematic approach to work', and demonstrated that 'great things in theatre are only achieved by the shared convictions of permanent companies: something that became the central tenet of Peggy's faith'.[3]

In 1925 she saw her first Chekhov play, when J. B. Fagan's production of *The Cherry Orchard*, with Gielgud as Trofimov, transferred from Oxford to the Lyric, Hammersmith. Gielgud made the 'most devastating impression' on her,[4] while the play seemed 'much more real' than any other she had seen, and the characters 'more alive and full'.[5]

An even greater revelation was Theodore Komisarjevsky's Chekhov season at the Barnes Theatre in 1926. In *Uncle Vanya*, 'a brilliant production, tremendously moving',* Ashcroft remembered most vividly Jean Forbes-Robertson's Sonya (*CC*). *Three Sisters* was 'brilliant', even though Ashcroft was extremely puzzled by Gielgud's Tuzenbakh – 'a kind of handsome juvenile'* – and horrified by Komisarjevsky's explanation that the English could not have understood Tuzenbakh as actually written by Chekhov (*CC*).

This early exposure to Chekhov convinced Ashcroft that 'there *are* no plays like Chekhov's plays' (*CC*): 'It opened new windows on what theatre could be about – its reality, its poetry, its comedy ... So there was the Chekhov world which ... one longed to enter and try to perform' (*CC*). 'Then I knew that – apart from always wanting to play Shakespeare – I would most like to play in Chekhov.'*

Ten years elapsed, however, before Ashcroft entered the 'Chekhov world'. After her professional début in 1926, she played some forty parts, manifesting a touching innocence and vulnerability, integrity and purity. Her Juliet at the New Theatre (from October 1935) was hailed as a 'flawless miracle', and established her as a 'star'.[6] Her Chekhovian breakthrough came in 1936 when Gielgud invited her to play Nina in *The Seagull*, directed by her ex-husband, Komisarjevsky.[7]

'THE SEAGULL' AT THE NEW THEATRE (20 MAY 1936)

During the previous quarter-century *The Seagull* had gradually gained acceptance with British audiences, and was ranked in 1936 'among the supreme masterpieces of the theatre'.[8] Komisarjevsky's 'endlessly beautiful production'[9] proved an immediate success, leading one reviewer to suggest that Chekhov 'will begin to rival Shakespeare as the West End's new best-seller'.[10]

Gielgud recalls: 'This was the first Chekhov production in the West End to be given the full honours of a star cast and expensive décor.'[11] Komisarjevsky firmly believed that 'the ensemble of the actors ... makes a Theatre and not the producer' and that actors and producer must share a 'mutual sympathetic understanding'.[12] A journalist watched him rehearse *The Seagull* in early May:

He is the quietest of producers. I have never heard him give an actor an 'intonation', or say how a line should be spoken. He will discuss what the character is thinking or feeling, and leave it to the actor to work out. But at the end of a few weeks with him there is more underlying unity and rhythm in everything that happens on the stage than most other producers approach.[13]

After only three or four weeks rehearsal (*CC*), this 'unity' had been attained. 'Here is British acting at its best: balanced, creative and individual, yet devoted to the dramatist's ends'.[14] 'It was a wonderful cast',* said Peggy Ashcroft, and the subsidiary parts were almost universally praised.

The major quartet proved more controversial. Edith Evans' Arkadina was 'terrific in its peacock vanity' (Brown[1]), but struck some as too heartless. Ashcroft found Edith Evans 'unforgettable': 'She was wonderfully comic, totally sort of megalomaniac, selfish, foolish.'* Stephen Haggard's Konstantin was sensitively drawn, if perhaps slightly monotonous, but Gielgud's Trigorin split the critics. Gielgud recalls that Komisarjevsky insisted he play Trigorin as a 'smartly dressed, *blasé* gigolo'.[15] Ashcroft commented laconically: 'Komis, probably taking into account John's personality, made him a dapper, fashionable writer. You can take it or leave it, can't you?'*

As the fourth member of the leading quartet, Peggy Ashcroft approached her task with trepidation:

I was deeply insecure and terrified at the prospect of playing Nina, because not only is it a gigantic role but I knew that Komis's sister had been the original Nina and I had a photograph of her and reverenced her memory very much ... It's a colossally difficult part because you have to encompass the young girl and then her disillusionment and desolation at the end.*

Gielgud describes her during actual performances, sitting alone in the wings with a shawl over her head, 'working herself up for her entrance in the big hysterical scene at the end of the play'.[16] Ashcroft later confessed, with a laugh: 'I used to take a sip of brandy before I went on in the fourth act, which was a very immoral thing to do ... Because I was so insecure.'* Encouragement from Jacques Copeau helped her to feel confidence, and to play the last act with enjoyment.*

The result was a triumph achieved in adversity. Critics acclaimed her: 'Miss Ashcroft has done nothing better than her Nina; the part is perfect in its growth from the dewy innocence of the first acts to the pale, storm-pelted desperation of the last' (Brown[1]). 'Miss Ashcroft's Nina has an enchanting freshness in the early scenes, and her tragic return has the supreme quality of being indeed not the coming of a stranger, but the return of the girl we have known, changed by suffering but not obliterated by it, so that what she was is visible always through what she has become' (*The Times*). In production photographs,[17] Ashcroft's Nina looks delightful: pigtailed, pure, serene in Acts 1–3, short-haired and strained in Act 4.

Her performance was deeply moving. 'She speaks the lines of Constantin's play with a charming simplicity, and in the last act, when she repeats them with his arms about her, she touches the very heart of her audience.'[18]

Agate (frequently critical of Ashcroft) found her 'heartrending' in the earlier acts: 'But alas, when she came to the last scene there was not enough power in her to carry it through.'[19] J.G.B. reproached her for acting 'too well and too competently': 'Nina should be played by the right sort of bad actress, amateurish but ardent, whereas Miss Ashcroft is the wrong sort of good actress ... She cries beautifully in the last act, but Nina's tears are not beautiful; they should be dreadful paroxysms of sobbing.'[20]

Agate's claim that *The Seagull*'s 'thundering good parts' can all be interpreted 'in almost any number of ways' may be applied particularly to Nina in Act 4. Has she, or will she ever, become a good actress? Is she broken as a person?

Ashcroft, never having seen *The Seagull* on stage (she missed the 1925 and 1929 productions[21]), relied heavily on Komisarjevsky's interpretation. She believed that Nina is 'destroyed' (*CC*):

Why the title – *The Seagull*? Trigorin's 'a subject for a short story' ... which was the seagull's destruction. And the actual meeting of Constantin with Nina – his witnessing her despair is what prompts his suicide – he believes in nothing any more. Komis's view of Nina's protestations of belief in her future career – only a covering up of her *dis*belief ... similar to Sonia's at the end of *Vanya* ... and I suppose the belief in the future as reiterated by the three sisters.[22]

'In my view – mind you, of course I was tremendously influenced by Komis' point of view about the character – I think she wasn't any more than a rather second-rate provincial actress, and I doubt if she would ever have succeeded in being anything else.'*

Ashcroft's recollection of Komisarjevsky's view is somewhat contradicted by a press report, which attributes to him the following remarks:

Certain French and English critics – quite wrongly – have said that all Chekhov's ... characters are inactive failures ... Nonsense! Look at *The Seagull* alone. Most of its characters are highly successful in their own

4   Stephen Haggard (Konstantin) and Peggy Ashcroft (Nina) in Act 2 of
The Seagull, 1936

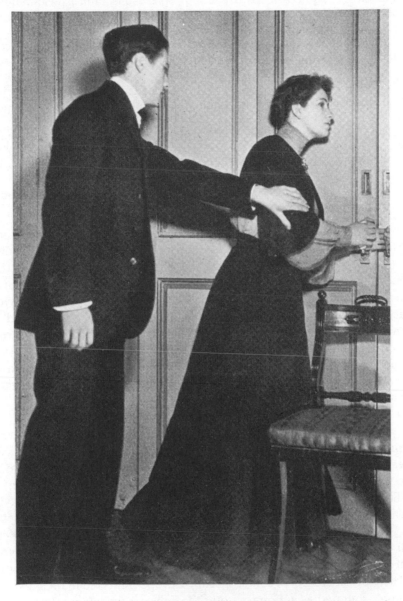

5   Stephen Haggard (Konstantin) and Peggy Ashcroft (Nina) in Act 4 of
The Seagull, 1936

lines [*sic*] ... Even of the two young people, Konstantin is beginning to attract attention as a writer, and Nina, after her early struggles, is going to have success as an actress.

No. What probably interested Chekhov more was the idea that success didn't bring happiness to these people.[23]

Ashcroft observed in 1989:

You can't be black and white when you talk about Chekhov ... I think he was a bit of a pessimist really. He was a pretty sad man himself ...

He combines comedy and tragedy to the full in each play ... When I say he's a pessimist, I mean that he doesn't think that suddenly it's going to be all lovely for any of the characters. He knows that it's going to go on being very, very difficult ...

Komis's production certainly was full of comedy ... You can be comedic as well as pessimistic, can't you?*

'I think Komisarjevsky is very much responsible for the love that English people have for Chekhov. His approach was what I believe Chekhov requires ... He brought out the comedy as well as the poetry and the sadness' (*CC*).

Ashcroft remembered the part, the play and the production with deep affection. Playing Nina was 'a great experience, I enjoyed it enormously'.* 'I love *The Seagull* very, very much.'* She remembered Komisarjevsky, too, with gratitude: 'Whatever pain he caused, he was a great inspiration to me both as an actress and a person ... I learned from him how to approach a part, how to analyse a role, how important it was to understand the director's whole conception of a play ... He made me realise that to be an actor is to be a perfectionist.'[24]

Above all, perhaps, she learned the true value of a permanent company when working with Gielgud at the New Theatre: 'John ... wanted an ensemble of acting, which he managed to achieve ... and it was by far the most formative part of my acting experience.'[25] 'There was a great feeling of ensemble. There were no stars ... It was a lovely atmosphere' (*CC*).

The Seagull ran for 109 performances, establishing a 'once-derided dramatist as the most successful of international playwrights'.[26] Ivor Brown welcomed Chekhov's new-found popularity but, seeing the 'Heartbreak House' of contemporary Europe 'reflected in the Russian glass', sounded a cautionary note: 'Tchehov is for our sombre years; a generation which can look forward to a brave new world instead of to bigger and more sanguinary chaos may some day be surprised that we so doted on the Russian dramatist'.[27]

'THREE SISTERS' AT THE QUEEN'S THEATRE
(28 JANUARY 1938)

The 'sombre years' were lightened by an even more illustrious event in 1938. Michel Saint-Denis' *Three Sisters* has been deemed 'the definitive production of this play in our profession ever since'.[28] It was 'the most legendary of all English Chekhov productions'.[29]

Long familiar to British audiences, *Three Sisters* was welcomed in 1938 as 'a work of art which exalts like a beautiful piece of music'.[30] Agate was reminded of conductors, poets, and painters (Manet, Vuillard, Utrillo): 'It is part of this drama's genius to make you think in terms of other media – of lilts and cadences, of brushwork, of wind and strings.'[31]

Production and acting, costumes and scenery, sound effects and lighting blended in rare perfection. This harmony was achieved after meticulous rehearsal. The Queen's Theatre programme emphasized the season and time of day: 'Act 1: Midday. Spring'; 'Act 2: 8.15 p.m. Winter'; 'Act 3: 2 a.m. Summer'; 'Act 4: Midday. Autumn'. Ashcroft recalled the unprecedented seven weeks[32] of rehearsal:

One of the wonderful things I remember was the spring of the first act, the winter of the second act – the cold, the coming back from work tired, the coming in out of the streets in the carnival, the sleigh arriving to take Natasha off into the snow – and then the hot, hot summer of the fire in the third act, and the autumnal beauty of the fourth act. And, because we had so much time to rehearse, we would have rehearsals when we only concentrated on that feeling of the seasons, or the general mood ...

And the marvellous effect he got from the band playing. We must have spent hours and hours and hours getting the coming of the sound just exactly right in the climax.*

'A Chekhov play is so much a director's creation', she remarks.[33]

In 1938 Saint-Denis was fortunate to work with a more or less permanent company. *Three Sisters* was the third piece in Gielgud's season at the Queen's Theatre, following *Richard II* and *The School for Scandal*, but preceding *The Merchant of Venice*. The value of a settled band of players – reinforced, as in *Three Sisters*, by guest artists such as Gwen Ffrangcon-Davies and Carol Goodner – was universally recognized. 'This lovely presentation of Chekhov may fairly be described as an all-star cast in a no-star play, and the stars, in their modest courses, behave admirably ... It is all real acting and no egotistical nonsense.'[34]

It seemed invidious to single out individual performances. 'The aim of an actor should not be the part, but the whole.'[35] Peggy Ashcroft recalled the entire ensemble:

Gwen Ffrangcon-Davies was marvellous as Olga. She's a beautiful Chekhov actress, a beautiful actress altogether ... And we had a wonderful Masha, Carol Goodner, who was American by birth. She was very handsome and rather voluptuous-looking, and she was, I thought, dead right – but *not* played, as I have seen her played, as a kind of almost nymphomaniac in her sexiness ... Vershinin is a windbag, without very much heart. I think he's a bit of a ladykiller, and Masha suffers at his hands. Gielgud never was quite happy, I think he didn't feel totally rightly cast. I thought he was awfully good ... George [Devine] as Andrey was remarkable. Because George was a *fat* man in those days, rather heavy. I can see him now, pushing that pram ... Freddie Lloyd was absolutely wonderful as the doctor. And Leo Quartermaine was the schoolmaster ... Michael Redgrave as the Baron was one of his finest performances ever. It made Michael as an actor – it was an extraordinary performance. He created this bumbling, plain, shy, talkative, not-meaning-anything character. He's *intensely* lovable, and Irina *wants* to love him, but she can't really ... Solyony is a mysteriously wonderful character, isn't he? ... Natasha is unredeemable. She was brilliantly played by Angela Baddeley, because she never overdid it, but she was totally awful. She's vulgar, selfish – after all, she really destroyed Andrey.*

Ashcroft had been eager to work with Saint-Denis, having admired his achievements with the Compagnie des Quinze and his 1935 production of *Noah*. She was relieved to discover that his approach to Chekhov was similar to Komisarjevsky's: 'Michel had a completely comedic view of the plays, particularly, I would say, of *Three Sisters*, although the tragedy was there too.'*

Moreover, Ashcroft considered Saint-Denis 'a very faithful director of Chekhov ... much more faithful than Komis' (*CC*). Whereas she had felt daunted by Komisarjevsky, Saint-Denis 'gave one the feeling – although he *was* directing precisely what he wanted – that you were really doing it yourself' (*CC*). 'I like a director who works very systematically.'[36] In 1970 Ashcroft named Saint-Denis and Komisarjevsky as the two greatest influences in her youth.[37]

As Irina, the youngest sister, Ashcroft was again required to make the transition from youthful naivety to the frontiers of despair. Yet, whereas Nina's transformation is abrupt, dominating the final act, Irina changes gradually and, compared with Nina, was not a difficult part.*

6 Peggy Ashcroft (Irina) and Michael Redgrave (Tuzenbakh) in Act 2 of
Three Sisters, 1938

7   Peggy Ashcroft (Irina), Gwen Ffrangcon-Davies (Olga), and Carol Goodner
(Masha) in *Three Sisters*, 1938

Ashcroft's performance this time was universally acclaimed. Critics admired her aura of 'pathetic hopefulness'[38] and 'wistful dreaminess'.[39] 'We have no other actress who suggests so effectively the forlorn quality that underlies the aspiration and exuberance of youth; the foreknowledge that all radiance is doomed to darkness, all power to defeat.'[40]

Ashcroft subsequently rejected L. Senelick's view that 'Irina is remarkably unpleasant to both her suitors' and that the sisters lack real values, culture, and sensitivity.[41] She felt 'enormously sympathetic' (*CC*) towards Irina and her sisters, regarding them all as 'frustrated by provincialism, by the society they lived in, by the fact that they were an impoverished family, and they *had* seen better days':*

They're not marvels of perfection, they all have their weaknesses, but that they are like Natasha seems to me total nonsense ... There is an enormous gulf between Natasha and the three sisters, and that's part of the tapestry of the play ... Certainly, they don't achieve. But that people don't succeed doesn't seem to me to make them monsters. They are impoverished, unhappy, longing – like most people. (*CC*)

Although the end of *Three Sisters* is 'pretty despairing',* Ashcroft did not think that 'any great work of art such as this – or any of Chekhov's plays – is "dispiriting" or "depressing" – true tragedy is too cathartic surely, to be "depressing"'.[42] *Three Sisters* was her favourite Chekhov play, and she 'most enjoyed playing Irina'.[43] The 1938 production was 'almost perfection', a 'great experience for us all'.* 'They were halcyon days in which was created almost a family of actors.'[44]

Three Sisters proved so successful that its run was extended by three weeks, until 13 April. The Queen's season ended on II June 1938, with the last performance of *The Merchant of Venice*. Findlater observes: 'When the nine months were over the company was dispersed, never to be reassembled, leaving the vision of an English Compagnie des Quinze to haunt a generation of playgoers and performers'.[45]

In the autumn of 1939 Saint-Denis began rehearsals of *The Cherry Orchard* with another brilliant cast, in which Ashcroft was to play Anya. After the collapse of this ensemble venture because of the war, 'Ashcroft was an actress in search of a company ... It took over twenty years to find what she was looking for, in the Royal Shakespeare Company'.[46]

'THE CHERRY ORCHARD' AT THE ALDWYCH THEATRE
(14 DECEMBER 1961)

Peggy Ashcroft's next appearance in Chekhov was with the Royal
Shakespeare Company, in Michel Saint-Denis' production of *The
Cherry Orchard*.[47] Three years before there had been the remarkable
Moscow Arts Theatre season at Sadler's Wells, in which the production
of *The Cherry Orchard* was hailed by Tynan as a 'total spring-cleaning',
offering comedy and sanity instead of the typically English 'pathetic
symphony'.[48] Ashcroft, however, disliked in this Moscow *Cherry
Orchard* the 'tremendous political emphasis' on the 'breaking of the
awful old order' (while finding their *Uncle Vanya* 'marvellous', and
Three Sisters 'very, very good').*

In 1961 *The Cherry Orchard* was greeted as Chekhov's 'masterpiece',[49]
'the greatest play of the century',[50] but Saint-Denis' deliberately
anti-romantic interpretation split the critics into conflicting camps.[51]

Peggy Ashcroft's Ranevskaya also divided the critics, albeit less
stridently. Muller praised Ashcroft's 'harrowing truthfulness and
ardour', while Brien saw this Ranevskaya as 'pretty enough to have
been immoral, sparkling enough to charm', yet basically as silly as
her brother.[52] She was the 'silver drift of a woman, indolent, feckless,
loving, and lost',[53] displaying a 'flirtatiousness' which Hobson had
never noticed in other Ranevskayas.[54] Trewin wrote:

I shall remember her on the morning of her arrival when she sits back on
her chair in weary comfort, her feet upon a stool; relaxation is complete,
and while her eyes look languidly about the room we know that, luxuriating
in her home-coming and in the wistful remembrance of things past, the
dear, foolish woman has no thought of the future, the October that must
follow May.[55]

In her remembrance of the past in Act 2 she scored a 'wonderful
piece of that Chekhovian acting which is poised on a razor edge
between absurdity and pathos'.[56] 'The part suits her grace and her
quick comedy, and at the end, when the old house is shut up for
the last time, she wrings our hearts with her gentle sorrow.'[57]

If that were all, Ashcroft would seem to have captured the essence of
Ranevskaya, including her fecklessness and flirtatiousness, her tender-
ness and tiresomeness, her absurdity and pathos. However, many
critics were unconvinced. 'A woman of Ranevsky's sudden impulses,
both sexual and financial, could afford to be more flamboyant.'[58]
Whiting thought her 'rather too aware ... Dame Peggy listens too

well for a play by Chekov [*sic*].'[59] Tynan, commenting caustically
that 'there is far more to Ranevsky than the distracted hostess that
Dame Peggy conjures up', suggested that 'this gifted actress ... be
forbidden, for a number of years, to accept any part of which gracious-
ness was an essential ingredient'.[60]

Several reviewers sensed that Ashcroft was acting to Saint-Denis'
instructions. She 'seems forbidden to exhibit the warmth of heart underlying her weaknesses'.[61] 'She is really too cool, too much of a piece –
and that is the general fault of Michel Saint-Denis' production.'[62]

In 1989 Ashcroft confirmed that her conception of Ranevskaya had
conflicted with that of Saint-Denis, and she had been constrained
to perform the part contrary to her inclinations. She had greatly
admired the 'quicksilver volatility'* of Gwen Ffrangcon-Davies'
Ranevskaya in 1954, while finding Alla Tarasova 'far too big and
heavy' in the role in 1958.*

Ashcroft regarded Ranevskaya as an 'intensely volatile' character,
warm, generous, lovable, but 'hopeless', deserving to lose the orchard:

She's a ludicrous character, really. That's why Chekhov calls it a farce,
perhaps. She's so over-the-top about everything. She's all surface things.
And I think that I was made to try and deepen it, which was not totally
right.

Michel made me feel that I'd got to be somehow heavier. I didn't want
to be heavier ... and so I had a battle with myself, in playing it with my
own feeling for it, and satisfying Michel.*[63]

Ashcroft's appreciation of the 1961 *Cherry Orchard* was tinged with disappointment. It had been partly at her suggestion that Peter Hall invited
Saint-Denis to direct the play – Saint-Denis was the 'most instructive
director' she had ever worked with.[64] Yet, whereas Gielgud and
herself, having played in the 1938 *Three Sisters*, 'knew what it was
like to work with Saint-Denis' and felt 'very free' in 1961 (*CC*), the
younger actors 'found it quite difficult to take so much direction
from Saint-Denis, and it was not in a way as happy a production as
Three Sisters' (*CC*). The young actors felt 'overpowered by Michel,
whereas in *Three Sisters* none of us ever did' (*CC*).[65] 'The production
... hadn't the overwhelming success that *Three Sisters* had, and I think
rightly so, because we were a bit acting to orders ... Of course, he
was still a great director, but I think he wasn't as in touch with his
company as he had been in *Three Sisters*. There was something out
of joint.'*

The Cherry Orchard ran in the Aldwych repertory until 17 March

8   Peggy Ashcroft (Ranevskaya) in Act I of *The Cherry Orchard*, 1961

1962. Michael Elliott's studio adaptation of the production was shown on BBC television on 13 April 1962.

'THE SEAGULL' AT THE QUEEN'S THEATRE (12 MARCH 1964)

Peggy Ashcroft's fourth Chekhovian appearance was in Tony Richardson's production of *The Seagull*, which formed part of the English Stage Company's season at the Queen's Theatre.

In 1964 *The Seagull* was welcomed as an established classic on the London stage, and many critics admired the new production. Most ecstatic, perhaps, was Cain, who declared it 'an interpretation which will go down in history': 'Tony Richardson's production is funny, sad, and terrible: beautiful, but not pretty, and never sentimental'.[66] The production impressed as 'almost perfect',[67] 'beautifully graduated',[68] a 'revival richly accomplished'.[69]

Several reviewers, however, voiced serious reservations. Hope-Wallace was particularly disappointed by the first two acts, in which the 'all-important overtones ... fell dead'. It seemed to him 'a deliberate and curiously heartless performance'.[70] Brien condemned the 'general pall of defeatism and depression' imposed by Richardson: 'In flattening the surface and darkening the colours, he has also obscured much that Chekhov surely meant a director to bring to light.'[71] Bryden described the production as a 'failure', a 'toned-down, naturalistic affair', meticulously expunging romance and exhibiting a 'sluggish pace and coldness'.[72]

Laurence Olivier's production of *Uncle Vanya* in 1962–4 had set towering standards for Tony Richardson to emulate. Esslin declared both productions in the world class, bearing comparison 'even with the Moscow Art Theatre'.

Everyone agreed that Richardson had assembled the 'most classic cast' (Cain), and the ensemble's achievement was widely acclaimed. Yet several reviewers felt that something was missing. The 'fine players' were not yet acting with 'perfect "ensemble" ease'.[73] 'It is an evening of sensitive acting. But at the moment it doesn't all coalesce into one big unhappy family.'[74]

Within the ensemble, Vanessa Redgrave's Nina attracted most attention. Many found her magnificent, particularly in the last act. Redgrave's conception of Nina in Act 4 differed fundamentally from Ashcroft's in 1936. Whereas Ashcroft considered Nina 'destroyed', Redgrave declared: 'The audience must believe that Nina has found a source of strength which will pull her through, but it will take some time before she really *is* strong. It's a difficult tightrope to walk and is different every night.'[75]

From 'a very good cast'* Ashcroft singled out George Devine as an 'absolutely masterly' Dorn: 'I can't imagine it better played ... I think Dorn is quite a bit like Chekhov – "Ah, youth, youth!"'[76] I think that Chekhov deliberately detached himself.'* Devine offered a 'most pleasingly and teasingly composed portrait of hedonistic serenity'.[77] Peter Finch as Trigorin gave 'a perfect miniature performance', 'dead right', but 'a bit *under* in projection' after his long absence from the theatre.*

Peggy Ashcroft played Arkadina, an established, forty-three-year-old actress. Reviewers characterized Arkadina as self-centred, tiresome, miserly and shallow, one of Chekhov's 'silly women – Arkadina, Elena, Madam Ranevsky – trailing their Moscow dresses and sexual provocation' (Bryden). Ashcroft conveyed Arkadina's egoism and arrogance with a 'richly comic sense and authority' (Shorter), revealing 'how bourgeoise a little woman Arkadina is behind the glitter of the seemingly successful actress'.[78]

Ashcroft's achievement was much appreciated. 'Peggy Ashcroft's Arkadina is superlative: she never lapses into caricature, remains firmly within the realm of comedy and yet reaches the confines of the tragic' (Esslin). Ashcroft chose to emphasize in Arkadina the 'ageing beauty' rather than the 'provincial actress': 'Her monopoly of the limelight is not achieved imperiously; it is done with pouts, with coy wheedles of the voice, with a fidgeting of her bare shoulders when she is forced to watch Nina in Konstantin's play. Her boast that she could still play a 15-year-old girl is reinforced by the fact that she spends most of her time doing so.'[79] 'It is a great improvement on her comparable performance in the Aldwych *Cherry Orchard.*'[80] Cain called it 'one of her finest performances', but, surprisingly, added: 'Dame Peggy has always been mannered and idiosyncratic, and here she is playing just such an actress, so constantly, and consciously, playing her part.'[81]

There was much to savour. Lambert admired her in the first half of the play, 'sitting by the lake, the lady of the manor for the moment, idly patronizing, insensitive yet utterly charming'.[82]

Act 3, however, is Arkadina's act. 'Her great scene is the reconquest of Trigorin, who has fallen for Nina; Dame Peggy makes a wonderful moment out of it with her cheap leer, "He's mine!". She then walks

9 Peggy Ashcroft (Arkadina) in Act I of *The Seagull*, 1964

over to the mirror and preens herself before it like the second-rate actress which Arkadina is.'[83] 'For once, it is justifiable to see Arkadina's reclamation of her lover handled as near-comedy' (*The Times*).[84]

Seymour was impressed by the few moments just before the final curtain when she 'laughingly shakes off her fears that her son has killed himself',[85] and Levin hailed the culminating pistol-shot and 'Dame Peggy's momentary glimpse into the abyss of what she has done'.[86]

Several adverse criticisms were voiced. 'Richness of nature and a certain animal stupidity are the essence of Arkadina. The keen brilliance and eagerness of Peggy Ashcroft do not serve the role, as I see it ... It seemed petulant where it needed to be egocentrically voluptuous' (Hope-Wallace). Some condemned Ashcroft's restraint: 'Peggy Ashcroft could have done with more emotional rouge ... Rather more flamboyance would have been permissible' (Barker).

In 1963–4 Ashcroft had played Margaret of Anjou in John Barton's Shakespearean adaptation *The Wars of the Roses*. She enjoyed the role: 'I rather like slightly nasty women, having been overfed with *ingénues* in my youth.'[87] Ashcroft enjoyed Arkadina, too, with her 'brashness' and 'egocentricity', her 'cheapness, in a way': 'She's a much easier character to play than Ranevskaya. She's rather nasty, she's petty, she's superficial, and wants to be loved, wants to be the centre of the stage ... I like playing characters that are unsympathetic. They're easier to do, in a way, because you can be more objective about them, and you can invite the audience to detest you – whereas you can't invite an audience to love you.'*

Tony Richardson's production was not an altogether happy experience for Ashcroft, who disagreed with his interpretation of Nina.

I was very aware, having been in *The Seagull* before, of what Tony Richardson was missing. He's a very brilliant director, but I don't think he's totally suited to Chekhov ... He couldn't really orchestrate. And the trouble was that I knew that there was George [Devine] who knew exactly how to orchestrate the whole thing ... And only at the end did George help in the last act, which is a very difficult act to direct, and so we got through it, but it was a bit of a struggle ...[88]

I didn't find the help that I'd been used to in Chekhov. At the same time when it came to the performance I felt that it came to life, that it had a life of its own, and it was that '*Seagull* world' whether you interpret it that way or the other. I think that's what I missed in *The Cherry Orchard*. One was striving in *The Cherry Orchard*, and I think we'd more arrived in *The Seagull*.*

The play ran until 30 May.[89]

Arkadina was Ashcroft's last stage appearance in a Chekhov production, although in 1968 she played Chekhov's wife, Olga Knipper, in a television compilation, *From Chekhov with Love*.[90]

Ashcroft continued her keen interest in Chekhov by reading books about the writer, with her favourite 'undoubtedly the life by

Ernest J. Simmons'.[91] She also saw many productions, greatly admiring, for instance, Trevor Nunn's *Three Sisters* at Stratford-upon-Avon in 1979, but finding Boris Livanov's *Seagull* (performed by the Moscow Arts Theatre at the Aldwych in 1970) an 'agonizing experience': 'Masha was played like Nina, and Nina – Masha, and the settings were not as Chekhov directed ... I prefer to forget that, because I have such a wonderful view of the Moscow Arts Theatre.'*

Looking back in 1989 on her four Chekhovian roles, Ashcroft remarked: 'I think I'm very lucky to have had them.'* She appeared in four Ibsen productions as well – *Hedda Gabler* (1954), *Rosmersholm* (1959–60), *Ghosts* (1967), *John Gabriel Borkman* (1975) – and reflected on differences between the two dramatists: 'Chekhov is instinctive, poetical, impressionistic, and therefore one finds a Chekhov character in a much more intuitive way than in Ibsen.'[92]

Ashcroft did not believe that the 'Russianness' of Chekhov's characters causes particular problems for British actors, for his characters are 'universal':

I think the thing that Chekhov demands of an actor or actress is something that should be demanded in every play ... In Chekhov the character has to be alive all the time, reacting to everything that goes on around him or her ... You can't do Chekhov unless you are aware of that and able to inhabit that character throughout the whole time you appear on the stage. (*CC*)

If Chekhov's plays are meant for ensemble acting, with permanent companies, Ashcroft constantly 'disproved the superstitions that a major artist cannot work in an ensemble'.[93] In her work she perhaps 'found the permanent alliances sometimes lacking in her life'.[94] Gielgud confirms that she was the 'most perfect partner', and her influence in a company was 'extraordinary'.[95]

Notes

1 Interview, January 1971, in David Addenbrooke, *The Royal Shakespeare Company: The Peter Hall Years* (London: William Kimber, 1974), p. 194.
    For assistance with source material, I thank Christopher Robinson (Keeper of the University of Bristol Theatre Collection), Douglas McVay, Patrick Miles, Michael Sanderson, and Nick Worrall.
2 *The Times*, 1 February 1960; republished in Laurence Kitchin, *Mid-Century Drama* (London: Faber and Faber, revised edition 1962), p. 201.
3 Michael Billington, *Peggy Ashcroft* (London: John Murray, 1988), pp. 19–20.

4 Ashcroft, 5 August 1987, at the Anglo-Soviet Colloquium, 'Chekhov on the British Stage'. Ashcroft conversed with Irving Wardle before answering questions from the floor. Further quotations from the Cambridge Colloquium are identified thus: (*CC*).

5 Interview with G. McVay, London, 5 January 1989. Further quotations from this conversation are indicated by an asterisk.

6 See Robert Tanitch, *Ashcroft* (London: Hutchinson, 1987), pp. 44–7.

7 Komisarjevsky directed Ashcroft in four productions in 1931–5, becoming her 'guru and husband (in that order)' (Billington, *Peggy Ashcroft*, p. 21). By mid-1935 he had left her.

8 *The Times*, 21 May 1936.

9 James Agate, *The Sunday Times*, 24 May 1936.

10 Ivor Brown (Brown[1]), *The Observer*, 24 May 1936.

11 John Gielgud, *Stage Directions* (London: Heinemann, 1963), p. 88.

12 Theodore Komisarjevsky, *Myself and the Theatre* (London: Heinemann, 1929), p. 160.

13 *The Observer*, 10 May 1936.

14 P. L. M., *Daily Herald*, 21 May 1936.

15 *Stage Directions*, p. 89. See also John Gielgud, *Early Stages* (London: Heinemann, 1974, revised edition; first published 1939), pp. 168, 171.

16 *Early Stages*, p. 172.

17 By Houston-Rogers, *Play Pictorial*, no. 409 (1936).

18 *The Bystander*, 3 June 1936, p. 402.

19 Agate, *The Sunday Times*, 24 May 1936.

20 J. G. B., *The Evening News*, 21 May 1936.

21 Letters from Peggy Ashcroft, 3 February and early March 1990.

22 Letter, postmarked 21 December 1981.

23 *The Observer*, 10 May 1936.

24 Billington, *Peggy Ashcroft*, pp. 72, 53, 54.

25 Ashcroft, talking to David Jones, in Hal Burton, ed., *Great Acting* (London: British Broadcasting Corporation, 1967), p. 91.

26 *Theatre Arts Monthly*, October 1936, p. 770.

27 Ivor Brown (Brown[2]), *The Illustrated London News*, 6 June 1936, p. 1017.

28 Laurence Olivier, introduction to Michel Saint-Denis, *Theatre: The Rediscovery of Style* (London: Heinemann, 1960), p. 11.

29 Irving Wardle, Cambridge Chekhov Colloquium, 5 August 1987.

30 Desmond MacCarthy, *The New Statesman and Nation*, 5 February 1938, p. 206.

31 James Agate, *The Sunday Times*, 30 January 1938.

32 Gielgud claims they had eight weeks for rehearsals, 'instead of the usual three or four' (*Stage Directions*, p. 90).

33 *The Times*, 1 February 1960. See also Gwen Ffrangcon-Davies, 'The Players's View', in R. D. Charques, ed., *Footnotes to the Theatre* (London: Peter Davies, 1938), pp. 240–53.

34 Ivor Brown, *The Observer*, 30 January 1938.

35 Ashcroft's words in 1961, quoted in Richard Findlater, *The Player Queens* (London: Weidenfeld and Nicolson, 1976), p. 209.

36 *Great Acting*, p. 92.

37 Interview with Margaret Tierney, *Plays and Players*, December 1970, p. 20.

38 A. V. Cookman, *London Mercury*, March 1938, p. 534.

39 Clive MacManus, *The Daily Mail*, 29 January 1938.

40 P. T., *The New English Weekly*, 10 February 1938, p. 355.

41 See Laurence Senelick, *Anton Chekhov* (London: Macmillan, 1985), pp. 108–11.

42 Letter, postmarked 21 December 1981.

43 Letter, postmarked 21 June 1980.

44 Ashcroft, in Ronald Harwood, ed., *The Ages of Gielgud* (London: Hodder and Stoughton, 1984), p. 73.

45 Richard Findlater, *The Player Kings* (London: Weidenfeld and Nicolson, 1971), p. 183.

46 Findlater, *The Player Queens*, pp. 217–18.

47 Ashcroft had become a Dame of the British Empire in 1956, and a founder-member of the Royal Shakespeare Company in 1960.

48 *The Observer*, 18 May 1958.

49 Bernard Levin, *Daily Express*, 15 December 1961.

50 Robert Muller, *Daily Mail*, 15 December 1961.

51 See Patrick Miles, *Chekhov on the British Stage 1909–1987* (Cambridge: Sam and Sam, 1987), p. 34.

52 Alan Brien, *The Sunday Telegraph*, 17 December 1961.

53 J. C. Trewin, *The Illustrated London News*, 23 December 1961, p. 1118.

54 Harold Hobson, *The Sunday Times*, 17 December 1961.

55 Trewin, *ibid.*; see the photograph in Burton, ed., *Great Acting*, p. 153.

56 Philip Hope-Wallace, *The Guardian*, 15 December 1961.

57 Eric Keown, *Punch*, 27 December 1961, p. 950.

58 Bamber Gascoigne, *The Spectator*, 22 December 1961, p. 928.

59 In *John Whiting on Theatre* (London: Alan Ross, 1966), p. 81.

60 Kenneth Tynan, *The Observer*, 17 December 1961.

61 *The Times*, 15 December 1961.

62 V. S. Pritchett, *New Statesman*, 22 December 1961, p. 966.

63 Saint-Denis deliberately avoided underlining Ranevskaya's 'charm, warmth and elegance', in order to sound the required 'note of comedy' (Michel Saint-Denis, introduction to Anton Chekhov, *The Cherry Orchard*, English version by Sir John Gielgud (London: Heinemann, 1963, many reprints), p. xi).

64 Ashcroft, in Addenbrooke, *The Royal Shakespeare Company*, p. 197.

65 See Gerald Jacobs, *Judi Dench* (London: Weidenfeld and Nicolson, 1985), pp. 32–3.

66 Alex Matheson Cain, *The Tablet*, 21 March 1964, p. 329.

67 Martin Esslin, *Plays and Players*, May 1964, p. 32.

68 J. W. Lambert, *Drama*, 73, summer 1964, p. 20.

69 J.C. Trewin, *The Illustrated London News*, 28 March 1964, p. 500.

70 Philip Hope-Wallace, *The Guardian*, 13 March 1964.

71 Alan Brien, *The Sunday Telegraph*, 15 March 1964.

72 Ronald Bryden, *New Statesman*, 20 March 1964, p. 464.

73 Felix Barker, *The Evening News*, 13 March 1964.

74 Eric Shorter, *The Daily Telegraph*, 13 March 1964.

75 Letter, between 13 and 17 March 1964.

76 Dorn's words in Act I.

77 Harold Hobson, *The Sunday Times*, 15 March 1964.

78 Alan Seymour, *The London Magazine*, May 1964, p. 65.

79 Bamber Gascoigne, *The Observer*, 15 March 1964.

80 *The Times*, 13 March 1964.

81 Cain, *The Tablet*, 21 March 1964, p. 329. In contrast, Harold Hobson, in his profile, 'Dame Peggy' (*The Sunday Times*, 15 March 1964), characterized Ashcroft as 'less given to tricks, gimmicks and artificial surprises than any other considerable actress, playing always in straightforward obedience to her authors ... seeking nothing flashy or meretricious'.

82 Lambert, *Drama*, 73, summer 1964, p. 20.

83 David Pryce-Jones, *The Spectator*, 20 March 1964, pp. 379–80.

84 See Ashcroft's comments, *Great Acting*, p. 93.

85 Seymour, *The London Magazine*, May 1964, p. 65.

86 Bernard Levin, *Daily Mail*, 13 March 1964.

87 In Addenbrooke, *The Royal Shakespeare Company*, p. 201.

88 See Billington, *Peggy Ashcroft*, pp. 210–11. Tanitch mistakenly believes that Devine *was* the director (*Ashcroft*, pp. [III], 154).

89 The present writer saw the production at the New Theatre, Oxford, on 2 March and 6 March 1964, before its London opening. Several performances seemed outstanding (Ashcroft's Arkadina, Paul Rogers' Sorin, Devine's Dorn, Finch's Trigorin), but Redgrave's Nina in Act 4 was unforgettably moving.

90 This portrait of Chekhov, compiled from his correspondence, was televised by Rediffusion (London) on 14 June 1968. Gielgud played Chekhov.

91 Letter, 3 February 1990.

92 *Great Acting*, p. 93. See also *The Times*, 1 February 1960.

93 Findlater, *The Player Queens*, p. 227.

94 Billington, *Peggy Ashcroft*, p. 5.

95 John Gielgud, *An Actor and His Time* (London: Sidgwick and Jackson, 1979), p. 113.

CHAPTER 9

Far from the West End: Chekhov and the Welsh language stage 1924 – 1991

W. Gareth Jones

When Chekhov presented Nemirovich-Danchenko with a medallion inscribed 'You gave life to my "Seagull". Thankyou!',[1] in recognition of the first successful production of *The Seagull* by the Moscow Art Theatre, he was acknowledging that the Chekhovian play had required a new form of theatre to animate it. In turn the adoption by the Moscow Art Theatre of a seagull as its emblem signalled its debt to Chekhov's revolutionary text. If *The Seagull* had failed to be realized by the commercial, entertainment theatre of its day, it was rescued by the combined endeavours of a dedicated amateur, Stanislavsky, who had been nurtured in a 'Little Theatre' movement enjoying substantial private patronage, and by the insights of the studious Nemirovich-Danchenko with his academic Conservatoire background.

In Wales, the same union of the amateur and academic, prompted by the Russian experience, was to prepare the Welsh-language stage for Chekhov. The dramatic challenge from young amateurs of talent, commitment, and private means, such as Konstantin Treplev, to the commercial theatre, represented by his mother Arkadina, was played out within *The Seagull*. Yet the complex mother–son relationship in that play must to some extent mirror Chekhov's appreciation of the essential familial bond between the two contending kinds of theatre. And today, whenever a Chekhov play is performed, the same tension between old and new forms of drama, embedded in his theatrical vision, is still communicated. In the reshaping of twentieth-century drama, Chekhov's contribution has not been limited to an initial push at the beginning of the century, but has been in the nature of a permanent revolution.

As he thanked Nemirovich-Danchenko in 1900 for giving life to *The Seagull*, Chekhov could not have foreseen how in the twentieth century his plays would in turn breathe new life into the European theatre, soon affecting even a distant minority culture on the Western shores of the continent. Although a Chekhov play in Welsh had to wait until 1941 for a public performance, the foundations of the new theatre associated with him had already been established, and henceforward Chekhov was evident at every important turn in the development of the Welsh language stage.

The foundation-stone was laid when Lord Howard de Walden, who had striven to foster a Welsh national theatre on the Irish example in the early years of this century, commissioned Theodore Komisarjevsky to produce a play at the National Eisteddfod in Holyhead in August 1927.[2] The previous year Komisarjevsky had demonstrated the Russian cooperative approach to acting and directing at the Barnes Theatre with his staging of *Ivanov*, *Uncle Vanya*, *The Three Sisters*, and *The Cherry Orchard*.[3] The main aim of inviting Komisarjevsky to Holyhead, however, was not to bring Russian plays to the Welsh stage, but to make Wales' amateur companies more conscious of standards other than those of the London West End.[4] The novelty of the costly venture (production expenses were between £3,000 and £4,000), was apparent to all. In its guarded report *Yr Herald Gymraeg* wrote: 'Something completely new in the history of the Eisteddfod and in the history of the theatre in Wales was the grand performance of such a drama as this evening's'.[5]

The choice of Ibsen's *The Pretenders* for this grand performance was more predictable. For Welsh audiences at that time, Ibsen was the foremost European dramatist. The Norwegian's plays with their portrayal of the conflict between man and his society, and the unmasking of pious hypocrisy, had a clear resonance in non-conformist, Welsh-speaking Wales on another part of Europe's Western seaboard.[6] Ibsen stood in the way of Chekhov. By collaborating with Lord Howard de Walden, Komisarjevsky was not promoting Ibsen, but acknowledging once again the leading role taken by committed non-professionals – 'Antoine, the Duke George II of Meiningen, Stanislavsky, Diaghileff, Vera Komisarjevsky, Gordon Craig, Copeau, and the founders of The New York Theatre Guild'[7] – in the encouragement of new ideas on the stage. The intelligent amateur from his position in the front of the house, argued Komisarjevsky, could have a broader view of the total theatre than the professional actor's 'narrow point of view, i.e. from the stage itself'.[8]

With this invigorating amateur perception went a growing awareness of the potential of a serious academic approach to new ways of staging the theatre's literary repertoire. Chekhov's texts were certainly appreciated by young members of post-war senior common rooms and *The Bear* and *The Proposal* had been performed by staff of the University College of North Wales at their musical evenings in the spring of 1924.[9] One of those present was T. Hudson-Williams, Professor of Greek, who enjoyed the performance of his friend John Mabbott, later President of St John's College, Oxford. Hudson-Williams was in time to produce a Welsh version of *The Bear*, which by 1943 was the only one of Chekhov's plays published in Welsh. That *Bear*, however, owed much to Komisarjevsky.

The Russian's production at Holyhead had been exemplary in demonstrating to the Welsh that drama could be as 'serious' an art form as music. Until then, drama in Welsh had been perceived as a didactic tool or sociable pastime with little of the prestige that the chapel, eisteddfod, and university had bestowed on music making. If the eisteddfod had been forced to acknowledge the artistic power of drama by Komisarjevsky, the university was now pressed to give it due academic status. In 1929 The Little Theatre journal *Y Llwyfan* noted that 'Following the presentation of the Welsh translation of Ibsen's play *The Pretenders* at Holyhead, August 1927, the Welsh University Union discussed the development of drama in Wales. Mr. J.J. Williams, M.A., Bethesda, advocated that the University should take the fostering of dramatic art under its aegis, as it has already taken music.'[10] Within a short time, in 1931, the University of Wales responded with the appointment by the University College of North Wales to its Department of Extra-Mural Studies of a Lecturer in Drama and Welsh Literature. It was no surprise that the non-conformist pulpit, with its tradition of dramatic declamation, provided the first lecturer. The Reverend Albert Evans-Jones, however, like many other Welsh writers with their indiscriminative surnames, had adopted a historic bardic *nom-de-plume*. A popular lyric poet, he was better known as 'Cynan', and it was under this bardic name that, ten years later, he was to take his bow as the first Welsh 'Bear'.

This may be seen as another remarkable instance of how the personal example of the original members of the Moscow Society of Art and Literature, which had sustained Chekhov as a playwright, had continued to exert its influence on the development of European drama.

Russian avant-garde ideas had penetrated the Welsh dramatic consciousness, as was revealed in another article in the issue of *Y Llwyfan* that had called on the University to foster dramatic art. While complaining that the English theatre was still flirting with the ghost of realism, Ifan Kyrle Fletcher declared: 'Twenty years ago the Russians began to experiment with new theories of the theatre. Tairoff worked at his theory of Cubism; Komisarjevsky preached the gospel of "the theatre theatrical"; Meyerhold, the greatest of them all, began to adapt his production to the conditions of modern life, thus developing the valuable theories which are hidden under the foolish names of Constructivismus and Mechanismus.'[11] Fletcher also noted, a little peevishly, that the theatre was being exploited in the renaissance of Welsh-language culture: 'So widespread have become the evidences of dramatic expression that the Welsh-language enthusiasts have seized on it as the most potent means of propaganda.'[12]

Cynan, whose considerable natural histrionic powers had been developed by the eisteddfod's pageantry and bardic tradition of verse declamation, had come to his appointment prompted by Komisarjevsky and his 'theatre theatrical', at a time when the growing popularity of the theatre succoured Welsh culture with translations of dramas. This was particularly apparent in the repertoire of the Welsh Drama Society at the College which was in the forefront of the drama movement.[13]

A happy coincidence would soon make translations of Chekhov's plays available. It was as a student at Greifswald in 1895-6, when Dostoyevsky was the rage among his German contemporaries, that Thomas Hudson-Williams, by now Professor of Greek, was first attracted to Russian literature. He had relished the performances of Chekhov at his college's musical evenings in 1924. By June 1931 a yearning to read Pushkin in the original had finally persuaded him to buckle to and learn Russian; before Cynan began to give his drama classes in the autumn, Hudson-Williams had managed to read some Tolstoy stories and St John's Gospel in Russian. Translations from the Russian followed, and by the time that Cynan wrote an article on 'Russian literature in Welsh translation'[14] in the magazine *Wales* in 1945, his output was considerable. His Chekhov translations were particularly commended. Cynan wrote:

With Pushkin, Dr. Hudson-Williams ranks Turgenev and Chekhov among his favourite Russian authors. He has done all Chekhov's plays into Welsh. Having already produced some of them, I am amazed at the sheer dramatic perfection of their Welsh dialogue. The sonorous cadences of the Welsh Bible and the 'Mabinogion' – our ancient mythological romances – give the right atmosphere in Welsh to Nina's famous moonlight speech in the play within the play in Act I of 'The Seagull'; while a dash of the colloquialism of the Caernarvon streets and of Welsh farmsteads gives conviction and verve to such a character as Lopakhin in 'The Cherry Orchard'. For Dr Hudson-Williams is no cloistered scholar writing the literature that smells only of other literature. He is nothing if not of the soil; he delights in the customs and the conversation of the common people ... [He has an] ear as sure as Synge's for a fresh un-hackneyed, and colourful phrase in the speech of the common people [which is] absolutely essential in translating drama.[15]

If Cynan, the producer of Chekhov, was well served by his translator, the fluent translator would be just as well served by Cynan in the theatre. Indeed in a commemorative article on Cynan as director and actor, it is as Grigory Stepanovich Smirnov in *The Bear* that he was best remembered: 'that role suited his style perfectly. He created a character who is still alive in my mind. One of the reasons for that perhaps was that he succeeded at the same time as a catalyst who brought out the best in his fellow actors.'[16]

He was obviously a catalyst in his energetic drama class of twenty-four who had spent the winter of 1940–1 preparing for a production of *The Bear* at the attenuated wartime National Literary Eisteddfod, Colwyn Bay, by studying Russian drama: Hudson-Williams had translated for them Ostrovsky's *Orphan* and *The Storm*, and Gogol's *Inspector General*, as well as Chekhov's plays. Reading Cynan's lecture notes for those classes reminds one again of the way in which the Welsh stage had been prepared for Chekhov. There was the acknowledgement of the debt to continental innovation exemplified by Komisarjevsky: 'some of us unfortunates', he fulminated, 'were sufficient fools ... to believe that London would be the saviour of the drama movement in Wales without realising that the London commercial theatre was a hundred years behind the German and Russian theatre, and that therefore we were following professional models in the West End which were completely profitless as a pattern for any nation which was serious about the art of the Theatre'.[17] The point was made that, by embracing Chekhov, Welsh drama could move through the Ibsen barrier: 'Perhaps you feel as actors reading his plays "Oh! if only he would give me something to do – slamming the door on an exit like Nora in *The Doll's House*".'[18] During the study and practical work on their production of *The Bear* it is clear from Cynan's lecture notes that, although he conveyed the conventional view of Chekhov's society 'sinking into the mire of the Slough of Despond',[19] great stress was laid on the humour and comedy.

The thorough preparation had its reward. 'Success of Chekov in Welsh' was the headline to an enthusiastic letter from Sara Roberts of the Unity Theatre, London, to the *North Wales Weekly News* of 14 August 1941:

On Friday evening last at the Church House, Old Colwyn, I spent the most exhilarating three hours I have known since the war began. It was the performance of four one-act plays by students of drama at rural W. E. A. classes under the direction of 'Cynan' ... I cannot write of the four plays but feel that I must mention the high spot of the evening, the Welsh version of Chekov's 'The Bear' ... How this Welsh audience rocked with laughter at the shouting, blustering 'Bear' himself admirably played by Cynan! Chekov is certainly a success in Welsh. I hope that we may see more translations of this great dramatist's work on the Welsh stage.[20]

Chekhov had at last arrived on the Welsh stage – as he had first appeared to Russian theatre audiences – with his original variation on a one-act farce. *The Bear* was a piece well suited to the tradition of Welsh play-making. It fitted the needs of Wales, as Saunders Lewis had seen them in 1919 when he applauded Lord Howard de Walden's courage in declaring, as he stood blinking behind the footlights of the Albert Hall, that Welshmen should not make the popular English theatre their model. Saunders Lewis, later to be Wales' most authoritative critic and foremost playwright, argued that 'our plays must be village plays ... they must belong to the people and portray the people's life and dream; and ... this folk art should never be divorced from our own familiar civilisation'.[21] He hoped that, as the local companies flourished, they would not 'allow the footlights to separate them from the friendliness of their hearers'.[22]

Although the success of *The Bear* had whetted the appetite for more Chekhov in Welsh, the resources were lacking for stage productions of the longer plays. It was radio that first presented one of the Hudson-Williams translations to a wider audience when *The Seagull* was broadcast on the BBC Welsh Home Service on 27 June 1952 in a production by John Gwilym Jones. Not until 1954 were *The Seagull* and *Uncle Vanya* first performed on stage; significantly, the task fell to the college drama societies in Bangor and Aberystwyth respectively. Although Bangor had the good fortune to have John Gwilym Jones as their guest director, he admitted that Chekhov presented the sternest of challenges to a student cast. The nature of the challenge was reflected in the programme note:

It is not to excuse itself that the Company wishes to say that undertaking *The Seagull* is a great venture. Its background is alien and its atmosphere difficult to catch, but the Company thought that it would be good to endeavour to stage it and so pay homage to Dr Hudson-Williams for his service to the literature of our country by broadening the horizons of our knowledge of the literature of other countries.

It is difficult to say whether it was exhaustion brought on by their staging of *The Seagull*, or unbridled enthusiasm for Chekhov that led to an unprecedented decision by the Society. The students' record book reads: 'It was agreed not to have a dinner for the company after the performance this year, but instead to travel to Aberystwyth on the 8 February to see the college company acting *Uncle Vanya*, another drama by Chekhov translated by Dr T. Hudson-Williams.'[23]

An encouraging review in *Baner ac Amserau Cymru* sympathized with the Aberystwyth students in their grappling with 'a difficult drama, a brave choice for young people'. The difficulty presented by Chekhov was well explained by the reviewer:

It was in the ordinary, unimportant circumstances of everyday life that his main interest lay. He liked to portray the unhappy, unsuccessful characters he saw around him, and through his strong, but simple and direct style he managed to make these people alive and interesting. Life's burdens are predominant with him. Sadness and depression are the themes of his song. As a consequence his plays are not amongst the simplest to perform.[24]

The following year, however, a fillip was given to the Welsh-language theatre by an Arts Council decision to set up a touring company. Its director was Raymond Edwards, whose admiration for Hudson-Williams' translations led him to choose *Uncle Vanya* for this pioneering venture. The actors invited to join the Cardiff-based company were those who had made a name for themselves in radio drama, and who also had extensive stage experience. Vanya and Astrov were played respectively by Hubert Hughson and Glanffrwd James who had both worked under Tyrone Guthrie, while the part of Yelena was taken by a talented student at University College, Cardiff, Siân Phillips. The designer of set and costumes was David Tinker. The tour ended with a performance at the National Eisteddfod in Pwllheli in August 1955.[25] 'A consummate performance', wrote Emyr Edwards in *Baner ac Amserau Cymru*, noting the beneficial results of frequent playing. 'It is fair to say after seeing it three times that the standard of performance has matured considerably particularly in the successful conveying of the sense and feel of pre-revolutionary Russia.'[26] A sturdy production allowed Edwards to criticize the director's conception of *Uncle Vanya* as a tragedy, and to argue that it was rather 'a realistic, elastic fresco' which Saunders Lewis had suggested should be played as a farce.

Chekhov had shown the way for the National Eisteddfod, now fortified with Arts Council subsidies, to become a showcase for European and American theatre in Welsh, and the sixties and seventies saw productions of plays by Lorca, Brecht, Sartre, Pirandello, Anouilh, Beckett, Ionesco, Arthur Miller, Tennessee Williams, Synge, and Dürrenmatt. Concurrently, the Welsh Arts Council also fostered the publication of translations of the world's classic plays. *The Seagull* appeared in a new translation by myself in 1970.[27]

Why should Hudson-Williams' translations need to be superseded?

If Chekhov's plays continually challenge their producers to strive towards new forms of theatre, his texts too present a continual challenge to their translator to find a new language for the stage. This accounts for the number of translations from him in any language, the apparent failure to find a single received version. For the Welsh translator, Chekhov is especially elusive, since the nature of the language to be used for the stage is a particular problem for him as for the Welsh playwright. In the thirties, when the early versions of Chekhov were made, T. Gwynn Jones, the leading poet of his time, pondered the question, 'What is the wisest course for the author of a drama, to speak nothing but dialect or to mix dialects according to his whim, or to devise a new dialect which has never existed?'[28] Hudson-Williams responded with the one-dialect opinion, by putting Chekhov into 'racy Caernarvonshire Welsh' which was undoubtedly the right solution for Cynan's WEA class. It eminently suited characters like Smirnov, or Telegin in *Uncle Vanya* who struck the Pwllheli reviewer as 'a poor landowner, more at home in a conventional Welsh kitchen comedy'.[29]

In the same review, in which he had recognized the continuing presence of homespun Welsh situation drama, Emyr Edwards had praised the company's success in conveying the atmosphere of pre-revolutionary Russia. The apparent contradiction points to one of the persistent problems of producing Chekhov on the Welsh stage: where is the action to be located, and in what epoch?

The basic quandary of time and place facing any British interpreter of Chekhov is felt particularly keenly in Wales. Does the Cherry Orchard await the axe in Southern Russia or in a recognizable Welsh community? Was it chopped down in 1904, or is the axe still poised to strike today? Are the class tensions still alive? As Cwmni Theatr Gwynedd planned a production of *The Cherry Orchard* for the Spring of 1991, would its entrepreneurial Lopakhin be rooted in pre-revolutionary Russia, or would he relate to contemporary *perestroika*, or to the local problem of second homes?

Answers to these questions determined the kind of Welsh that Chekhov's characters spoke in 1991. Hudson-Williams, with his Mabinogion prose and racy Caernarvon colloquialisms, had certainly recognized both the timelessness of Chekhov's vision and its need to be rooted in a distinct community. He had avoided the trap of 'routine smoothiness' (*rutinnaya gladkopis*) against which Korney Chukovsky warned Chekhov's translators (a warning which I had tried to heed).[30] A racy, colloquial version, however, can only be achieved at the expense of that plainness of language which is also a Chekhov hallmark. It is the avoidance of colourful dialect in favour of what Mayakovsky recognized as Chekhov's genius for 'simple, "grey" words' that is so striking in the original.[31]

The new translation of *The Seagull* was performed in March 1971 by Theatr Fach Llangefni after members of the Little Theatre company had been given an object lesson in producing the play by the Moscow Art Theatre during the 1970 World Theatre season in London. The experience of staging the play reinforced the awareness of the translator's problem: to strike the delicate balance between the naturally colloquial and the careful stylization which is Chekhov's genius. The translator's dilemma of rendering a 'good' or 'faithful' translation is particularly acute with Chekhov, and is the reason why there cannot be a canonical translation.

Conscious of the continuous need for new versions to match new interpretations, the National Eisteddfod has acted as patron in encouraging fresh new translations and giving them a stage. At the 1980 Dyffryn Lliw Eisteddfod, Elin Wyn Roberts' version of *Uncle Vanya* was commended,[32] revised, and performed the following year at Theatr y Werin, Aberystwyth, by the Drama Department of the University College of Wales as part of the Maldwyn National Eisteddfod.

Two years later Elin Robots' translation of *Three Sisters* was produced by Ceri Sherlock for the Llangefni Eisteddfod, and went on tour in the autumn. Between the Eisteddfodau of 1955 and 1983 Chekhov demonstrated how the circumstances of Welsh-language theatre had changed within a generation. *Uncle Vanya*'s short tour through town and village halls had aimed to climax at the National Eisteddfod; *Three Sisters*, after using the festival as a proving ground, was able to tour the network of small community theatres established with the support of the Welsh Arts Council in recent years. Its reception at Theatr Ardudwy, Harlech, was reflected by a note in *Y Ffynnon*, the Lleyn Peninsula community newspaper, commenting on 'the best audience, the truly voluntary one' who had come 'from their own choice and for positive reasons': 'At ten minutes to eight the lights rose on "The Three Sisters", and the first half went on without an interval until ten o'clock. Throughout the whole time, not a cough or a rustle of sweets paper was heard. Everybody listened intently enough to hear the actors think.'[33]

Chekhov was won over for his Welsh audience thanks to the sympathetic perception of Hudson-Williams, his first translator, who had the good fortune to work alongside drama enthusiasts, immersed in their community drama, with an understanding of the new theatrical trends, and links, however tenuous, with the Moscow theatre which had sustained Chekhov. These enthusiasts spoke to a friendly audience who, undazzled by the glare of alienating professional footlights, listened intently. Through their listening – and they were helped to do so by Cynan – they heard the humour in the plays, the plain but poetic speech of Chekhov's characters, and recognized the magical transmutation of those elements which had been the crude stuff of the homespun Welsh kitchen comedies, the quiet dramas of ordinary people leading ordinary lives, what Saunders Lewis had called 'the people's life and dream'.[34] For his part, whether it be in the eisteddfod, the college societies, radio drama, Arts Council ventures or the recently established professional companies and television productions, Chekhov has been a creative presence at each salient in the development of the Welsh-language stage.

Notes

1 A. P. Chekhov, *Polnoye sobraniye sochineny i pisem v tridtsati tomakh (Complete collected works and letters in 30 vols)*, XII (*Pisma*) (*Letters*) (Moscow: Nauka, 1983), p. 194.
2 Theodore Komisarjevsky, *Myself and the Theatre* (London: Heinemann, 1929), pp. 172–6.

3 *Ibid.*, p. 42.

4 Elsbeth Evans, *Y Ddrama yng Nghymru* (Liverpool: Gwasg y Brython, 1947), p. 55. See also 'Notes of the month', *Welsh Outlook*, January 1927, p. 5: '... one of the lessons which Wales is most in need of learning at the present moment. Hitherto its culture has been either a "home industry", or a thing borrowed exclusively from England ... A new step in the right direction is to be taken in the 1927 Eisteddfod, when Ibsen's play, "The Pretenders" will be acted in Welsh.'

5 *Yr Herald Gymraeg*, 9 August 1927, p. 8.

6 Evans, *Y Ddrama*, p. 45.

7 Komisarjevsky, *Myself and the Theatre*, pp. 20–1.

8 *Ibid.*, p. 22.

9 I am indebted to Harvey Pitcher for this information confirmed in a letter from J. D. Mabbott.

10 *Y Llwyfan*, 1:8 (1929), p. 122.

11 Ifan Kyrle Fletcher, 'A thought for the immediate future', *Y Llwyfan*, 1:8 (1929), p. 123.

12 *Ibid.*

13 See *Y Ford Gron*, 1:3 (1930), p. 18. The drama correspondent in reply to a letter from Idris Foster, Secretary of the Welsh Drama Society at UCNW, Bangor, who had complained that an account of the development of Welsh drama had failed to mention the College Society, apologized for not having listed the College Players in the 'First Division in the North'.

14 Cynan, 'Russian literature in Welsh translation: the brilliant and immense work of Professor Hudson-Williams', *Wales*, 5:7 (1945), pp. 81–4.

15 *Ibid.*, pp. 82–3.

16 Eric Wynne Roberts, 'Yr Actor a'r Cynhyrchydd', *Llwyfan: Cylchgrawn Theatr Cymru*, 5, n.d., p. 22.

17 Bangor MS 22469.

18 Bangor MS 22463.

19 Bangor MS 22463. Cynan here was possibly thinking of an observation made by T. Hudson-Williams in his note on Chekhov in the journal of the Calvinistic Methodists, 'Bardd a Llenor', *Y Drysorfa*, 92 New Series, (1938), p. 251: 'There is more hope for the salvation of the soul in the man driving wildly towards the City of Destruction than the man lying fast asleep in the mire in the Slough of Despond.'

20 Sara Roberts, 'Success of Chekov in Welsh', *North Wales Weekly News*, 14 August 1941, p. 3.

21 J. S. Lewis, 'The present state of Welsh drama', *Welsh Outlook*, December 1919, pp. 302–3.

22 *Ibid.*, p. 302.

23 *UCNW Student Record Book*, No. 5, 1953–4, p. 18.

24 R. E. Griffith, 'Ewyrth Ifan (Tsiechoff)', *Baner ac Amserau Cymru*, 17 February 1954, p. 3.

25 *Rhaglen Swyddogol Eisteddfod Genedlaethol Frenhinol Cymru Pwllheli a'r Cylch: Awst 1, 2, 3, 4, 5a 6* (Cardiff: Hughes a'i Fab, 1955), p. 196.

26 Emyr Edwards, 'Y Dramau ym Mhwllheli', *Baner ac Amserau Cymru*, 10 August 1955, p. 8.

27 Anton Tshechof, *Gwylan*, translated by W. Gareth Jones (Cardiff: Gwasg Prifysgol Cymru, 1970).

28 T. Gwynn Jones, 'Gwnawn inni "Fap" Newydd o Gymru yn dangos y tafodieithoedd', *Y Ford Gron*, 5, November 1934, pp. 3–4.

29 Edwards, 'Y Dramau', p. 8.

30 *Gwylan*, p. x; Korney Chukovsky, *O Chekhove (About Chekhov)* (Moscow: Khudozhestvennaya literatura, 1967), p. 199.

31 Vladimir Mayakovsky, *Polnoye sobraniye sochineny v trinadtsati tomakh (Complete collected works in 13 vols.)*, I (Moscow: Khudozhestvennaya literatura, 1955), p. 300.

32 *Eisteddfod Genedlaethol Frenhinol Cymru, Dyffryn Lliw, 1980: Cyfansoddiadau a Beirniadaethau*, ed. W. Rhys Nicholas (Llandysul: Gwasg Gomer, 1980), p. 182.

33 *Y Ffynnon: Papur Bro Eifionydd*, October 1983, p. 6.

34 Lewis, 'The present state of Welsh drama', p. 303.

CHAPTER 10

Chekhov re-viewed: the Moscow Art Theatre's visits to Britain in 1958, 1964, and 1970

Cynthia Marsh

The three visits made by the Moscow Art Theatre (MKhAT) to Britain between 1958 and 1970 took place at an important time both politically and culturally. As the newspaper reports of 1958 show, Britain was suspicious of the Russians: the cold war was still a reality. MKhAT's visits, however, were to contribute substantially to a thaw in the political climate. Culturally, the British theatre was experiencing its own crisis, which not only determined attitudes to the visitors, but was also affected by their presence.

In the West MKhAT was regarded as the cradle of Chekhov and, equally importantly, as the home of Stanislavsky. Attitudes to both were to undergo considerable change as a result of these opportunities to see Chekhov performed in Russian by the company co-founded by Stanislavsky and regarded as the inheritor of his techniques. These visits also offered the opportunity of a fresh look at Chekhov's own cultural context. This insight led to a reassessment of the British style of playing Chekhov. In the process there was a move to disentangle Chekhov's plays from Stanislavsky's versions of them, and also the opportunity to compare the modern, Western, sometimes distorted concepts of Stanislavsky's theories with those preserved in the practice of the Moscow company.

MKhAT seemed to wish to confirm their advance reputation as the foremost exponent of Chekhov by filling their programme with his plays. In 1958 they brought *The Cherry Orchard, Three Sisters*, and *Uncle Vanya*, and Rakhmanov's *The Troubled Past*; in 1964 *The Cherry Orchard*, Gogol's *Dead Souls*, and Pogodin's *Kremlin Chimes*; and in 1970 *The Seagull* and Pogodin's *Lenin – The Third Pathétique*. Five out of the nine plays London saw were by Chekhov. However, perhaps more importantly for gauging his impact on the British theatre, Chekhov's participation in the MKhAT programme steadily diminished. Of the three Chekhov plays performed in 1958 Viktor Stanitsyn's production of *The Cherry Orchard* was new; Iosif Rayevsky's *Three Sisters* dated from 1940 when it was originally mounted by Vladimir Nemirovich-Danchenko, the co-founder of MKhAT; *Uncle Vanya*, produced by Mikhail Kedrov, dated from 1947. The latter two, however, had recently been recast with younger players, notably in the female roles. In 1964 MKhAT returned with one Chekhov – the same production of *The Cherry Orchard* with a few cast changes – while Boris Livanov's *Seagull* of 1970 was entirely new. In other words, after the first visit London saw only one new production of Chekhov, in 1970. All the productions, however, had been treated in the rigorous manner inherited from Stanislavsky.

I

These visits had important consequences for the British reputation of both MKhAT and Chekhov. MKhAT never failed to impress with its ensemble playing; Stanislavsky was a controversial figure in the debate over interpretation of the plays; British and American scholarship began to tackle Chekhov's dramatic style; and finally, the British theatre mounted some new productions of Chekhov which suggest that a new vision of his drama was being born.

In Britain the theatre was going through a transition of its own. After Osborne's *Look Back in Anger* of 1956 a minor revolution in taste and expectation occurred. The demotion of star and promotion of company implied in ensemble playing particularly suited the new mood. MKhAT impressed British theatre in both 1958 and 1964 with the suitability of the ensemble style for highlighting the complex counterpoint of the dramatic structure of Chekhov's plays. The 1970 production of *The Seagull*, though disliked generally by the critics, none the less united them in admiration of the acting quality and the ensemble playing. Enhanced as it was by the ensemble concept, the counterpointing of Masha and Nina within the dramatic structure was a new feature, increasing the irritation of those who saw it as a departure from Stanislavky's interpretation, but confirming others in their view that the Stanislavsky line should not be regarded as prescriptive.

MKhAT was not, of course, the only company to bring this mode of performance to London. A highly successful visit by the Berliner Ensemble in 1956, masterminded by Peter Daubeny who was also responsible for the MKhAT visits, had created an enormous stir with its committed ensemble playing.[1] Some British actors and directors had periodically dreamed of establishing a permanent company. The theatrical system of Russia was newly admired for its permanent companies, state subsidies, the security offered to the actor, and the variety and opportunity of the repertoire. MKhAT's standards of teamwork reinforced the desire: the dream became reality with the establishment of the National Theatre at the Old Vic in 1963. At the same time, though, the reviewers' comments identified some of the disadvantages of this system, such as the difficulty for older actors, however good they may be, of relinquishing the younger parts, and the consequent lack of opportunity for younger players.[2] In 1964 this stultification was exemplified when the same production of *The Cherry Orchard* returned with only a very few cast changes. Nevertheless, even with these reservations, the Moscow company had provided some stunning examples of the potential of such a system.

Stanislavsky is a key figure. Again and again the reviewers remark on the painstaking technique: clear evidence not only of thorough rehearsal, but also of years of training in the Stanislavsky system. The revelation in 1958 was to see this system catalysing Chekhov. The mistake, and one which was mostly understood by 1964, was to see this system as germane to Chekhov. It was difficult at first to differentiate between the two, partly because of lack of understanding of Chekhov, and partly because of the misinterpretation of Stanislavsky's theories in the West and their subjugation to other theatrical influences.

The 1958 MKhAT visit demonstrated the difference between what was commonly assumed to be the Stanislavsky heritage in the West and its Russian counterpart. The general trend in the West towards more naturalistic productions had been achieved at the expense of, or even in denial of, theatricalism. As Ivor Brown pointed out in 1960, the modern fear of bravura acting had led to avoidance of expression of emotion and a tendency to underplay comic potential. Modern actors tend not to exploit their voices, and lines are thrown away. Stanislavsky dismissed the old rhetorical style, but never failed to communicate and always exploited the theatrical.[3] The naturalistic style, in other words, does not imply an abandonment of theatrical skills. Ivor Brown was advocating a return to the principles of theatre that underlay Stanislavsky's teaching and practice. Modern acting, much of it claiming to derive from Stanislavsky, is in fact a distortion of his theories. Many thought that MKhAT had preserved the Stanislavsky system untouched, and that in this confrontation with his company lay the chief value of the visits.

However, the Stanislavsky system had been modified in Russia too. In 1959 a group of theatre educationalists from America paid a study visit to MKhAT. Their conclusion was that, although MKhAT declared that they were adhering to Stanislavsky's methods and had maintained the tradition faithfully, Stanislavsky's system had been added to and certain impractical parts omitted. The Soviet approach was now marked by too puritanical a concern with pedagogical theatre. Technical training remained paramount, but strict sub-ordination to the director's demands and a (putative) policy of fidelity to the text disallowed any flexibility of approach.[4]

A minority of British critics, though, tried to disentangle their Chekhov from their Stanislavsky. In the preface to his study of Chekhov as a dramatist David Magarshack convincingly argued that MKhAT demonstrated by their 1958 visit that the Stanislavsky version represents only one interpretation of the Chekhov play.[5] An article in *The Times* the same year summed up the English view of Chekhov and defended the slightly sentimentalized version the English stage had made its own. This anonymous critic disliked the robust Chekhov offered by MKhAT.[6] Laurence Kitchin gave the credit to Chekhov rather than to Stanislavsky for the enormous impact the plays produced during the first visit by MKhAT.[7]

The 1970 production of *The Seagull*, however, failed in its mission to Britain. It was a deliberate attempt to rethink the play and remove it from the strait-jacket imposed, not only by Stanislavsky, but by decades of repression preventing theatrical innovation and experiment. The blame for the failure should not be laid too heavily on British audiences and critics. They had had no opportunity to view Russian productions of Chekhov's plays other than those of MKhAT, largely inspired by Stanislavsky and staged by a theatre noted for the tradition-alism of its views within a conservative system. Nevertheless, the point should be made that some reviewers of the earlier visits had tried to convey the changes wrought to Chekhov in the Soviet period.

Most of the comments focussed on *Three Sisters*. In 1958 Nicholas Nabokov had found the 'strained optimism' of the production a major difference from the Chekhov plays he had seen in their original stagings.[8] The ending was cut in the MKhAT production and was defended by Rayevsky on the authority of a manuscript in the Stanis-lavsky museum in Moscow. Gerhardie protested to *The Times* about this 'vandalism' and 'injury'.[9] J. W. Lambert felt that the cuts and staging left the sisters 'looking like a tableau at an old-fashioned revivalist meeting'.[10] One view ran in the opposite direction. In the 1964 version of *The Cherry Orchard* Stanislavsky's interpretation was felt to mask the socially significant aspects of Chekhov's 'essentially Marxist' play.[11] Such a view, despite its singularity, was among the first to distinguish between Chekhov's plays and Stanislavsky's versions of them.

British and American scholarship also began reassessing Chekhov the dramatist. In 1953 Charles Meister summed up what he saw as the attitude to Chekhov in the English-speaking world. Chekhov was regarded as a social prophet pleading for humanitarian principles; a dramatist of limited appeal who, despite his rapidly increasing period character, had written on themes of modern interest; and a short story writer who had engaged a considerable following.[12] By the end of the 1950s, however, comparisons were being drawn with modern dramatists including Pirandello and Tennessee Williams.[13] A recurring theme in reviews of Chekhov productions had been the treatment of the comic aspects. To some they remained a mystery, only explicable in terms of the Slav character; to others they were fundamental to Chekhov's dramatic mode and to his perception of life. Towards the end of the 1950s, several articles attempted to explore this particular problem.[14] Chekhov was linked to the theatre of the absurd on the basis of the nexus of comedy and tragedy in his works.[15] One Slavist argued that this perception had at last made Chekhov intelligible to the French![16]

Analysis of the dramatic structure of Chekhov's plays was undertaken, notably by Magarshack, whose study published in 1960 remains a classic of its kind. He evolved the theory of the play of indirect action, and traced its evolution through the major works.[17]

From these remarks it can be seen that the West was ready to disentangle Chekhov from Stanislavsky, and was poised to learn from the cultural model it had been offered, but equally anxious to develop its own interpretation of Chekhov's plays. And indeed, between 1958 and 1964, three key productions were mounted on the British stage, which suggest that not only reviewers and scholars, but also directors and performers were adjusting their views.

In his 1961 version of *The Cherry Orchard*, according to the *Times* reviewer, Michel Saint-Denis tried to find a compromise between the 'slightly sentimentalised' Chekhov the English were used to and the more robust figure the Russians had presented. He went on to say that emphasis on the positive aspects of Trofimov entailed intensifying the farcical elements of the other characters to ensure the absence of sentimentality. There were certainly less tears and sighs, and many of what he referred to as the 'poetic values' had disappeared.[18]

The second key production, *Uncle Vanya*, directed by Olivier in 1963 for the recently founded National Theatre, was almost universally acclaimed as magnificent. The anonymous reviewer in *The Times* found here all the 'inconsequence and spontaneity of life'; the sense of ensemble was very strong; the expression of the emotional under-tones overwhelming; and precision of detail in the characterization remarkable.[19] It seemed to add up to a manifesto production for the naturalistic style, and clearly lessons had been learned from MKhAT actors: particularly in attention to detail and in the expression of emotion.

Where was the comedy, we may well ask? Was Britain to persist in denying the comic in Chekhov? After all, in the MKhAT version Yelena was 'poised on the knife-edge of comedy' throughout.[20] Even the critic Kenneth Tynan, famous for his mocking comment on British theatre, found nothing to laugh at here. For him the abiding power of Chekhov, arising from this production, was the 'constant nagging sense that things might have been otherwise'. The perfor-mances of Olivier as Astrov and Redgrave as Vanya, Tynan thought, were superlative. His description of Sonya's 'heart-rending' final speech suggests the assertion of a different style of playing Chekhov.[21] This production made an uncompromising appeal to the emotions.

The third production, *The Seagull*, directed by Tony Richardson, just preceded MKhAT's 1964 visit. 'F. S.' in *Theatre World* liked the realism of Richardson's production and the 'lived-in' look of the design by Jocelyn Herbert.[22] Alan Seymour compared the 'conscious Naturalism' of Chekhov's play (the theatrical tricks were all there, he argued) with the low key of this production. He saw Richardson's method was to display the ordinary side of the characters and avoid the obvious interpretations. This method gets close to 'life as it is lived'. However, he argued, a 'danger' of Naturalism lies in the denial of theatricality, exemplified in the misinterpretation of this stance by Vanessa Redgrave who, in the role of Nina, played ordinariness as no performance and remained flat and lifeless throughout. He felt that she was pulled through, however, by the strength of the ensemble (and perhaps the play).[23] This production is important in the debate in two different ways. On the one hand, the pursuit of ordinariness was new and was aimed against the usual English view of the play as a Romantic tragedy. On the other hand, despite praise for the ensemble playing, there was criticism of the lack of theatricalism which had been such a revelation in the MKhAT style and which was also so much a part of Chekhov's first major play.

The return of the same MKhAT production of *The Cherry Orchard* in 1964, though admired for its techniques, disenchanted some. The limitations of MKhAT's unchanging approach were made newly evident, despite the fact that this conservatism had been implicit in the company's ethos as known previously in the West. Out of disenchantment, though, grew the first seeds of change. 1967 saw two London productions of *Three Sisters*.

William Gaskill's production at The Royal Court was regarded as 'cold blooded in its surprises' (Wardle),[24] 'bland and milky' (Brahms),[25] 'lugubrious' and 'played in the manner which used to get Chekhov a bad name' (Lambert).[26] Despite emphasis on the forward-looking elements of Chekhov's play, the production seemed to wallow too deeply in the sentimental English style. It was admired for that by some, but was discounted by a proportion of the critics now seeking a newer approach. In contrast, the National Theatre production a few months later was 'down-to-earth' and 'sturdy' (Brahms),[27] showed a 'vivacious realism', but was not quite the equal of the same company's *Uncle Vanya* (Wardle).[28] Josef Svoboda's set was certainly an attempt to break free from the usual naturalistic design.[29] Irving Wardle felt that *Uncle Vanya* had been a 'show for stars', whereas *Three Sisters* was very much more laudable as an ensemble production: Masha and Vershinin, for example, were not allowed to usurp the central position. It seems that the style and techniques of playing were reminiscent of MKhAT, but a determined attempt had been made to remove Stanislavsky's stamp of authentic period Naturalism.

II

Implicit in the debate stimulated by the arrival of MKhAT and their productions of Chekhov is the issue of cultural transference. Modern thinking about theatre suggests that every performance of a play creates a new text, and that it is pointless to seek a definitive version of any play. In these circumstances, the possibility of perceiving what a dramatist had or has in mind, or of recreating an authentic period performance, or of reproducing an entirely correct cultural context, is remote. Perhaps the argument about cultural transference should begin from the other end, as it were – from a consideration of what is expected from the theatre as a cultural phenomenon. At one level theatre is expected to be responsive to its own cultural and temporal environment. Chekhov's plays contain enough that is universal about the *tragédie* or *comédie humaine* for them to be appreciated in different cultures, without extensive reference to their Russianness. At the same time, however, some specific problems did, and still do, arise in the transference of Chekhov to Britain.

In the British press, the most heated dispute was over character interpretation. Ranevskaya, Trofimov, and Lopakhin in *The Cherry Orchard* were considered the most problematic. Some reviewers were expressing their subconscious awareness of cultural difference by their 'disappointment' or 'surprise' at the character interpretations the Russians offered.[30] Others tried to analyse the cultural leaps that had taken place. J.W. Lambert was not alone when he laid the blame on the Russians, implying that a different political outlook was responsible for these deviations from the Chekhovian text.[31] Kenneth Tynan and V.S. Pritchett took the British to task. Tynan wrote that the British stage had turned Chekhov's characters into 'decadent aristocrats'. They should be seen, he suggested, as 'country gentry'.[32] Pritchett thought that a confusion of Chekhov's with Turgenev's characters had taken place in the British mind.[33]

Transplanting these characters from one cultural framework to another contributed to the disagreements. The family is not even the 'country gentry' of Tynan's description: some access to their relatively poor economic base and disintegrating family cohesion also needs to be given. The Russians projected a new view of Ranevskaya in Britain: her maternal instincts, and sense of guilt at the economic and moral impoverishment of the domestic set-up turned her into an unattractive '*Hausfrau*'.[34] And Pritchett was perceptively correct in distinguishing her from the elegant 'salon' women of Turgenev.

Tynan saw Trofimov as a misfit whose social miscasting was as crucial to his adherence to idealistic prophecies, as to his awkward buffoonery. In my view Lopakhin's different social origin was also instrumental in the misconception: to the rigidly class-structured English mind he appeared as the villain of the piece. MKhAT showed, at least in the 1958 production, that he is a character of maturity, who is unwillingly, and perhaps tragically, caught between his own generosity and self-assertion. Perhaps even more significantly, Tynan pointed out that the British had also invested these characters with the nostalgia they had for their own gentry and comfortable 'English' country life. From these attitudes had derived the prominently sentimental British view of Chekhov.

Two further issues which proved stumbling blocks in the cultural transference were Naturalism and Stanislavsky. In its day, around the turn of the century, Naturalism had implications for both the content and style of new plays. Its limitations, however, were soon discovered, and have become ever more obvious since. On the one hand, Naturalism represented a set of new and disturbing ideas which derived largely from positivist philosophy and from Darwin's theories on evolution. The impact of the 'new' theatre became socially and politically increasingly explosive. On the other hand, here was a laudable attempt to make theatre relevant to the lives and concerns of its audiences, as opposed to a contemporary theatre preoccupied with escapism and hollow entertainment. However, the attempt to imitate reality had important consequences for theatrical style and performance. The result was a kind of freeze-framing of the contemporary situation. Naturalism did not, or could not, foresee that topicality and exact imitation of contemporary reality could, with the passing of time, act as a kind of mask, a distancing mechanism between the audience and the issues under discussion.

Whether Stanislavsky understood the transitory nature of Naturalism is less clear. His productions of Chekhov's major plays were undertaken in the admirable spirit in which the Moscow Art Theatre was founded, following the characteristics of the Naturalist style rather than its specific philosophy. Above all, his desire was to stage plays which were of direct relevance to its contemporary middle-class audience. The imitation of reality that Naturalism implied meant that motivation and verisimilitude were considerations high on Stanislavsky's agenda. As a result, he was dubious about anything that was not covered by these priorities or smacked of theatricalism. However, the paradox is that what was life-giving to Stanislavsky's productions could only with the passing of time come to be seen as part of a particular period, and present difficulties for actors and audience uninitiated in the habits of Russian life at the turn of the century.

Motivation and verisimilitude became ingrained in the MKhAT

performance style. However, in the new productions mounted in the 1950s they still masked aspects of Chekhov's work which failed to fit the naturalist framework. For example, in Act 1 of *The Cherry Orchard* there is the moment when Lopakhin utters an absurd bleat to Varya and Anya. Magarshack welcomed the attempt on MKhAT's part to break with Stanislavskian tradition, but argued that their treatment of Lopakhin's sudden appearance from off stage showed as little comprehension as Stanislavsky sometimes displayed of Chekhov's dramatic intention. In the 1958 MKhAT version a realistic motivation was provided for Lopakhin to be on stage: to deflect the absurdity and lack of context of the line, he was required to pull on a heavy suitcase.[35]

Stanislavsky devised naturalistic frameworks for Chekhov's plays. He was not always faithful to the text Chekhov had provided. He was, in fact, creating his own interpretation of the Chekhov play, as does any director. However, so strong were Stanislavsky's influence and reputation that his interpretations were regarded as definitive. What was needed, and still is, was the recognition that Chekhov's plays can successfully be dissociated from one performance style and from one historical period. There are other examples of absurd, unmotivated effects in Chekhov's plays (the breaking string in *The Cherry Orchard* is one) which bring him closer to modern dramatists such as Sartre, Camus, and Beckett, and which Stanislavsky's Naturalism tended to obscure. Chekhov's playtexts, however time-locked they may appear, are laced with theatrical devices which add an essential timelessness in performance. MKhAT's visits enabled the process of distinguishing Chekhov's plays from Stanislavsky's versions of them to begin.

It may also be the case that exposure to the West after such a long interval also stimulated debate in Moscow, if the innovations of the 1970 production of *The Seagull* are anything to go by. In this way London, and Moscow by 1970, were beginning to appreciate that Chekhov's plays would outstrip the naturalistic style and Stanislavsky in their international reputation.

The vexed question of translation and its role in cultural transference of the foreign dramatist was not broached in the criticism. An obvious reason lies in most theatre critics' ignorance of Russian. At least two critics were sensitive enough to refer to this area as a blank.[36] Moreover, scholarship tends to dwell on the written Russian text rather than on performance in English. Choice of idiom, register, and particularly accent in Britain is crucial to the building of character interpretation in performance. Equally crucial and difficult to transplant successfully is Chekhov's frequent literary allusion, his musical reference and his sound atmospherics. Chekhov was sufficiently well known for many people to have seen his plays in English, if not to have read them, and from 1964 simultaneous translation was available in the theatre. There were, though, two interesting reactions to the language which were mutually contradictory. One suggested that changes in language are a more important divisive factor in interpretations of Chekhov over different periods, even in his native land, than has been realized, while the other implied that cultural transference is possible.

Nicholas Nabokov was Russian-born, and had seen the original MKhAT productions. In some ways this discredits him as an objective reviewer of the later MKhAT performances but it did allow him to make some rare revelations to those who knew no Russian, and to those Russian speakers who had no experience of spoken Russian in the first part of the twentieth century. He found that in the gap of 30 or more years since 1922–3 when he had first seen these plays, the language had changed sufficiently to affect interpretation. For example, he commented, in the 1958 version of *Three Sisters* Natasha appeared a 'vulgar half-breed, a provincial coquette', while she actually belonged to the provincial middle class. With the type of Russian now spoken, if only on the stage in the USSR, she had lost her 'fluttering superciliousness and even grotesqueness', and sounded unconvincingly peasant-like. Irina (*Three Sisters*) and Trofimov (*The Cherry Orchard*) were similarly affected.[37] William Gerhardie, also born in Russia, wrote at the time that the 'miracle' of Chekhov lay in the 'lyrical undertones of his perfectly colloquial, even humorously trivial lines'. He then added that these undertones are penetrable by the foreigner and that, leaving aside the inimitable performances of Lukyanov (Lopakhin) and Yanshin (Pishchik), John Gielgud's Vershinin was probably better than the native interpretation in catching them.[38]

In conclusion, the visits made by MKhAT to Britain were valuable because they gave rise to a cultural and temporal confrontation between the British and Russian views of Chekhov. British theatre was able to appreciate for the first time how much Chekhov had been assimilated to English culture. Subsequently, the balance was redressed in favour of a more authentic Russianness. Furthermore, these visits demonstrated clearly to the British theatre that even though Stanislavsky had placed his period stamp on Chekhov, he could not obliterate the originality and modernity of Chekhov's theatrical genius. All due praise was given to him for having enabled Chekhov's plays to survive. However, his 'system' founded on the principles of Naturalist theatre could only perpetuate that particular view of Chekhov. Finally, Chekhov himself emerged with honours as a dramatist: this confrontation proved that his plays can transcend the cultural and temporal divides, and his international stature and timelessness as a dramatist were confirmed.

Notes

1 Peter Daubeny, *My World of Theatre* (London: Jonathan Cape, 1971), pp. 45–64, provides an unselfish account of the labyrinthine difficulties of the 1958 visit.
2 Kenneth Tynan, review of Faubion Bowers, *Broadway, USSR, Entertainment in Russia*, republished in *Curtains* (London: Longmans, 1961), p. 441.
3 Ivor Brown, 'After Chekhov', *Drama*, 56, Spring 1960, pp. 28–30.
4 John D. Mitchell, George Drew, Miriam P. Mitchell, 'The Moscow Art Theatre in rehearsal; *Educational Theatre Journal*, 12, December 1960, pp. 276–84.
5 David Magarshack, *Chekhov the Dramatist* (New York: Hill and Wang, 1960), p. vii.
6 'Chekhov on the English stage', *The Times*, 16 January 1960.
7 Laurence Kitchin, 'Chekhov without inhibitions. The Moscow Art Theatre in London', *Encounter*, 11:2, August 1958, pp. 68–72.
8 Nicholas Nabokov, 'The Moscow Art Theatre: old and new', *The Listener*, 5 June 1958, pp. 933–4.
9 W. Gerhardie, Letter to the Editor, *The Times*, 11 June 1958.
10 J. W. Lambert, 'Plays in performance', *Drama*, 51, Autumn 1958, p. 17.
11 Ronald Bryden, 'Heart', *New Statesman*, 5 June 1964, p. 887.
12 Charles W. Meister, 'Chekhov's reception in England and America', *American Slavic and East European Review*, 12, February 1953, pp. 109–21.
13 Alvin B. Kernan, 'Truth and dramatic mode in the modern theatre: Chekhov, Pirandello and Williams', *Modern Drama*, 1, 1958, pp. 101–14.
14 Jacqueline E. M. Latham, '*The Cherry Orchard* as comedy', *Educational Theatre Journal*, 10, March 1958, pp. 21–9; Norman Silverstein, 'Chekhov's comic spirit and *The Cherry Orchard*', *Modern Drama*, 1, 1958, pp. 91–100.
15 Walter Stein, 'Tragedy and the absurd', *The Dublin Review*, 233, Winter 1959–60, pp. 363–82.
16 S. Sobolevitch, as reported in 'Chekhov and West European Drama', ed. V. Ehrlich, *Yearbook of Comparative and General Literature*, XII, 1963, pp. 56–60.

17 Magarshack, *Chekhov the Dramatist*.
18 'Uneasy compromise on Chekhov', *The Times*, 15 December 1961.
19 'Acting as natural as breathing', *The Times*, 20 November 1963.
20 'Moscow Art Theatre's Uncle Vanya', *The Times*, 21 May 1958.
21 Kenneth Tynan, review of *Uncle Vanya*, published in *Tynan Right and Left* (London: Longmans, 1967), pp. 110–11.
22 F. S., *'The Seagull'*, *Theatre World*, 60:471, April 1964, p. 11.
23 Alan Seymour, 'Summer seagull, winter love', *The London Magazine*, 14:2, May 1964, pp. 63–7.
24 Irving Wardle, 'Chekhov produced with fidelity', *The Times*, 5 July 1967.
25 Caryl Brahms, 'My twenty-first-and-a-half-sister', *The Times*, 28 June 1969.
26 J. W. Lambert, 'Plays in performance', *Drama*, 86, Summer 1967, p. 27.
27 Brahms, *ibid.*
28 Wardle, 'Chekhov produced with fidelity'.
29 See the article by Arnold Aronson (ch. 17) in this volume.
30 'Chekhov's characters' subdued style', *The Times*, 30 May 1964.
31 See Lambert, 'Plays in performance', p. 16; Nabokov, 'The Moscow Art Theatre', p. 934.
32 Kenneth Tynan, 'Review of *The Cherry Orchard* and *Three Sisters*', republished in *Curtains* (London: Longmans, 1961), pp. 433–4.
33 V. S. Pritchett, 'More than method', *New Statesman*, 24 May 1958, pp. 662–4.
34 Lambert, 'Plays in performance', p. 18.
35 Magarshack, *Chekhov the Dramatist*, pp. ix–x.
36 Kitchin, 'Chekhov without inhibitions', p. 72; V. S. Pritchett, 'More than method', p. 663.
37 Nabokov, 'The Moscow Art Theatre', p. 933.
38 Gerhardie, *The Times*, 11 June 1958.

CHAPTER 11

A path to Chekhov

Oleg Yefremov

I

I might never have become an actor and director if during the war, in 1943, when I was still a teenager, I had not seen the famous Moscow Arts production of *Three Sisters*. The impression it made was overwhelming. I did not understand much at the time, but I was so excited, so fascinated by it. For days afterwards I was under the kind of spell that Chekhov probably *should* cast. Then I started thinking how I might join the theatre profession myself, and in 1945 I became a student at the Moscow Arts (MKhAT) Studio School.

Meeting Mariya Pavlovna Chekhova and Olga Leonardovna Knipper also drew me closer to Chekhov. I was only eighteen when I went to Yalta and met Mariya Pavlovna, but she, the sister of Chekhov, received me as an equal. Several times we had breakfast together and she would tell me about the early years of her nephew, the actor Michael Chekhov; she assumed that since I wanted to become an actor this was what would really interest me. She and Michael Chekhov had been very close. They were always joking and playing tricks on each other, but, I recall, they obviously had a deep respect for each other as well. She also told me things about Anton Pavlovich, this very tall man with the very deep voice, that brought him alive for me.

In 1948 Olga Leonardovna invited friends to come and stay with her at the little Tatar house at Gurzuf on the Black Sea coast which had been left her by Chekhov. This was where he wrote *Three Sisters* (in 1987 it was opened as a museum). It was set in a bay, had a small garden, and that summer Svyatoslav Rikhter, Nina Dorliak, Pavel Markov, Genrikh Neygauz, and others came there for a rest. And the fact that they had gathered here, in Chekhov and Knipper's house, created a very special atmosphere. Olga Leonardovna, then nearly eighty, was a remarkable woman. She kept open house and I went there several times that summer even though I was still a student.

The impressions you have when you are young stay with you. From those remote years I carried away something that is still alive in me: an image of Chekhov's home, and the atmosphere of Chekhov, an idea of what a genuinely Chekhovian production is, and what Chekhov himself was like, lively and unpredictable. Then, slowly, I began to stage Chekhov's plays myself. I must admit that all my MKhAT productions of Chekhov cost me great effort. I had, of course, to arrive at my own understanding of Chekhov, and I could only do this by overcoming the lure of the tradition, the legends, the clichés even. I did not want to repeat these clichés.

Nemirovich-Danchenko's 1940 staging of *Three Sisters* is still running at MKhAT! The cast has changed several times over, of course, but if I went and saw this production today I doubt whether I would want to become an actor ...

II

I find it difficult to talk about my own productions. Perhaps it is best for me to describe what we were trying to do in our work with the plays and the problems that came up.

Ivanov (1976)

Chekhov wrote *Ivanov* at a time when he was deeply preoccupied with the meaning of life and the behaviour of people in society. It seems to me a very personal play.

The first thing I was criticized for was altering its shape. I opened with the second act. That is to say I opened with part of the second act then went back to the first. We had a short scene at the Lebedevs' in which the guests discuss Ivanov's moral conduct, so to speak, and Sasha stands up for him, and that was all. It was an exposition: the audience discovered something about Ivanov, then went back to Act 1 and saw Ivanov himself. Here, on Ivanov's estate, the act ran straight through to the point at which he actually leaves for the Lebedevs. Now his arrival at their house seemed natural and the second act resumed.

To be honest, I felt that Anton Pavlovich had written Act 2 in the old manner. There is no complex inner life going on, everything is much simpler – possibly because of the nature of the characters themselves. Dividing Act 2, however, slightly softened this impression.

This is my favourite production. I was very lucky with my actors: Ivanov was played by Innokenty Smoktunovsky, Lebedev by Andrey Popov, and the Count by Mark Prudkin. It was a very rich and very strong ensemble, but not without its problems.

The criticism has been made that Smoktunovsky played Ivanov as a depressive, that his Ivanov was a man who was finished, that the part could not develop. Of course what is happening to Ivanov is partly physiological (he says in Act 3 that he is 'suffering from strain', that he 'took on too much'). And yet he does a number of things that suggest a rather *strong* personality. For instance, there is his scene with Sasha in Act 2 when he suddenly burns bright again with a 'what if?' ('Can I start a new life then, Sasha?'), and the vehemence of his scene with his wife in Act 3. These show that his character is a passionate one, one that can be set on fire. Smoktunovsky could not give me this. He acted the part extremely interestingly, but it is true that I wanted him to show Ivanov getting out of his depression more.

I think the reason *Ivanov* is staged less often abroad than Chekhov's other plays is that it portrays a very Russian phenomenon. It hinges on a particular characteristic of the Russian intelligentsia – its need to serve, to give itself (dare one say it) to the people. Ivanov's tragedy is that nobody wants this from him. Society is too apathetic, its interests are too low. Ivanov cannot understand what the matter is, but he is destroyed more by the fact that he and his abilities are not needed than by his own morbid introspection. It would be wrong, I think, to play him as a neurotic, and Chekhov constantly stresses this.

In one of his letters Chekhov says that whereas in Europe people commit suicide from overcrowding, in Russia it is because there is too much room and they have to go so far to reach the nearest person. In my production I wanted a particular space, not naturalistic with fields and forests on a backdrop etcetera, but basically what the audience would see as the squared-off forecourt of the house itself. To my mind, Borovsky produced a very fine design[1] which forced the actor to exist in a particular way. Smoktunovsky had nothing to lean against, nowhere even to sit down, it was just an uncomfortable, empty stage with a lone man suffering and fretting on it, looking for a place for himself but not finding it. He was being very precisely propelled into the physical and mental state of the character. Smoktunovsky was not happy, however, he wanted the traditional Chekhovian table, chairs, and comfort. We have now revived this production with a different cast: Ivanov is played by Stanislav Lyubshin, and Smoktunovsky plays the Count.

The Seagull (1980)

Again we adopted a free approach. Instead of four acts with three intervals, we had one interval between Acts 3 and 4, when 'two years pass'. This meant that we had to move one or two things, for instance the scene in which Masha tells Dorn of her love for Treplev. With the first two acts run together, this scene bunches up Masha's fate too much, her whole stage existence; so in our version we put it at the end of Act 2 rather than Act 1. We also added various things from the earlier versions of the play, especially lines of Medvedenko. This part was greatly reduced by Chekhov in his final version. We more or less reconstructed it.

The last act was also slightly altered. In the final version of the play Nina and Treplev are alone for their classic *Concertstück*, they have the stage to themselves. In the earlier text Sorin is also on stage, asleep in his chair, but Nina and Treplev are so preoccupied with each other that they barely notice. Suddenly she asks: 'Is he very ill?'. He replies: 'Yes'. That is all they say; but it is very Chekhovian. So we used that version.

The main question at the end, of course, is whether Nina is broken, finished as a person, or has attained a wisdom that will help her to believe. We have to understand why she has come, why she is seeing Treplev again. As soon as the reason is clear to the actress the scene will succeed, because then she will understand what is the main thing about this scene and indeed the play. Nina has come because she and Treplev once started together. She subsequently committed a mistake, she betrayed him, and must absolutely come back to see him now before she can go on – it is as though he were her director. So she has come; but he no longer believes in anything ...

Before Nina appears, Treplev has a soliloquy. This is sometimes delivered rather casually, but it is very important. He says that it is 'not a question of old or new forms' and that his life is a failure. He has not stuck things out. He did not have the strength. But one has to. And even though Nina has been mangled by life, even though she is barely alive, she *is* alive and has faith ('I am an actress'). Anastasiya Vertinskaya played this powerful scene in a very interesting way, I think. Here Nina had not yet suffered everything through, attained wisdom, but she did want to carry on, to be an actress. And that is the vital thing.

I think Chekhov went through something very similar in those years. He was preparing himself for something, there was something he had to achieve. *The Seagull* is very personal – it is about him, about a very disturbed period of his life. Hence all the arguments about art in the play, the depression, and the outbursts. Everyone wants to change something and to change themselves. Some can, some cannot. In *The Seagull* Chekhov was dealing with the important problem for him of a creative state in which art and duty combine. To bear one's cross and believe in what one is doing is one's duty, one's calling, one's life. In this sense *The Seagull* was an achievement, a breakthrough in art, and he knew this, which is why he took its flop so badly.

Uncle Vanya (1985)

Actresses sometimes feel that the part of Yelena in this play is cold. I do not agree. If they understand how she lives and what she lives for, they will discover that she has warmth, and a very interesting part can emerge. As always with Chekhov, it is a question not only of looking at the stage life of a character, but of studying its past.

He has pitched such a beautiful woman into life, but her character and her previous existence do not enable her to dare to do anything. Should she have an affair with a country doctor, Astrov? But she is from a different background and upbringing. Although she admits to him in Act 4 that she found him attractive, there can be nothing between them. She is honest with herself. If Yelena is acted as though she does not like Astrov, however, there will be nothing to play at all, nothing to fill the part. The more attractive she finds him, the better.

Similarly Serebryakov should not be played merely satirically, as we need to understand how Yelena made the mistake of marrying him. (She is not stupid; it is quite wrong to make her stupid.) He considers himself an opinion-maker, a 'master of men's thoughts'. This is his character, and he behaved towards Yelena accordingly. She believed it all and married him ... Now, of course, he is unbearable, as the night scene in Act 2 accentuates. Even here, though, he talks of himself in the same breath as Turgenev, as if to say 'I may be old and sick, but I'm still a major figure', and this is not merely funny:

he is continuing to fight for Yelena. If the actor playing Serebryakov does not put on a performance for her here, it will be boring. His heart may be breaking, he may be in pain, but he is still trying to win her, and he is pleased with the success of this self-made image of the 'wounded lion'.

Complex states of mind are frequently expressed in Chekhov by characters 'acting' like this. The classic example is Arkadina's scene with Trigorin in Act 3 of *The Seagull*, where her line 'Now he is mine' seems to me far less important than her elation at the performance she has given. Such stratagems are quite different from the beginning of *Uncle Vanya*, where Astrov would never have rambled on so much to Marina if he had not been trying to hide something. The sub-text here is: that woman is here, Yelena, and I am totally disconcerted.

III

Komisarjevsky has been criticized for cutting and altering Chekhov for his English productions in the 1920s.[2] The work of any writer, however, takes an extremely complicated route to its reader or audience. Chekhov himself was 'to blame' for the disastrous reception of *The Seagull*: how was the Russian audience to know of the upheaval that had occurred in him? They knew him still as the author of humorous stories and vaudevilles. Even Stanislavsky, I am convinced, did not understand Chekhov when he first staged *The Seagull*. If you look at his director's copy, you will see that he imported all kinds of business into this 'boring' play to make it more interesting for the audience. He staged the opening scene as farce. Front of stage he had a swing-seat which Sorin was sitting on, Treplev kept running back and forth from this seat to his theatre, then he leapt up onto it, and Sorin nearly fell off. Why? Obviously Stanislavsky did not trust his author. He wanted the play to have more action and interest. But he was still trying to bring it before an audience. Similarly Komisarjevsky made his changes, I am sure, out of love for Chekhov and so that these plays would at least be seen on a British stage. I for one then am prepared to forgive him.

On the other hand, I believe that in the twentieth century we have let the art of the director go to our heads. We have subordinated to it everything. In fact, though, life on the stage is created by the actor, and this is the only way to discover the secret of Chekhov or any other great writer.

I believe that, if a director approaches Chekhov from areas exterior to the art of the actor, he will fail; or he will be left with a production exterior to the life that only actors can create. I think sweeping directorial interpretations of Chekhov kill something in him. The director's work with his cast must be profoundly two-way: let all take the initiative. We so often underestimate the wonderful energy that the complex art of the actor generates, and the magnetism of the actor's playing. Such energy is possible only in the theatre and can only be apprehended through the actor.

Together, the actors and I try to discover the basic forces of the play. We then translate these into a line of action, which in turn gives birth to staging, design, the production. This is how we arrived at our conceptions of the symbols, for instance, in *The Seagull*. In addition to the bird itself, the 'magic lake', and others, I found the image forming of a theatre situated in a gazebo, which would serve as Treplev's theatre, Arkadina's theatre, Trigorin's theatre.[3] The symbols exist on various planes of the play and make their appearance at key moments, when the director has somehow to reveal a character's inner state or other people's attitude to him. They were realized for me by Valery Levental, who also did the design for *Uncle Vanya*.

Here the set presented a huge house with all its rooms, passageways, nooks, and corners. When it opened up, an outdoor space was created centre stage, with an autumn landscape in the distance.[4] Let me tell you how the production ends, though, and why. The lights fade downstage and the whole house can be seen upstage. Then the house too is plunged in darkness, but one window in it glows brighter and brighter. There is a light. For me this is associated with Uncle Vanya. Yes, he has discovered that he has wasted his life, but he still seems to me a man of truth. Of course his life is not easy, but he will carry on living for others whatever he has to suffer. He will continue to bear his cross. Again a production image is born from within, and has to be vindicated by the actor.

Somerset Maugham said that Chekhov was not a dramatist, because his plays could only be performed by actors of genius.[5] This is almost true: Chekhov demands discoveries, revelations, from his actors, and only when they make them do his plays come alive, only then do they light up. Of course the overall interpretation and stage design are important, but if the meaning of the play is not focussed in the art of the actor the whole play falls apart and cannot be understood. Chekhov's principal secret, however, is *life* on the stage. The more

10   Act 3 of *The Seagull* at MKhAT, 1980, directed by Oleg Yefremov, designed
by Valery Levental

11   Model by Valery Levental for *Uncle Vanya* directed by Oleg Yefremov at
MKhAT, 1985

subtle and living the images we can create, the closer we are to Chekhov;
and I believe this is one of the top priorities in Chekhov's theatre
today.

Notes

Oleg Yefremov (b. 1927) was leader of the Sovremennik Theatre in Moscow
from 1956 until 1970, when he became Artistic Director of MKhAT. His
productions include the trilogy *The Decembrists*, *The Narodovoltsy*, and *The
Bolsheviks* (1967), Bokarev's *The Steelfounders* (1972), Gelman's *A Sitting of the
Party Committee* (1975), and Vampilov's modern classic *Duck Hunting* (1979), in
which he acted the main part. Since 1976 Yefremov's work has been especially
associated with Chekhov. In 1986 he headed the formation of the breakaway
Union of Theatre Workers of the USSR, relinquished control of the new
MKhAT building on Tverskoy Boulevard, and together with his supporters
moved into the old, 1902 theatre. The latter company, led by Yefremov,
is now (1992) known as the Chekhov MKhAT, and the former, led by Tatyana
Doronina, as the Gorky MKhAT. *Nick Worrall*

1 See the illustration in Arnold Aronson's article (ch. 17) in the present volume.
2 See the article (ch. 7) by Robert Tracy in the present volume.
3 See illustration.
4 See illustration.
5 W. Somerset Maugham, *The Summing Up* (Harmondsworth: Penguin Books, 1963), pp. 84–5.

CHAPTER 12

Subsequent performances: Chekhov

Jonathan Miller

At last, to the pleasure of us all, Anton Pavlovich sent the first act of the new play, still unnamed. Then there arrived the second act and the third. Only the last act was missing. Finally Chekhov came himself with the fourth act, and the reading of the play was arranged, with the author present. As was our custom, a large table was placed in the foyer of the theatre and covered with cloth, and we all sat around it, the author and the stage directors in the centre. The atmosphere was triumphant and uplifted. All the members of the company, the ushers, some of the stage hands and even a tailor or two were present. The author was apparently excited and felt out of place in the chairman's seat. Now and then he would leap from his chair and walk about, especially at those moments when the conversation, in his opinion, took a false or unpleasant direction. After the reading of the play some of us, in talking of our impressions of the play, called it a drama, and others even a tragedy, without noticing that these definitions amazed Chekhov.[1]

The unnamed play Stanislavsky refers to is *Three Sisters*. Chekhov was not only 'amazed' but 'left the meeting'. When Stanislavsky sought out the unhappy playwright, he discovered that the reason for his anger 'was that he had written a happy comedy, and all of us had considered the play a tragedy and even wept over it. Evidently Chekhov thought that the play had been misunderstood and that it was already a failure.'[2]

Although Chekhov is a very different playwright from Shakespeare, his work similarly enjoys an afterlife and shares some of the problems common to works of art when they outlive their authors. This story, however, indicates that his intention was problematic even when he was alive and superintending a play reading. What has happened since Chekhov's demise? Initially his work was cared for by his widow who took on the dramatist's mantle and acted as the custodian to his intention. His plays have now become intricately connected with the slice-of-life realism and method of Stanislavsky. In England the misunderstanding of genre evident in Chekhov's time has been compounded by what I call the Keats' Grove genteel, well-mannered school of acting that flourished in the late 1930s and post-Second World War period. His plays have often been performed by the English theatrical Royal Family – with leading actresses like Peggy Ashcroft – and a certain style of acting has been so consistently associated with them that people begin to think of the melancholy, pausing version as the only permissible one. When another style is introduced, and Chekhov's work is played much more rapidly, casually, even shabbily, they think that a beautiful work has been violated. This seems to me to misunderstand what is remarkable about Chekhov – that his work takes such pleasure in what is un-beautiful and mundane about life. I have directed *The Seagull*, *Three Sisters*, and *The Cherry Orchard*, and in each case I reacted against the genteel approach, trying to make the work much coarser and more comic.

Three Sisters is a comedy in which someone is killed in a rather farcical and idiotic accident. Solyony has never struck me as a wonderful, sinister, duelling villain who with unerring aim kills Tuzenbakh. I've directed him as a rather drunken, resentful, solitary, and harassed figure who was dangerous precisely because he was unexpected. Similarly, the sisters' failure to get to Moscow is *not* tragic; they simply have to continue having a dull suburban life – with an affair now and again – as time passes by. Chekhov says somewhere that in most of his plays people just have conversations and drink tea, and most of our lives are filled up doing that. In a sense, the feeling in the plays is rather like Beckett – it passed the time and it would have passed anyway. This element together with the comedy needs to be brought out. The plays float on a rather indolent tide of un-directed chit-chat, and unless time in rehearsal is given to that, we find people trumpeting and elocuting the lines as if singing arias.

In the process of rehearsing *Three Sisters* we discovered the recurrent themes of time and memory. There are references to the passage of time and the impermanence of strong feelings on almost every page. Starting with the first speech when Olga says, 'It's exactly a year ago that Father died, isn't it? This very day, the fifth of May ...'[3] we learn that Irina was prostrated with grief but that she is now radiant with happiness. The characters then attempt to date the significant moments in their lives ('... your Saint's day, Irina') and later Andrey asks Natasha when it was he first began to love her. 'Eleven years have gone by', says Olga, remembering when they left Moscow, 'yet I remember everything about it, as if we'd only left yesterday'.[4]

For some of the characters the past seems vividly present, but to others it seems lost altogether. When Vershinin is reintroduced to the sisters, he has to admit, 'I don't really remember you, you know, I only remember that there were three sisters.'[5] But he remembers their father: 'I remember your father, though, I remember him very well. All I need to do is to close my eyes and I can see him standing there as if he were alive.'[6] And the memory of Vershinin himself is incompletely distributed between the three girls. 'I don't remember you, at all', says Masha, and then a few speeches later she says, 'Do you remember, Olga, there was someone they used to call "the lovesick major"?'[7] With the return of this memory she adds, 'Oh, dear, how much older you look! How much older!' This raises the second issue with regard to time, and that is how things, especially people, are altered. 'Yes, I was still a young man in the days when they called me "the lovesick major",' says Vershinin, 'I was in love then. It's different now.' Again in the opening lines, 'It's exactly a year ago that Father died ... I felt then as if I should never survive his death ... And now – a year's gone by, and we talk about it so easily.' Even grief, it seems, will be forgotten, both those for whom we grieve and even the bereaved themselves: 'You know, I'm even beginning to forget what she looked like. I suppose people will lose all memory of us in just the same way. We'll all be forgotten.'[8] And then there is the effort to try and visualize what the oblivious future will be like: 'Let's try to imagine what life will be like after we're dead, say in two or three hundred years time.'[9] And although, of course, they will be forgotten and no one will remember who they were or what they were like, they all, as Vershinin points out, have a stake in the forgetful future, for each one of them will have contributed to everything that follows. They cannot experience the posterity they imagine, but it will not come into existence without their actions. The happiness that Vershinin confidently anticipates is brought into existence by the suffering that we have to endure. In other words, it does no good to suppose that one could enjoy future happiness by hibernating until it comes into existence of its own accord, since it is brought into existence only by the misery that has to be endured.

As in Proust, the metaphor of photography is used to emphasize the experience of time. A group photograph is taken at the end of the first act and at the beginning of the last – two moments enjoyed and perhaps remembered by the participants, but whose visual record will be impenetrable and enigmatic to anyone looking at it hereafter.

When they pose for the photograph, it provides a moment at which strange and unexpected smiles will be recorded, but they do not look like anyone's smile because they are half-way between, their lips caught either on the way up or on the way down. When I directed this scene, the characters applauded themselves when the photograph was taken as though they had just performed and would see themselves on camera later.

Another metaphor of time is provided by the spinning top that briefly silences the company at the end of Act 1 while each of them contemplates his or her mortality as it spins, slows, falls silent, wobbles, and finally topples to a standstill. Suddenly the company see their lives winding down in miniature. The fact that things that seem so important at the time are soon forgotten pervades Chekhov's work. In *The Seagull*, there is a similar effect to that of the opening of *Three Sisters* when Dorn says, 'By the way – where is Zarechnaya now?' and the response, equally casual and throwaway, is 'I suppose she's all right.'[10] Things are soon forgotten, our lives pass with someone growing ill, having a stroke or dying. One of Trigorin's lines captures Chekhov's preoccupation with time: 'So we are going? More railway carriages, stations, refreshment bars, veal cutlets, conversations.'[11] That is the world of the plays – idle chatter, and the comic surface of social interaction.

While it is widely accepted now that genteel, pausing melancholy is not the only way to perform Chekhov, I have always been very stringent about the amount of comedy that can be included in his work. Again, as with Shakespeare, the director has to be careful not to follow, or fall into, stereotypes. Those in Chekhov are much less famous than they are with a play like *Hamlet*, precisely because Chekhov's work has been with us for a much shorter time and it is not written on the heroic scale that attracts simple, prototypic outlines in performance. Even so, for years Trigorin has been played as a rather silvery, distinguished figure, reminiscent of a slightly disreputable English gynaecologist. Arkadina also invites stereotypes. She is usually played in a very English-actressy way, whereas it would be rather interesting to show her as a rather pudgy little spitfire played by an actress like Prunella Scales. This would bring out a particular sort of raucous, Russian vulgarity which is usually neglected. There should be a lot more of the eruptive gaiety that is characteristic of Russians – floods of tears followed immediately by hysterical laughter. Masha in *Three Sisters* is also a part that has fallen into a cliché by being seen as a star performance that should be played by a 'great actress'. In fact, Masha is a rather unlikeable provincial girl with ideas that would have suited the Bloomsbury set. She thinks she is much more sensitive and intelligent than she is – after all she falls in love with the most boring, dull cavalry officer.

Another example is little Irina, a part that is often played as a sweet innocent child, as indeed she is described by Chebutykin who, as it happens, is a sentimental old fool. I have always imagined her as a very hard woman, and discovered that this was realizable on stage by re-designing the delivery of one short line at the end of the play. This came about in rehearsal with Angela Down playing Irina. Usually when the Doctor enters with the news that Tuzenbakh has been shot, there is a melancholy and sad surrendering 'I *knew* it, I knew it . . .'[12] Instead I had her suddenly bite and slam her fist down on the ground, spitting out the words as though shouting an expletive. This totally transformed the character and retrospectively we had to reconstruct her.

Chekhov is quite clearly more realistic than Shakespeare. The characters speak lines that are very like those that ordinary people speak when conversing with one another. There are ways of enhancing that sense of being in the presence of reality, and it is most important to attend to what are called 'the rules of conversation'. These have been identified only in the last twenty years or so by psycholinguists who are very interested in what is called 'turn-taking' in conversation. Conversation has a certain internal structure which is determined by rules that we all somehow know without understanding how we acquire this knowledge. There are rules of listening, of not speaking until the other person has finished, learning how to take your turn, and all sorts of mutually understood rules for establishing how to become the next speaker, and how floor space is allocated. If the actors pay great attention to this, the plays can possess a glittering sense of social reality. Otherwise the speeches simply follow one another and become stale because they do not reproduce the rhythm of ordinary speech. I found it essential to be more slipshod, and allow more hesitation and pauses of the kind you find in any ordinary conversation. It is also useful to allow for things that Chekhov has not written, by which I mean interruption, reduplication, and overlap with people starting to talk when the previous speaker has not finished and then having to apologize. All these little characteristics of speech take a long time to re-create on stage but when the actors manage it the audience feels as if it is in the presence of a real conversation.

On the other hand, we have to recognize that there is a certain artificiality about the organization of the scenes in Chekhov's plays. Despite the fact that they are much nearer approximations to spoken conversation than Shakespeare, for example, they are still what we might call 'fourth-order approximations' and not real speech. In Chekhov's writing there is a hidden sonata structure. This draws your attention, as a director, to thematic recurrences and the shape of the plays. Certain themes are stated, developed, reduplicated, inverted, and then returned again to the main theme. The sonata structure can still be preserved while encouraging the actors to speak in ways that are not written into the text. This is a rather complicated idea that needs some explanation.

When an author writes down a speech that he thinks of as being a genuine record of how people might speak, he inadvertently does something similar to what psychologists have recognized in perception and called 'regression to the real object'. This means that when we look at a scene we are not aware of the fact that the objects arranged in space create images on the retina that are very much smaller as they get more distant. All that we are aware of is that the objects appear as we know them to be. Similarly, in recording speech a naive draughtsman writes down the speech as it is understood, its clear meaning, rather than its actual sound. On the page, we see the meaning of what is heard and not what is *actually* heard. So the speech appears to be much more grammatical than it would if it had been spoken, and lacks the hesitations, the incompletenesses and the overlaps you might find on a tape-recording of the conversation. In a strange way, if you want to make the speeches seem real you have to overlook the way in which they are written down and try to remember how people actually sound, recognizing that what you have on the page is something that has regressed to the real object.

In order to return Chekhov's over-clarified speeches to the state of real conversation it is necessary to break them up and pay very close attention to the processes involved in conversation. This means having to listen to all the verbal and non-verbal accompaniments of conversation that regulate the process of turn-taking. This can be captured only from memory and most actors do *not* remember. They remember what the speeches mean, and everything else, which is so vital to the production and belongs to social exchange, is disregarded. Most people will reproduce what is on the page without realizing that the text provides only a clarified picture of what the characters mean. They forget that the lines do not convey how they might actively be spoken. In Shakespeare's play, we are not presented with this problem because writing in the particular verse form and rhetorical idioms that he did there was no need to pay attention to the dynamics of conversation. The verses follow one another with their metrical structure, and we cannot insert hesitations and interruptions, nor can we have people mumbling and interjecting with agreements. Yet Chekhov invites these little details which have been rinsed out of the script because they are actually inaudible.

With great care and attention, these details must be consciously restored to the speeches, and when this happens successfully Chekhov's lines take off and become animated. It also means you can shorten the playing time by allowing for overlap. One of the reasons that Chekhov traditionally takes so much time is that pauses, instead of merely indicating lack of response, are self-indulgently wallowed in and given melancholy significance.

Chekhov's dramas are often family affairs and when silence falls in the home, it is not felt to be an enigmatic pause but simply a moment when no one speaks. In contrast, there is an unease about silence in a social situation such as the scene where Vershinin enters; everybody tries desperately to make conversation and feels tremendously relieved every time Vershinin says something, as it fills in the gap. In order to show that they are not being inhospitable, the family goes on reacting long beyond the need to respond to his remarks. Erving Goffman describes the very complicated requirements placed on each of us in a social scene.[13] These not only require us to show ourselves in the best possible light, but to support other people involved in the exchange. What often happens in conversation is that if somebody rather rudely or abruptly interrupts, they then have to overcompensate and apologize to the speaker they have stopped by over-agreeing and denigrating what it is they actually want to say. The dynamic of conversation is not scripted in Chekhov, so the director simply has to remind the actors that this is what happens. It can be very exciting when actors suddenly understand what you are asking them to do, and again it is an element that is very variable in performance.

By simply remembering what the idioms would be in a normal conversation, the actors have access to a generative grammar. It is not something you can learn rigidly line by line, what happens is that the cast understands the rules of conversation and generates the sequences accordingly. These rules, very loosely, are what Grice describes in his 'Rules of Conversation Relevance'.[14] This means that whatever contribution somebody makes should be relevant and not redundant, and should not overload the listener with information. These very simple understandings are built into any conversation. Similarly, there are rules of courtesy that require us not endlessly to interrupt other people unless we have extremely good reason to do so. Actors have to internalize these habits in a performance, and then they can generate these differently every night. It was an intuitive awareness that prompted me to rehearse Chekhov in this way. I have since read a great deal about the structure of conversation, and listened to yards of carefully analysed tapes made by specialists so that my hunch as a director was later informed by other more authoritative sources.

Far from imposing his or her will on the actors, the director should be simply reminding, and releasing performances that only the actors' competence can bring to life. Most of the points I am making about Chekhov are familiar to us all; we do these things unthinkingly when we behave according to rules of conversational decorum. Off stage we never go through conversations without, in fact, offering a constant barrage of remedies – apologies, excuses, glosses – for potential, or actual, offences.

I have already mentioned many points with regard to intonation and inflexion that are not written into the script, but there are also interstitial features that are not part of what is being said, but rather linguistic and paralinguistic performances that affect how something is being said. Again, this is usually done without thought, but it affects the audience's perception and understanding of the various relationships – familial and social – in Chekhov's plays, which are so full of the comic surface of social interaction. Often actors become more sure of a character when they discover for themselves the sort of performances that their fictional part might give of these remedial actions. For example, they might find that one particular character violates turn-taking procedures more than another and never apologizes for the violation, or does so in a way that heightens the offensiveness of his or her social behaviour. This aspect of performance is much more revealing than any produced by the archivist director who researches historical setting in minute detail. Obviously, certain details need to be checked to avoid anachronism, but Chekhov's short stories are probably the best prefaces to his plays. Descriptions of people's conduct and their mannerisms are conspicuous by their absence from the plays, and in reconstructing them it is very helpful to read the stories, which are full of accounts of gesture, and tiny physical detail. It is as if, confronted by a play script by Dickens, you found inspiration for details in its performance by looking at the novels, which are full of wonderful vignettes, like the one of Mr Pocket, Herbert Pocket's father, who is seen picking himself up by the hair. It is possible by looking at the stories to effect a kind of internal transfusion of personal mannerisms – those little touches that are rarely written down in plays. A playwright like Shaw does include such details but he is such a bad observer that his descriptions of personal mannerism are just as much regressions to the real objects as the conversations he writes down. Dickens and Chekhov both excel in providing unexpected oddnesses of behaviour, which, incorporated into a play, can be quite breathtaking. One detail that Chekhov does provide in *Three Sisters* is an odd description of Solyony, who is described as constantly dabbing his hands with cologne. It is an interesting and rare little foible in the script, and a very odd gesture that he makes because he hates the smell of his own hands – rather a Dickensian oddity. What makes any Chekhov production lift off is this morbid sparkle of tiny subliminal details, idiosyncrasies that are curious but never extraordinary.

Another example of this occurs again in *Three Sisters* where, idling away an evening, they are sitting over the samovar and drinking tea, gossiping while Irina sits playing patience. Chebutykin says something as he turns over a book. 'Balzac's marriage took place at Berdichev.'[15] A moment later, Irina repeats this phrase to herself, but she is not responding; she has not been listening attentively. There is no connection between the two speakers, they are merely talking along-side one another, but people often struggle to find some profound significance in this repetition. It is, in fact, what is called echolalia, and, unless it is treated as such, the effect is lost. It is a masterly inclusion of something that gives the genuine rhythm of undirected speech. Irina is preoccupied with turning over a card and the phrase has simply gone in one ear, and she faintly repeats the sound. Chekhov's plays are simply concerned with showing the chronic coming and going of fairly undirected discourse. Often the so-called philosophical conversation suggested by characters is treated with too much reverence. When Vershinin says 'Let's do a bit of philosophizing', the response reads 'Yes, let's. What about?' 'Well … let's try to imagine what life will be like after we're dead, say in two or three hundred years.'[16] This is usually played with pace, firm intention, and ferocious academic enthusiasm, but people rarely talk like this. It is a game, and they are merely trying to fend off boredom and pass the time. The line might go: '[yawn] What about? [pause] well [pause] let's – try to – imagine – what – life – will – be – like [yawn] – after we're dead, – say – in two – or three hundred years.' Then there might be a long gap.

Chekhov has been performed too often by people trying to sing the lines. There are no arias in Chekhov – only a diminishing sonata that is written in very atonal music. Subsequently, the characters need to be fairly radically redesigned so that they are neither too romantic, nor too attractive, nor too melodramatic. The ordinariness must be emphasized with the humour, although I have allowed some eccentricity in casting when in one production of *The Seagull* we had Fenella Fielding playing Arkadina. In another production it was Irene Worth, who was very funny but perhaps too grand. Arkadina is, after all, rather vulgar. Chekhov's characters are very provincial, smalltown people, not really gentry, who while away the time playing lotto and going on uneventful journeys. Conversation and veal cutlets – that's all there is to life.

Notes

This essay is reprinted with the kind permission of the author from his book *Subsequent Performances* (London: Faber and Faber, 1986).

1 Constantin Stanislavski, *My Life in Art* (London: Geoffrey Bles, 1962), pp. 370–1.
2 *Ibid.*, p. 371.
3 *Plays. Anton Chekhov*, translated by Elisaveta Fen (Harmondsworth: Penguin Books, 1978), p. 249.
4 *Ibid.*, p. 250.
5 *Ibid.*, p. 257.
6 *Ibid.*, p. 258.
7 *Ibid.*
8 *Ibid.*, p. 259.
9 *Ibid.*, p. 280.
10 *Ibid.*, p. 170.
11 *Ibid.*, p. 162.
12 *Ibid.*, p. 329.
13 Erving Goffman, *Forms of Talk* (Oxford: Basil Blackwell, 1981), pp. 1–77.
14 See H. P. Grice, 'Logic and conversation', in *The Logic of Grammar*, eds. D. Davidson and G. Harman (Encino: Dickinson, 1975), pp. 67–8;

'Further notes on logic and conversation', in *Syntax and Semantics: Pragmatics*, IX, ed. P. Cole (New York: Academic Press, 1978), pp. 113–27; 'Presupposition and conversational implicature', in *Radical Pragmatics*, ed. P. Cole (New York: Academic Press, 1981), pp. 183–97.

15   *Plays*, p. 282.
16   *Ibid.*, p. 280.

CHAPTER 13

'The dwindling scale': the politics of British Chekhov

Vera Gottlieb

For the British General Election of 11 June 1987, the Conservative Party displayed an election poster which urged the voter to: 'Take the politics out of education – Vote Conservative'. There are several important assumptions behind this election statement: first, it perceives the Tory approach to education to be unpolitical; second, it implies that the only politics to be found in connection with education are Socialist; third, it assumes that education and politics are somehow separable.

My reason for using this as a starting-point for an exploration of the politics of British Chekhov is not an arbitrary one. All of these assumptions are to be found underlying the common approach, whether critical or theatrical, to Chekhov's plays on the British stage. It has been assumed that the majority of British productions have been somehow 'non-political', and that where a production or version of a Chekhov play has overtly brought out political significance – such as Trevor Griffiths' 1977 version of *The Cherry Orchard* – then this has been a forced or unnatural 'grafting' purely for the sake of left-wing ideology. Chekhov is commonly regarded in this country as a non-political writer, but my argument is that *all* productions have been political, by omission if not by commission; that there is no such thing as 'non-political' theatre, and that the majority or 'norm' of British productions of Chekhov have been both political and generally reactionary in their unquestioning assumptions about the values and the issues raised by the plays. Equally, there is an often unspoken assumption about what constitutes 'political theatre': a distinction must be made between political theatre which is self-avowedly didactic or *agitprop*, and theatre which is political in that it questions reality, inhibits audience escape into fantasy or dream, and places characters in an historically definable social milieu. Each kind of political theatre is differently motivated, utilizes different styles of writing and presentation, and has a different emphasis in its use of dramatic components – such as treatment of character. In the political theatre which is deliberately didactic or *agitprop*, character is often two-dimensional; in the other kind of political theatre, psychological depth of character may be an essential requirement for engaging with social reality so that the role and nature of the individual character is questioned within a defined environment and social context. This kind of political theatre not only does not preclude the psychological dimension, but may indeed create a complete osmosis between the political and the psychological. In the British theatre, both kinds exist under the same label, hence it is all too easy to assume that the use of the word 'political' (as in the Tory election poster) necessarily denotes something strident and didactic.

All of Chekhov's plays are located in a very specific period of historical time; his characters are defined and definable in terms of social class, economic and cultural factors, and trapped in an historical moment between their individual aspirations and their class limitations. The ideas voiced in all of Chekhov's work, whether literary or dramatic, are certainly not those of a reactionary, nor indeed of a revolutionary, but of a progressive and humanist. The *leitmotif* of play after play is *'tak zhit nelzya'* – one cannot and must not live like that. The solutions are not provided, but the questions *are* posed. As Chekhov himself put it: 'You are confusing two concepts: answering the questions and formulating them correctly. Only the latter is required of an author.'[1] This view was shared by Ibsen in his famous poem *A Letter in Rhyme*: 'I only ask. My task is not to answer.'[2] In their formulation of major questions about their contemporary reality (social *and* psychological), both Chekhov and Ibsen may be seen as political dramatists. But the majority of British productions of Chekhov have not posed the questions, and generally do not treat the plays as if they contain crucial and relevant issues. In this sense, many British productions have been much more reactionary or retrograde than Chekhov was in the writing of the plays.

The political 'norm' may be traced through 80 years of productions: the plays have frequently been viewed as tragedies; in more recent productions, such as Lindsay Anderson's innovatory 1975 *The Seagull*, or Jonathan Miller's 1976 *Three Sisters*, the comedy has been played up, but only as an aspect of dramatic form – not as a method of raising the issues through ironic detachment or as a source of political questioning through distancing and to counteract empathy. Chekhov has usually been regarded as a pessimist, and his characters presented as individual eccentrics impotent in the face of circumstances beyond their control. The circumstances, however, have been 'depoliticized' through unfamiliarity with or ignorance of social, political, and even geographical context. 'Circumstance', in the majority of British productions, has been either 'mysteriously Russian' or philosophically abstracted in terms of life and death and the passage of time (as in Peter Brook's 1981 Paris production of *The Cherry Orchard*). The consistent approach to characterization has been that of charming and blameless victims, and it was only with Trevor Griffiths' version of *The Cherry Orchard* in 1977 that an opposing interpretation was offered which suggested some measure of responsibility, even culpability, on the part of the characters. The 'norm' of approach was seen yet again in the 1987 production of *Three Sisters*, directed by Elijah Moshinsky. The moment when Natasha rounds on Anfisa with the line 'How dare you sit down in my presence?' was met by a shocked and delicate silence from the actress playing Olga. In this production, Olga was interpreted *uncritically* as powerless to intervene – but in the script Olga's silence, her non-intervention, and her inability really to engage with the harsh reality of Natasha's class attitude, does carry some measure of culpability and collusion, even granted Olga's bewilderment and refinement. The role of the servants in the plays is treated as picturesque rather than significant, even though Chekhov presents a class cross-section in all of the full-length plays. In the majority of productions, therefore, the characters' culpability is personalized into individual fecklessness or irresponsibility, rather than failure on the broadest and deepest level to recognize realities. This over-emphasis on individual characteristics trivializes social significance and contributes towards reactionary interpretations of Chekhov.

The dominant mode of translation, production, performance, and criticism in this country has enforced the idea that Chekhov's plays deal nostalgically with 'the tragedy of dispossession' and that (in the words of Chekhov's *émigrée* biographer, Princess Nina Toumanova, in 1937) his was 'the voice of twilight Russia' – the twilight before the darkness of the Bolshevik Revolution. These are political assumptions, and given the official British view in 1917 it is scarcely surprising that the plays were seen as tragedies. This official view manifested itself in the British intervention and invasion of Russia in 1918, and was expressed by much of the British press which characterized the Revolution as 'a danger as grave as was the invasion of Ghenghis

Khan or Tamerlane' (*Daily Chronicle*, 18 December 1918). Even in
1912 the *Times Literary Supplement*, reviewing Calderon's translations
of *The Seagull* and *The Cherry Orchard*, had stated that Chekhov's
characters 'are incapable of helping the life-force or the force of circumstance ... Futility is the characteristic which all his people share ...
Implicitly they deny the greatest force in the many of which what
we call Life is composed – the spirit and the will of man.' It is ironic
that this anonymous reviewer fails to see that this is exactly where
Chekhov's own implicit criticism of many of his characters lies, and
why none of his plays are subtitled 'tragedies', but the same reviewer
continued: 'Russian melancholy we know; the futility may be another
side to it – a tragic helplessness.'[3] This confusion of Chekhov's
views with those of his characters has continued until the present time.
After 1917, however, the characters were seen as even more tragic
when events from a British viewpoint seemed to have swept them
irretrievably into the dustbin of history. Viewed as individuals, the
pathos of some of the characters should be presented – but, viewed
also as social beings with the potential for 'spirit and will', other
questions should be explored and presented.

Other factors, however, also influenced the politics of British
assumptions about Chekhov. The period of increased productions
coincided, and not accidentally, with the mood of disillusionment
and dejection which partly characterized the inter-war years. As Ivor
Brown put it in 1935:

Was not Chekhov, after all, a kind of sublime crooner, continually cultivating
his Muscovite Blues? And may not that be the reason why, neglected in
England for a quarter of a century, he recently became 'box-office'? He
spoke for the defeated, for the self-pitying, for the parlour philosophers
whose babbling of -isms and -ologies is only a veil for inertia. The mood
of our English nineteen-twenties was doleful enough. Rich girls had to be
pitied for their poverty, and popular melody was all boo-hoo-hoos and
blue-hue-hues. Self-pity was the note and sourness the flavour ... But the
young people of the nineteen-twenties and thirties ... could be far more
responsive to Chekhov's compassionate studies of defeatism; his samovar
gave them just their cup of tea ...[4]

The economic crisis of the twenties and the stark economic contrasts
of the thirties all increased an identification with Chekhov's characters
which said much more about Britain than about Chekhov's Russia,
and made it difficult for directors and audiences alike to distance
themselves. In a sense, many British admirers of Chekhov's plays

became 'Chekhov characters in a Chekhov situation'. The tone and mood of production after production illustrated a sorrowing evocation of a valuable way of life gone for ever: nostalgia, resignation, futility, defeatism.

These political attitudes were reinforced by the translation in the inter-war years of Chekhov's stories, of Dostoyevsky and Gogol (most of them by Constance Garnett) in which English views of 'the Slav soul', of the 'typically Russian', and of 'Russian philosophizing' seemed to be confirmed by Chekhov's plays. The emphasis, then, was on 'tragic character' to the virtual exclusion of 'social comedy'. The plays were produced as either 'doom and gloom' *or* trivialized as in Theodore Komisarjevsky's edited productions between 1925 and 1936 – trivialized in a way perhaps best expressed by his famous comment that 'the English public always demand a love interest'.

Another influential factor must be mentioned, however, in attempting to analyse the origins of British attitudes to Chekhov, and that is the effect and influence of Stanislavsky on the British theatre: character exploration rather than an exploration of the *ideas* in a play. As in America, it was assumed that Stanislavsky's productions of Chekhov were the definitive ones, and Chekhov's own often-expressed unhappiness with Stanislavsky's detailed naturalism and tragic tone was either unknown or, until recently, simply ignored. In the West few knew of Vakhtangov's 1921 production of *The Wedding*; of Meyerhold's experiment in 1935 with *The Bear*, *The Proposal*, and *Jubilee* in his production *33 Swoons*, or of Tairov's Symbolist *The Seagull* in 1944 – 5. It was assumed that the authentic approach to Chekhov was through naturalism, but it became naturalism without the ensemble orchestration of the Moscow Art Theatre, given the financial pressures of British rehearsal time and the need for a 'star' actor to ensure good box-office returns. The Stanislavsky approach, compounded by the misleading translations into English of his writings and teachings, offered *carte blanche* for detailed character filigree – the significance of the play as a whole was largely lost.

So a strange anomaly has arisen: the plays are always staged within a period setting or, at least, with period costuming, but with very few exceptions the period and social context of the plays has been ignored. We are presented with 'the period' visually, but almost never in substance. The characters wear late nineteenth-century dress, but the plays do not 'voice' the economic, social, philosophical, and political conflicts and issues of Chekhov's Russia. Character is isolated from milieu and context in a way which is peculiarly British. The plays have been 'naturalized' – as Kenneth Tynan has written: 'We have remade Chekhov's plays in our image.'[5] Or as Caryl Brahms wrote in an article entitled 'Chekhov, the dramatist of fare-wells': 'The English, in their productions, have taken over Chekhov. They have hung his drawing-rooms with their own decently faded chintzes. They have peopled his decaying estates with Aunt Lillians and Uncle Vincents ... the peasant as quaint as those toy-shop Russian families; brightly painted wooden Papoushkas and Mamoushkas complete with facsimiles in dwindling scale ...' This 'dwindling scale' relates not only to class but also to location: 'Moscow, Kharkov, St Petersburg – why, are they not quite simply Maidstone, Cheltenham, Edinburgh? Indeed when the Moscow Arts Theatre plays Chekhov we half resent it. They all seem so vulgar – without Dame Edith, and Miss Seyler, and Sir John.'[6] The naturalization process has indeed created a 'dwindling scale', has trivialized the ideas of the plays, and politicized them into a British context, incorporating values which demonstrate much more sympathy for Ranevskaya than for Lopakhin (frequently presented as a kind of clichéd bluff Yorkshire businessman), and identifying much more with Gayev than with Trofimov. The naturalization process has ignored the nature of nineteenth-century Russian provincialism and geographical distance; remained ignorant of *poshlost* (virtually a theme in Russian literature which demonstrates the banality, tawdriness, pettiness, and destructive triviality of everyday existence); ignored the significance of the primitive conditions on and around the big estates – and ignored the implications of the fact that Chekhov was writing under censorship. Again and again the emphasis on individual characterization without an orches-ration of *meaning* operates at the expense of the play as a whole.

One of the most extreme examples of this recently was in Mike Alfreds' in some ways innovatory production of *The Cherry Orchard* at the National Theatre in 1985 – a production in which Trofimov was played as 'no true idealist – the voice of the people who will soon create a new social order – but a cold-hearted, self-regarding humbug'.[7] Trofimov is inadequate and even ridiculous, but to play him as a 'humbug' is to throw the whole balance of the play, to ignore his social and political role in the play, and it makes what was, in fact, a profoundly reactionary reading of the play, albeit perhaps without deliberate intent.

This often unconscious politically retrograde reading of the plays must also be seen in relation to the debate about tragedy and comedy in Chekhov's plays. Chekhov's own views were clearly and frequently expressed, whether in the sub-titles which he carefully gave each play, or in crucial and frequently quoted comments in letters and reminiscences, in which he consistently wrote of the interrelationship between the important and the paltry, the great and the base, the tragic and the ridiculous in life. This emphasis on 'sad comicality' is not only a profound characteristic of Chekhov's philosophy, not only a *leitmotif* in his writing, whether literary or dramatic, but is both source and motivation for the *form* of his work. In British critical debates and theatre productions, however, 'sad comicality' is rarely related to the ideas and content of the plays, and instead is generally viewed purely as a question of form. Thus the interpretation of the plays as tragedies simply ignores both the content *and* the form; while those productions which have recently played up the comedy have also failed to fuse form and content exactly because the comedy has not been seen as emanating from the philosophy and ideas of the plays – comic styles have been explored, but not the serious function of the comedy.

But the debate about tragedy and comedy goes deeper than questions of content and form, and becomes a philosophical and political debate. To put it perhaps crudely: the tragic view of human impotence in the face of seemingly inevitable forces, implies an *acceptance* of the world order as it manifests itself and works out its design in the characters on stage. The assumption of human impotence, the acceptance of 'that which is', the belief in ungovernable external forces, and the insistence on 'absolutes', all become part of a retrograde world view. This philosophy, I would suggest, was complete anathema to Chekhov, whose concern as a scientist and as a writer was with the exposure of contradictions, and not an annulment or denial of contradictions. His aim was to expose, and not to tranquillize, what Coleridge called 'the lethargy of custom'.[8] The main means at Chekhov's disposal was a rejection of simple catharsis and an injection of comedy. The British theatre has viewed its Chekhov as somehow offering a cathartic experience, but Chekhov would, I think, have agreed with Shaw's views as expressed in 1928: 'I do not want there to be any more pity in the world, because I do not want there to be anything to pity; and I want there to be no more terror, because I do not want people to have anything to fear.'[9] Chekhov's use of comedy, then, is a philosophical and political one, and not merely a characteristic of his form. It is closely related to the idea of *'tak zhit nelzya'* – it allows for the suggestion not only of what 'is', but also of what 'need not be' and what 'could be'. As Chekhov himself put it in a famous and much-quoted letter on the question of art and writers, to his publisher Aleksey Suvorin in 1892: 'The best of them are realists and depict life as it is, but because every line they write is permeated, as with a juice, by a consciousness of an aim, you feel in addition to life as it is, also life as it should be, and it is that which delights you.'[10] Chekhov had a 'consciousness of an aim' in his own writing – and that aim was not what Ivor Brown called 'compassionate studies in defeatism'. His use of comedy is both a denial of the inevitability of tragedy *and* a method of assessing his characters objectively – and hence their responsibility for their lives. This objective assessment functions at one and the same time politically and psychologically: human potential in Chekhov's plays is always related to the individual character's aspirations and limitations.

Thus the combination of what Trevor Griffiths called 'the subjectively painful and the objectively comic' is at the heart of Chekhov's work, but has rarely been explored in British productions. The affirmation of human potential is frequently treated comically on the British stage – Tuzenbakh or Trofimov may be personally inadequate, but their words should be treated seriously. And this relates to a particular reversal of approach in this country: 'doom and gloom' are treated tragically, and Chekhov's irony is ignored; positive affirmations of human potential are treated comically, and Chekhov's essential philosophy is ignored. We seem not to be able to hold a balance between sympathetic involvement and comic detachment. Yet when that balance is lost, the point of the plays is also lost.

Only when the theatre practitioner has sought to clarify the context have the ideas really been explored in production. Trevor Griffiths' version offers one example, while another is Thomas Kilroy's version of *The Seagull* in 1981, in which he transferred the action of the play to turn-of-the-century Ireland, and many of the social, philosophical, and political ideas of the play suddenly came into sharper focus – without loss of psychological depth of character. Versions of the plays have created a new emphasis on communicating the *ideas* of the plays to a British audience, rather than on a portrait gallery of individual eccentrics. The majority of productions, however, still fail to question their own assumptions about the plays, and hence repeat uncritically the retrograde characteristics of over eighty years of productions.

Notes

1 Letter to Suvorin, 27 October 1888. *Letters of Anton Chekhov*, trans. Michael Henry Heim and Simon Karlinsky (London: Bodley Head, 1973), p. 117.
2 In 'A Letter in Rhyme', quoted in Michael Meyer, *Henrik Ibsen*, II, *The Farewell to Poetry 1864–1882* (London: Hart-Davis, 1971), p. 210.
3 *Times Literary Supplement*, 1 February 1912, quoted in Victor Emeljanow, *Chekhov, the Critical Heritage* (London: RKP, 1981), p. 106.
4 *The Observer*, 17 November 1935, quoted in Emeljanow, *ibid.*, p. 385.
5 Kenneth Tynan, *Tynan on Theatre* (Harmondsworth: Penguin Books, 1964), p. 273.
6 *The Times*, 23 May 1966.
7 Frances King, *The Sunday Telegraph*, 15 December 1985.
8 Samuel Taylor Coleridge, *Biographia Literaria* (London: Dent, Everyman's Library, No. 11, 1962 reprint), p. 169.
9 George Bernard Shaw, 'An address before the Royal Academy of Dramatic Arts', delivered on 7 December 1928, printed in *The New York Times*, 6 January 1929. Reprinted in *Shaw on Theatre*, ed. E. J. West (New York: Hill and Wang, 1967 reprint), p. 197.
10 Letter to Suvorin, 25 November 1892. For a full translation of the letter, see *Letters of Anton Chekhov*, Heim and Karlinsky, pp. 242–4.

CHAPTER 14

'The Cherry Orchard': a new English version by Trevor Griffiths

David Allen

I did *The Cherry Orchard* because I felt that its meanings had been seriously betrayed, almost consciously betrayed, over some fifty years of theatre practice in this country. The English still cling wilfully to the idea that the play is an elegy for the decline of civilization. I do not read the history of the period in that way – and neither, moreover, do I read the *play* in that way. I wanted to break with a whole convention and tradition of reading the play; to create the space for a *new idea* of the play.

Trevor Griffiths

Trevor Griffiths' version of *The Cherry Orchard* continues to cause controversy. It has been attacked as a distortion of the play, an attempt by a Marxist dramatist to rewrite Chekhov. Written in 1977, it has still not received a London production.[1] It has been effectively marginalized, while other, blander translations continue to hold the stage.

The problem has not simply been Griffiths' approach to the text. In his introduction to the published version, he demolishes half a century of Chekhov on the British stage. It is a manifesto, a challenge to those 'high priests of the sacred art' in the British theatre, who have taken Chekhov to their breasts, and smothered him there.

Griffiths' version was commissioned by Richard Eyre, then Artistic Director of the Nottingham Playhouse.

'I believe *The Cherry Orchard* is the model play of the twentieth century', Eyre suggests.

It presents an entire spectrum of society, in which every social gradation, every class interest, is represented. Each of the twelve characters is equally important, and should hold the audience's attention and sympathy as they speak, but then be undercut by an entirely persuasive reply. Every 'voice' must be heard; every 'colour' in the spectrum must be clearly characterized. I felt that Trevor's own methodology as a writer made him the ideal choice as translator; in *Comedians*, for example, he attempts a similar spectrum of positions. The brief, then, was not to 'politicize' the play, but to strip away the varnish; to enable us to see the picture more clearly.[2]

In his introduction, Griffiths claims:

From the age of fifteen, when I had my first exposure to [Chekhov's] work *via* radio, I have always looked *straight through* the productions to the counter-meanings and counter-intentions screaming out to be realized. To come to cases, *The Cherry Orchard* has *always* seemed to me to be dealing not only with the subjective pain of property loss, but also and more importantly with its objective *necessity*. To present it as the first is to celebrate a pessimism; as to see it as both is to redress an important political balance potent in the text Chekhov wrote but in *practice* almost wholly ignored.[3]

The play was written in 1903 and produced in 1904. In 1905, the First Revolution occurred in Russia. The sense of a society in flux, and about to be turned upside down, is palpable in the play, but very seldom present in production. Griffiths comments:

As I worked on the translation, I began to feel the play more and more as a play about the past and future – or rather, pasts and futures. It speaks very specifically not only about the need for change, but also that change is going to occur. There is a change to society, to class relations, within the play itself. Lopakhin, the rising bourgeois entrepreneur, takes over the estate, and departs to dream his vision of the future. Trofimov and Anya bid 'goodbye' to today, and 'hello' to tomorrow. Trofimov's purchase on the future is rhetorical, but nevertheless pertinent. And Ranevsky almost evaporates, like water to air. She talks about going away, and she talks about returning – but it is all talk.[4]

It has been suggested that Griffiths has 'shifted the focus' of the play and 'reordered its inherent balances; so that, for example, Mme Ranevsky's pivotal role has been reduced while Trofimov's – and to some extent Lopakhin's – have been strengthened'.[5] Griffiths:

Ranevsky is usually seen as the centre of the action; the other characters revolve around her. If you look at how Trofimov and Lopakhin literally operate, that is a persuasive image of the play's movement. They do seem drawn to her, caught within her field of attraction. As I read the play, however, it seemed to me that its structure had, in the past, been mis-represented. Trofimov and Lopakhin represent two possibilities for the future: bourgeoisification and commoditization, or revolutionary change. These are the only futures available to these people. The ground of the present is like a building, and the pillars of the building are Trofimov and Lopakhin. Together, they form an arch over the other characters.

The key question in any discussion of Griffiths' version, and the issue which has caused most controversy, is his treatment of the character of Trofimov. He has been criticized for trying to turn Trofimov into the play's hero and 'an idealized leader of the revolution'.[6]

The British theatre has not always known quite what to make of Trofimov. Michael Frayn notes that he has often been portrayed as 'an inadequate and immature personality who is afraid to emerge from University and face the real world'[7] – an 'eternal student', endlessly following his Open University course. However, playing him as a fool or neurotic marginalizes the character. It trivializes his arguments: he is simply someone who talks a lot. 'To dismiss him in this way', Eyre suggests, 'seems to me a decision of Olympian arrogance. It makes Chekhov look foolish, in giving so much weight to the character. Trofimov's arguments are coherent and passionate. He describes contemporary Russia at length and in great detail, and his account is unimpeachably true. And yet, Chekhov *subverts* this, by showing that the character is someone who cannot deal with himself and other people on an emotional level. He is emotionally immature, but that does not mean his ideas are inherently wrong.'[8]

In a letter to Olga Knipper, Chekhov wrote: 'I am most worried about a certain unfinished quality about the student Trofimov. You see, Trofimov is in exile from time to time, and now and again thrown out of University, but how can these things be represented?'[9] The fact that Trofimov was unable to complete his studies because he had a criminal record for revolutionary political activity transforms our perception of him. Griffiths makes Trofimov's position clear, in a single line interpolated into the text. 'What do you do now?' Ranevsky asks him (in Act 1). 'I'm still a student', he replies; and Griffiths adds, 'if the authorities have their way, I suspect I'll always be one'.

In Act 2, Trofimov speaks of the appalling conditions in which people are forced to live in Russia. The bitterness in his voice, in Griffiths' version, is unmistakable:

Man *can* make progress, struggle for perfection. There *is* a discernible future in which we'll find solutions to the problems that confront us now; but we'll achieve it only through unremitting struggle, by working with all our strength to help those who are even now seeking the answers. Here, now, in Russia, very few are embarked on that course. The greater part of the intelligentsia seek nothing, do nothing . . . while all around them, right beneath their eyes, the workers eat scraps of rancid meat and sleep on bare boards thirty or forty to a room. Bedbugs, shit, leaking roofs, moral degradation.

It is interesting to compare this with Elisaveta Fen's translation of the same passage. Fen writes: 'Humanity is perpetually advancing, always seeking to perfect its own powers. One day all the things that are beyond our grasp at present are going to fall within our reach, only to achieve this we've got to work with all our might, to help the people who are seeking after truth.'[10] This is 'rarefied discourse, obsessed with ideas, metaphysics even'.[11] The language in Griffiths' version is noticeably different. It is more explicit that Trofimov is arguing the need for *political* change: 'Griffiths's Trofimov wants action, concrete and meaningful answers, not an abstract "truth". And this Trofimov knows exactly where these answers are to be found.'[12]

Has Griffiths distorted Trofimov's arguments, or simply accentuated certain implications latent in the text? In Griffiths' version, for example, Trofimov speaks not of 'work' but of 'struggle'. The difference is slight but significant. 'It is a question of nuance', Eyre suggests. 'The literal translation may be "work", but the context may well suggest "work – struggle".'

Griffiths comments:

Given the severity of the official censorship and the cravenness of theatres, Chekhov was very limited in what he could say about Trofimov's work at the University and his political activities. His own notes refer to the suppression of Trofimov, as a character, and as a set of meanings and statements. I had to imagine what those meanings and statements were, which Chekhov felt he had been denied the possibility of making. As a student in 1903, Trofimov could not have been unaware of what was happening in the political underground. *Iskra* groups were being formed throughout this period, all over Russia. In 1901, Lenin's *What is to be Done?* was published in Germany; and from 1902, the book would have been available and circulating in Russia. A new language was in the air: a new way of perceiving and accounting for the conditions of social reality and the possibilities of change. And that new language represents a huge break with the past. I was seeking to embrace that language, not comprehensively, but in oblique, tangential ways. It seemed to me not improper to give Trofimov a *hint*, at least, of a different kind of language from the traditional nineteenth-century bourgeois-liberal language that student intellectuals would have deployed.[13]

After Trofimov's speech, his audience is unable to speak at first. They have been silenced, by the force of his words, by the anger in his voice. A sound is heard: 'the sound of a string snapping and dying away'. Then, suddenly, a tipsy vagrant stumbles into their

12   Mick Ford as Trofimov in Act 2 of *The Cherry Orchard*, directed by Richard Eyre
at the Nottingham Playhouse 1977

midst. 'In most productions', Benedict Nightingale wrote, reviewing
the Nottingham production, 'this apparition is bizarre and rather
alarming, a reeling grotesque whose presence tells us less about the
society which presumably produced him than about the characters
he startles and intimidates, notably the prodigal Mme Ranevsky,
who randomly tosses him a gold coin. Not at Nottingham, though ...

There, the tramp is what he claims to be, a starving Russian citizen, a sickly, skeletal figure with a tubercular cough.'[14]

The term 'vagrant' may simply suggest to us the image of an ageing wino. Griffiths is careful to indicate that the figure has a different significance in a Russian context. He is dressed in a battered military hat and overcoat: a deserter, perhaps, or a political refugee. 'Brothers', he cries suddenly, after a fit of coughing, 'starving and suffering comrades, unite now by the river, let them *hear* your misery'.[15]

Nightingale concludes:

What performances like this do, and do without human sacrifice, is concentrate our minds on property, class, social discord, political crisis, the fading away of an old order and the absence of a satisfactory substitute for it, matters which, God knows, still preoccupy us today. The effect is not, I think, to diminish the play, still less shrink it into a Marxist tract: it is rather to remind us how large it is, how sweeping its interests and sympathies, how adventurous the interpretations it can safely contain, and how much of it we commonly miss. I, for one, will never be able to look at it in quite the same way again.[16]

'In commissioning a new translation', Eyre suggests, 'my basic premise was that the play should *live* in its own language. Translation means "carrying across", from one language and culture to another. It is not a straightforward equation. To earn its right on the stage, a translation has to "re-form" the meanings, nuances and images of the original in a new language.'

'The language of several existing translations seemed curiously old-fashioned and outmoded', Griffiths argues:

I did want to translate the play into a language, an idiom that was recognizably of our time. The first act poses a number of problems for the translator. The writing is often highly expositional: characters tell each other things they all know already, in order that the audience will gain a firm biographical picture of character, relationships, history. This method of introducing information now seems dated. There is a history of realism that spans some eighty years beyond Chekhov: a realism of the stage, but also a realism of film. The craft of realism, of shaping realist texts, has advanced in some ways beyond what Chekhov was able to achieve – particularly in levels of obliqueness.

In Act I, Anya, talking to Varya, recalls what happened, six years ago, that made Mme Ranevsky leave for Paris. Fen translates: 'It was six years ago that father died, and then, only a month after that, little brother Grisha was drowned in the river. He was only seven, such a pretty little boy! Mamma couldn't bear it and went away ... she never looked back.'[17] Griffiths translates the passage thus: 'Father dying. Grisha drowning in the river. Mother abandoning us, fleeing to Paris, all that grief, all that guilt flooding back.'[18] In Griffiths' version, we are less aware of the expositional nature of the lines. It seems as if Anya is simply recalling things to her own mind and reflecting on them. 'Father dying. Grisha drowning in the river' – each simple statement seems to suggest a whole history, and a wealth of buried feelings and associations.

Griffiths comments:

Fen's translation is probably closer to a *literal* translation. Many translators are meeting the demands of publishers, who want the text to be used in A-level or degree courses, where there needs to be a word-for-word or phrase-for-phrase correspondence. I was not concerned about that. I was looking for the bunched meaning of a phrase or sentence, rather than the extended literalized meaning. I was looking for a certain litheness and leanness of language, that eschewed floweriness or ornateness. I felt that was a proper and accurate intention, because I do not think Chekhov was about ornateness. I think he was about directness. There is, I think, a very special problem in translating the *emotionality* of Chekhov's text. There are national, cultural differences, lodged in particular histories. Ours is a history of emotional repression, self-denial, 'responsibility'. In Russian culture I suspect that emotion is expressed in a much less filtered or constrained way. There is a tremendous danger, for English actors performing Chekhov, of emotional overstatement. If the emotion is overstated, it can seem false, almost 'operatic', to an English audience. In performances I have seen or heard, Mme Ranevsky has always seemed highly volatile. The psychological movement between quite distant states of feeling can be very rapid. She may be laughing one moment and crying the next. I have attempted to tighten the language, and negotiate the shifts of feeling – to make the emotional life of the character *coherent*, rather than beyond the range of the English sensibility. The shifts of feeling are still there, but they have been narrowed to a certain extent.

Griffiths makes a significant intervention in the text in his use of stage directions to suggest the shape of a scene. In Act I, for example, Ranevsky is upset when meeting Trofimov again after so many years. Chekhov's stage-directions suggest that Ranevsky embraces Trofimov almost straight away, holds him, and weeps. In Griffiths' version, however, the moment Ranevsky recognizes Trofimov, she turns quickly away. She stands by the window, leaning fractionally on the frame, her back to us and to the people in the room. The emotion has taken her by surprise; she struggles to hold her feelings in. When she speaks, her voice is 'plain, very normal': 'Grisha. Little Grisha'.[19] Then she turns around. She has mastered her feelings, and yet we can guess what an effort this has cost her.

At one point in Act I, Ranevsky stands at the window in the nursery and looks out on the orchard. It evokes for her memories of her childhood and symbolizes for her the innocence she feels she has lost. Fen translates the speech thus: 'Oh, my childhood, my innocent childhood ... Oh, my orchard! After the dark, stormy autumn and the cold winter, you are young and joyous again; the angels have not forsaken you! If only this burden could be taken from me, if only I could forget the past!'[20] In Griffiths' version, the emotionality, the sentiment in the speech, is tempered a little. 'Childhood', she says simply. 'And innocence'. Then there is a long pause, in the hush of the house. 'My orchard gleams as white, as pure as ever, untouched by autumn's storms and winter's dead hand. Here you are again, and again, and again ... your own self. Some god watches over you. No ... past to weigh you down like a great stone.'[21]

Griffiths: 'There is something very contained about English, and when it does express deep emotion, it does so in simple rather than purple ways; in oblique and understated rather than rhetorical language. My translation is specifically called a new *English* version. To say that the play will be in the English language does imply – to me, at least – that it will be *anglicized* to a certain extent; that adjustments will be made to take account of a different history and a different national, cultural structure of feeling.'

One point in particular in Griffiths' text has caused some controversy. In Act 3, Yasha is talking to Firs. 'Grandad', he says, 'you're a bore. (Yawns) You're ready for the knacker's yard.' Firs turns to him and says deliberately, 'Up yours, butterballs.'[22] The Russian word Firs uses here, *nedotyopa*, poses quite a problem to translators. There is debate about the meaning of the word, even among Russians. It may be an obscure peasant word, collected by Chekhov; he may simply have made it up. It is usually translated very feebly: the various renderings have included 'ne'er do well', 'good-for-nothing', 'numbskull', 'silly billy'.[23]

'I don't know how I came up with "butterballs"', Griffiths observes:

It is not a word that anybody uses, as far as I know. But I definitely wanted
Firs to *score* at this point, and to score in a very surprising way – because
he is taking some really horrible shit from Yasha. Yasha is talking to him
as if he can neither hear nor understand what he is saying. 'You're ready
for the knacker's yard' – this is one human being to another. The shallow-
ness, the appallingness of what Yasha says seemed to me to need a corrective.
Firs wanders around, muttering to himself, '. . . you haven't got your coat
. . . here's your coffee . . . I remember when . . .' He seems deaf to the world.
And yet, the subtext here, perhaps, is that all the time, Firs has seen Yasha
and measured him – this man with his affected airs and his ridiculous
Paris suits. I wanted Firs's response to be quite explosive, but in a comic
way. 'Up yours, butterballs' – it is like a slap in the face for Yasha.

Eyre comments:

In translating a play into a new language, the best solution, at times, may
be to be very literal. In Act 4, Lopakhin says goodbye to Trofimov, and
tells him, 'Take care, little dove'. This line is usually translated in a variety
of whimsical ways.[24] Trevor's decision to use 'little dove' was, I think,
spot on, because it is a precise metaphor for Lopakhin's view of Trofimov.
It is benign, and encouraging, and patronizing at the same time. In this
instance, a more idiomatic translation would have strained the point. At
other moments, however, the process of translating may mean making
very bold, idiomatic 'jumps'. You have to accept that there are some words
and expressions in any language that are simply untranslatable. So, if you
are 'carrying them across', you have to find parallels. You will never find
the equivalents. To say any word is the equivalent is to deny the emotional
and social resonances that all language has. In the scene between Firs and
Yasha, one is looking for a colloquial insult, which has some force to it,
and some wit also in the context. The line was amusing and seemed effective.
To have opted for a form of archaic Victorianism, some false idea of rustic
peasant language, would have been quite wrong, I think.

Griffiths makes a major change to the text in the final scene between
Gayev and Ranevsky, when they are left alone together in the nursery.
Fen translates Chekhov's stage-directions as follows: 'They seem
to have been waiting for this moment, and now they embrace each other
and sob quietly, with restraint, so as not to be heard.'[25] In Griffiths'
version, Gayev simply walks to his sister's side, and puts his hand
in hers, 'as a child might'. The action is minimal, but evocative.
As we observe them, standing together, we can guess their thoughts
and feelings. The emotion is too strong for them to speak. Griffiths
has taken the bold step of cutting their lines here – except for a
single telling word from Gayev: 'Sister'.[26]

In the original text, Ranevsky surveys the room and says, 'Oh, my darling, my precious, my beautiful orchard! My life, my youth, my happiness ... goodbye ... Goodbye! ... For the last time – to look at these walls, these windows ... Mother used to love walking up and down this room.'[27] Griffiths argues:

Chekhov is here recalling, echoing, ideas and themes that have been heard throughout the play. My hope is that those ideas, those words, will resonate in that empty room, without the need for them to be spoken. To say less at this point is, I believe, to allow an English audience to feel *more*: to feel the depth and scale of the severing. I was not seeking to undermine the emotion in the scene, but to encode it, to encapsulate it, in a new and hopefully striking way. I like the idea of suggesting the deepest feelings by the slightest of movements, the tiniest of utterances.[28]

Griffiths' reworking of the scene has an additional effect. In the silence we are all the more aware of the voices of Anya and Trofimov, calling offstage. Their voices sound a note of optimism. 'Hello ... o ... o ... Tomorrow ... ow ... ow ... ow ...' echoes through the house; echoes around the two solitary figures in the nursery. Mme Ranevsky blinks, stirs, drops Gayev's hand. 'Yes!' she calls – and they leave.

'I wanted the play to taper at the end', Griffiths suggests, 'to pass almost into silence. All that could be said has been said. Now, history takes over. And, in the silence, the sound of an axe, cutting down the first of the trees in the orchard.'

And then Firs enters; tries the door and finds it locked. There is a solitary chair left in the room, its back broken. Painfully he drags it to the centre of the room and sits down. The axe starts up again, closer now. 'I don't imagine for one minute he's put his fur coat on ... No, no ... he'll be wearing the thin one ...' He mutters to himself unintelligibly for a moment. Then: 'It's gone ... it's gone ... as if I'd never lived it ... I might lie down in a minute. You've no strength left in you, have you ... you've nothing left, eh ... you've nothing ...'[29]

Griffiths:

I feel that what is important to me about Firs is that, through his age, his life, his experience, he stands as the representative of feudal Russia. He refers to the 'great disaster'. And what is he referring to? The emancipation of the serfs; the day people were given their freedom. He has been so shaped by serfdom that he still exists within it, his psychic formation derives from that experience. He may have been fifty before the serfs were emancipated.

Half his life had already gone. And he didn't want 'freedom'. He was secure within the old order, and its realities of dominance and subordination. In a sense, then, he represents a completely different era: an age which was not muddy and complicated, tense and full of fear. At the end, he reaches a moment of self-consciousness. He just sits there and asks, 'What has this life been about?' There is a transilient effect: he moves in and out of states of understanding and incomprehension. It is very stream-of-consciousness. He has never lived for himself, once. He has always been someone else's possession. And now, at the end, he sees his life summate before him. Where is his life? Where is *his* life? He sees that it adds up to zero. Nothing. That is very painful.

Firs begins to rock back and forwards, slowly at first, but the arcs grow longer. 'You silly old nothing', he says. 'Silly old nothing. Silly old nothing'.[30] The sound of the axe persists, closing in on the house. Firs rocks on, muttering. We hear, on tape, the sound of his voice, repeating over and over (in Russian): '*Nedotyopa! Nedotyopa!*'. Griffiths' translation, 'silly old nothing', suggests the emptiness of Firs' life, as he sits alone, in an empty room, in an empty house.

The sound of his voice suddenly cuts out. He topples to the floor, felled. The axe stops; silence. A distant sound is heard: the sound of a snapping string. And then, blackout.

Audiences will judge, Griffiths suggests, whether his version 'speaks to them more pertinently about the world they live in than other versions they've encountered':[31] 'I had no feeling that I wanted to impose contemporary meanings on the play. It just seemed to me that the spaces were there for contemporary meanings to emerge. What I was trying to say was that there will be changes in our own lives; and perhaps this English version of Chekhov's play will allow us to reflect on, and anticipate, some of those changes for the future.'

Notes

Anton Chekhov, *The Cherry Orchard*, a new English version by Trevor Griffiths, from a translation by Helen Rappaport (London: Pluto Press, 1978). First performance: Nottingham Playhouse, 10 March 1977. Directed by Richard Eyre. Set designed by John Gunter; costumes by Pippy Bradshaw. Subsequently produced for BBC Television by Ann Scott; broadcast 13 October 1981. Directed by Richard Eyre; designed by Susan Spence.

1   A production was planned for the Young Vic Theatre, London, for February 1990, but was cancelled because it would have clashed with a production of the play in Michael Frayn's translation at the Aldwych Theatre.

2   From an unpublished interview with Richard Eyre conducted by Stuart Young, 6 June 1985.

3   Griffiths, *The Cherry Orchard*, p. vi.

4   From interviews with Trevor Griffiths conducted by David Allen, 19 February 1987 and 1 April 1987. (Unless specified, all quotations from Griffiths are from this source.)

5   Griffiths, *ibid*.

6   From an interview with Mike Alfreds, conducted by David Allen, 5 October 1985.

7   Michael Frayn, Introduction to *Anton Chekhov: Plays* (London: Methuen, 1988), p. lxvi.

8   From an interview with Richard Eyre conducted by David Allen, 16 February 1988. (Unless specified, all quotations from Eyre are from this source.) Griffiths agrees that Trofimov *is* comic: in his relationship with Anya, for example, 'he doesn't have a clue. At the end of their scene together in Act 2, she looks at him and says, "Isn't it ... wonderful here ... today ...?". He doesn't understand her at all. "Yes," he replies. "Perfect weather".'

9   Letter dated 19 October 1903. Translated by Nick Worrall in *File on Chekhov* (London: Methuen, 1986), p. 69.

10 Elisaveta Fen, *Chekhov: Plays* (Harmondsworth: Penguin, 1959), pp. 363–4.

11 Mike Poole and John Wyver, *Powerplays: Trevor Griffiths in Television* (London: BFI, 1984), p. 154.

12 *Ibid*.

13 Chekhov himself, Griffiths acknowledges, is unlikely to have read Lenin's book. He was, however, very aware of the unrest that spread in the universities from 1899 onwards. The following letter, for example, was written to Chekhov the day after the Universities of Moscow and St Petersburg were closed and occupied by the police:

> The students are happy: the authorities are in total confusion, a new form of struggle has been introduced, a new weapon has become available, and the Marxists are hailing the triumph of the implementation of a practical Marxist programme ... It is time to set up a boundary between practical wisdom and faith in broad theories of the future. It is time to recognise the necessity of human sacrifice, for only by so doing can we live for the distant future, glorifying and idealizing those who sacrifice themselves ... This is a time when life is on its way to becoming pure pleasure. This is what the new age is like. (Mikhail Lavrov, Moscow, 18 March 1899. Translated by Michael Henry Heim and Simon Karlinsky in *Anton Chekhov's Life and Thought: Selected Letters and Commentary* (Berkeley: University of California Press, 1973), p. 350.)

14 Benedict Nightingale, *New Statesman*, 18 March 1977, p. 372.

15 Griffiths, *The Cherry Orchard*, p. 28. Cf. Fen, *Chekhov: Plays*: 'Oh, my brother, my suffering brother ... Come to mother Volga, whose groans ...' (Fen, *Chekhov: Plays*, p. 366).

16 Nightingale, *New Statesman*, 18 March 1977, p. 372.

17 Fen, *Chekhov: Plays*, p. 340.

18 Griffiths, *The Cherry Orchard*, p. 6.

19 *Ibid.*, p. 13.

20 Fen, *Chekhov: Plays*, pp. 347–8.

21 Griffiths, *The Cherry Orchard*, p. 13.

22 *Ibid.*, p. 38.

23 See the essay by Valentina Ryapolova (ch. 20) in the present volume.

24 Cf. Fen, *Chekhov: Plays*: 'my friend'; Ronald Hingley: 'my dear fellow'.

25 Fen, *ibid.*, p. 397.

26 Griffiths, p. 53.

27 Fen, *Chekhov: Plays*, pp. 397–8.

28 In both the Nottingham and television productions, Richard Eyre chose to restore the lines which had been cut by Griffiths in his translation.

29 Griffiths, p. 53.

30 *Ibid.*, p. 54.

31 *Ibid.*, p. vi.

CHAPTER 15

Changes of direction: Mike Alfreds' methods with Chekhov

Stuart Young

A lot of mythology creeps into the evaluation of most classic texts: there is an accretion of half-truths which need to be periodically scrubbed away.

Mike Alfreds, *New Theatre Quarterly*, 1986

Having directed four Chekhov productions between 1981 and 1986, Mike Alfreds has devoted to Chekhov an attention that is singular among contemporary directors, recalling the contributions of Komisarjevsky, Saint-Denis, Gielgud, Olivier and Fernald. Indeed the only recent, rival contribution in the British theatre has been that of the translator Michael Frayn. Alfreds' reputation as an interpreter of Chekhov was established in 1981 with Shared Experience's *Seagull* which, along with the Royal Court's production of the same play, was named Best Revival in the *Drama* awards.[1] Because of the success of his *Seagull* Alfreds was invited the next year to direct *The Cherry Orchard* for the Oxford Playhouse Company. That production was actually received with hostility, but his next *Cherry Orchard* (in fact his fifth), for the National Theatre in December 1985, enjoyed the sort of acclaim that greeted Olivier's *Uncle Vanya*. Clive Hirschhorn described it as 'the best, the funniest, the most lucid and unsentimental version of this enduring masterpiece' he had ever seen,[2] while Michael Billington wrote: 'I have seen *The Cherry Orchard* in Paris, Moscow, Chicago and at least nine times in Britain over the last two decades, but I have never seen such an emotionally full-blooded or deeply affecting version as Mike Alfreds's new production.'[3] Alfreds was named best director in both the *Drama* and *Plays and Players* awards for 1986.[4] Playing in repertoire for a comparatively short four-month run in the studio Cottesloe theatre, the production sold out completely. This critical and popular regard was due largely to its status as a National Theatre production featuring Ian McKellen,

Edward Petherbridge, Sheila Hancock, Hugh Lloyd, Roy Kinnear, and Eleanor Bron. Although it opened in London while his *Cherry Orchard* was still playing, Alfreds' next production, *Three Sisters*, did not receive the same recognition.[5] This was in part a consequence of its lower profile, as a Shared Experience production; it was also because of the production's length (three-and-a-half hours) and alleged lugubriousness, which drew adverse comment from critics.

AN ACTOR'S DIRECTOR

The invitation to direct at the National Theatre signalled the recognition of Alfreds by the 'Establishment' as one of Britain's leading directors. Coming from the McKellen–Petherbridge 'Actors' Group' the invitation also reflects his reputation as an actors' director. Maintaining that he is unique in asserting this priority,[6] Alfreds identifies the actor as the 'central creative energy' and 'generating force' of a performance:[7] 'scenery and all the other elements are incidental to [theatre]; they're extensions of the actors'.[8] It was to restore the actor's identity and freedom to create that Alfreds founded the Fringe touring company Shared Experience in 1975. Apart from emphasizing narrative and the theatrical possibilities of story-telling, Shared Experience's early productions stripped away all the 'accretions of theatre practice' such as scenery, costumes, sound, and lighting effects.[9] Given Chekhov's reputation in British theatrical tradition as very much the actor's playwright, it is not surprising that Alfreds' emphasis on the actor should lead to such assiduous devotion to Chekhov's plays.

Whereas Frayn has emerged as the chief apologist for that tradition, Alfreds takes issue with it. However, unlike Richard Eyre, he does not directly confront the ideology informing the established reading of the plays; he rejects the conventions of the *style* of their performance. Radically and persuasively redefining that style, his productions eschew 'pseudo-naturalism' and substitute for the traditional languid playing exuberance and intensity.[10] Alfreds repudiates the anglicization of the plays; instead his productions aim to emphasize the 'essential[ly] Russian quality of the writing and characters'.[11]

Alfreds' privileging of the actor and his concern to emphasize the 'Russianness' of Chekhov's plays have important implications for the function of the text in his productions. Like the scenic elements, the script is seen as an extension of the actor. For all his Chekhov productions Alfreds has written his own translations, with the help of a native speaker. The result is very much a working script which frequently offers alternative renderings for a particular phrase or sentence; the text is then finalized in rehearsals. The choice is generally between a more literal and a more idiomatic variant.[12] Because he wants the actors to capture the plays' 'Russianness' Alfreds tends to encourage the actors to use the more literal versions. The reliance on the language to engender the (appropriate) acting style has been implicit in Alfreds' several dramatizations, including *Arabian Nights* (1975 – 6), *Bleak House* (1977 – 8), *Handful of Dust* (1982),[13] and, at the National Theatre, *The Wandering Jew* (1987): just as Waugh's novel provided a pretext for arch, thirties-style playing, Eugène Sue's Gothic saga proved ideal for exploring an extravagantly melodramatic style. In staying as close to the original as possible, Alfreds' Chekhov translations sometimes sound slightly 'un-English'.[14] They faithfully reproduce the endearments and emotional language whose extravagance other translators readily curb: in this version of *Three Sisters* Solyony and Chebutykin call each other 'Angel of mine', and at one point Irina says melodramatically, 'my tears are flowing'. Consistent with Alfreds' privileging of the source text, the translations also retain all Russian names and forms of address, patronymics, and diminutives.

ALFREDS' METHODS

Alfreds insists that, no less in Chekhov than in work such as *Arabian Nights* or *Bleak House*, the actors' first responsibility is to tell the story: 'the story, the plot-line, the series of events are vital because they are the thread on which everything else hangs ... If the narrative is removed, or falters, there is nothing to hang on to, no spine to support the layers of images, themes, meanings.'[15] He insists that, far from being plotless mood pieces in which nothing much happens, Chekhov's plays must be recognized as having 'very solid plots containing the most vivid events'.[16] Before exploring the motivations of the characters, the first rehearsals are concerned only with establishing the 'actions' of the play, what the characters *do*. To facilitate this Alfreds breaks down each act into 'sections' and each section into smaller 'units': in *The Seagull*, for example, the first section of

Act I is 'Waiting for Konstantin's play to begin'; it comprises the units 'Masha rejects Medvedenko's love and values', 'Konstantin prepares for his play', 'Konstantin discusses his mother' and 'Konstantin and Sorin discuss Trigorin'.[17]

Once the details of the plot are established, each actor is required to isolate everything in the text that concerns his/her character, noting not only all biographical facts, but what the character says about him/herself, what others say about him/her and what he/she says about others. Only after these exercises are completed does the focus of rehearsals shift to personal motivations and relationships. To that end Alfreds runs each act over and over in its entirety, nominating for each run a particular 'point of concentration'. In Act I of *The Cherry Orchard* these included: the time, 2 a.m.; it is five years since Ranevskaya went away; Paris; Grisha's death; Ranevskaya and her lover; the cherry orchard; the nursery. Collectively these points of concentration help the actors to define the characters' objectives. They also help to clarify each character's 'superobjective', to which Alfreds insists that the actor should anchor his/her performance: for example, Chebutykin wants to justify his failure in life; Ranevskaya wants to be loved.[18]

By so informing the actor's consciousness with this series of exercises, Alfreds finds no need to prescribe a *mise en scène*. This means refraining not simply from blocking moves, but from fixing the interpretation of particular moments and scenes. This is to engender spontaneity, to allow the actors to be 'true to the moment' and to encourage them to be prepared to respond to the different impulses of the other actors. Most ambitiously, it is to encourage the actors to continue to explore the play in performance. Alfreds believes that a 'great play' defies the precise definition of particular scenes or lines:[19] performance can never be definitive; it is a matter of process, not product.[20]

The McKellen-Petherbridge group, unversed in Alfreds' methods, was less successful than the *Three Sisters* cast in achieving this objective. In *The Cherry Orchard* a number of moments which obviously 'worked well' became formularized, so fixing the interpretation of a particular episode. Sometimes, as in the case of the exceptionally elaborate search by Kinnear's Simeonov-Pishchik for his mislaid money, these became the sort of deadly routines Alfreds abhors. *Three Sisters*, on the other hand, remained considerably more fluid and flexible

13   David Blake Kelly as Sorin and Philip Osment as Konstantin in a dress
rehearsal of Act I of *The Seagull* directed by Mike Alfreds, 1981

in performance. For example, between performances of the *chekhartma/cheremsha* dispute, the tone of Philip Voss' Chebutykin ranged from nonchalance to anger while, correspondingly, Christian Burgess' Solyony moved between indignation and barely controlled hysteria. Similarly, depending upon the way in which the preceding moments had unfolded, Voss dropped the clock with varying degrees of deliberateness, sometimes doing so with defiance or even malevolence. This is the sort of variation which illustrates Alfreds' understanding of the essential 'roughness' of performance. That principle is not demonstrated by a detail such as whether or not McKellen ended up knocking over the table in Act 3; this detail, which so fascinated critics, did not signify any real shift of emphasis or interpretation in Lopakhin's victory scene and was, so to speak, 'cosmetic'.

Inherent in Alfreds' methods, which lay such emphasis on the exploration of character, is the danger of actors lapsing into gratuitous 'emotional states'. To avert this problem each of the characters also becomes, in turn, the point of concentration, with the result that the emphasis shifts very much to the relationships between the characters. Because attention is focussed on this interaction, Alfreds' productions reveal much more comprehensively than perhaps any other British production Chekhov's pervasive, and often cruel, irony. So, rather than experiencing a subjective identification with certain characters, the spectator is encouraged to retain an authentically Chekhovian, almost Brechtian, distance and objectivity. There can be no trace of the sentimentality Alfreds deplores. David Nathan described Shared Experience's *Three Sisters* as 'merciless',[21] while Eric Shorter, betraying his prejudices, complained that the production missed Chekhov's love for his characters.[22]

Just as the Prozorov sisters were de-glamorized, so stereotypes were challenged in the National *Cherry Orchard*. Having been 'pigeonholed as a vulgar comedienne', as she herself recognizes,[23] Sheila Hancock was considered by some unsuited to the part of Ranevskaya because of 'a certain lack of instinctive authoritative breeding'.[24] Precisely because the performance was not in the conventional mould of the *grande dame* the role was freed from its English aristocratic overtones. The production also completely denied any pathos to Varya, whom Eleanor Bron played as mean-spirited and rather stupid; there was no trace of the 'very kind-hearted' person Chekhov describes.[25] Because 'Bron's desolate Varya always knows that she is no consort for the life-affirming Lopakhin' there was none of the usual poignancy in the 'non-proposal' scene:[26] rather than suggesting that love has been disappointed, the performance implied that an issue which should never have been raised had at last been resolved.

'SLAVONIC EMOTIONALISM'

The distance Alfreds intends the audience to preserve from the characters is also encouraged by a heightened performance style. That style is the Shared Experience hallmark, its cue taken variously from the grotesque imaginations of Gogol and Dickens, the artifice and superficial elegance of Marivaux and Waugh, and the exotic world of the *Arabian Nights*. Although Chekhov's plays seem to offer little excuse for such theatricality, the acting in Alfreds' productions has been boldly physical and emotional, and indeed even verged on the grotesque. Departing so conspicuously from convention, the Oxford Playhouse Company's *Cherry Orchard* was decried as a music-hall burlesque featuring 'a bunch of neurasthenics'.[27] Not only does Alfreds take Chekhov at his word that the play is 'in places a farce', he points out that the text actually provides plentiful cues for such exuberance: the excited home-coming, Charlotta's conjuring, the dancing in Act 3, Yepikhodov's 'misfortunes', and the frequent states of nervous excitement experienced by a number of the characters.

Shaping and further legitimizing the exuberance is Alfreds' notion of the Slavic temperament, which he defines as volatile, prone to emotional display and physically expressive.[28] Reviewing the 1982 *Cherry Orchard*, Milton Shulman remarked that the cast had obviously been encouraged to be 'as Slavonic as a bubbling samovar'.[29] Of the 1985 production, however, Shulman remarked without sarcasm on the 'superb atmosphere of Slavonic emotionalism and exuberance' engendered by the endemic embracing.[30]

Alfreds' justification for such an approach to Chekhov is obviously extremely contentious: the Slavic temperament is construed as extrovert in opposition to the 'repressed' English character. Chekhov himself seems to corroborate the dubiousness of this argument. He objected to a performance of *Uncle Vanya* when the actress playing Sonya went down on her knees and kissed Serebryakov's hand after the line, 'Do show some understanding, Father': 'That was wrong. That's not what drama is. The whole meaning and drama of a person is inside, not in outward manifestations.'[31] Alfreds, however, is reacting to the codes of the society and the theatrical tradition to which he belongs: 'We English don't use our bodies, we don't gesticulate, we don't touch each other very much, and it affects our whole way of playing. We deal in irony and understatement.'[32] Therefore he encourages his actors to explore gesture and movement in order to externalize their characters' thoughts and feelings.

Evidently taking his cue from Charlotta, Alfreds visualizes *The Cherry Orchard* as 'a light elegant "clown show" … By "clown" I mean somebody whose unhappiness pushes him into ludicrous behaviour – who is somewhat idiosyncratic, but lost.'[33] Yepikhodov's description of himself as 'some sort of insect' proved uncannily apposite in the performance of Greg Hicks, who contorted his fingers with insectile angularity to suggest the pain in the character's struggle to express himself. Meanwhile Ian McKellen's Lopakhin roamed the stage not sure where to put his hands or himself and fidgeting with loose change in his pocket. Particularly hyperactive were Dunyasha, whom Selena Cadell played as extremely nervy and frenetic, and Ranevskaya, whose mercuriality was expressed in Hancock's extravagant gestures and twirls as well as extremes of joyous laughter and heavy sobbing.

In contrast to the general vivacity of his *Cherry Orchard*, the acting in Alfreds' *Three Sisters* was characterized by a sense of severe constraint which suggested 'suppressed hysteria'.[34] Occasionally, pent-up energies were released with great liveliness: for example when the sisters teased Andrey, and during the brief episode of singing and dancing in Act 2. Such moments served to heighten the impression of intense, repressed emotions and pain. The comparative stillness was not only intended to help to create for the characters a 'classical', almost 'heroic' stature[35] but, suggesting an apparent inability to move, it also provided a metaphor for their entrapment.

BUILDING A PERFORMANCE

Underlying Alfreds' approach to theatre is a fascination with the *process* of acting. Whereas Stanislavsky encouraged actors to create a 'role' or character, Alfreds wants them to build a performance. Shared Experience's productions have been consistently concerned with ' "the act of transformation" – the ability of an actor to transform himself or herself into someone else in the presence of an audience.'[36] Alfreds insists on the audience's awareness of this transformation; that awareness of course facilitates detachment from Chekhov's characters. As in all previous Shared Experience productions, the cast for *The Seagull* acted as ushers, carried out the scene changes and remained visible in the wings when their characters were 'off stage'. To emphasize further the 'duality' of the 'here-and-now' and the 'then-and-there',[37] the theatre remained evenly lit throughout the performance. Although Shared Experience's *Three Sisters* also observed the conventions of the actors being always on stage and carrying out the scene changes, at the Cottesloe it seems that 'National' practice prevailed: not only were stage-hands used but, because the set concealed the wings, the only world presented in *The Cherry Orchard* was the 'then-and-there'.

The risk inherent in Alfreds' approach to performance is that the acting may simply draw attention to itself. Billington identified the problem in *A Handful of Dust*: 'what you are asked to admire is actors' ingenuity'.[38] Shows like *Arabian Nights*, where the actors were required constantly to change roles, or Gogol's *Marriage* (1983), with its exaggerated and grotesque characters, justify and even demand such virtuosity. However, as his disputes with Stanislavsky suggest, Chekhov does not appear to invite the same virtuosity: in the plays' original productions, he disapproved of Natasha searching for burglars under the furniture and wanted 'no tricks' in Lopakhin's performance.[39] Nevertheless Alfreds says of *The Cherry Orchard*: 'All the characters are, to some extent, giving "performances" of themselves.'[40] Therefore, whereas Chekhov curtailed Charlotta's conjuring, Alfreds restored the original cues and even introduced additional tricks.

The expansion of Charlotta's repertoire nevertheless clearly served Alfreds' reading of the play. Not only is she the play's principal 'clown' but, as the governess, Charlotta presides over the nursery world which Alfreds sees as a metaphor for the relationships in *The Cherry Orchard*. Indeed, in spite of the scope Alfreds allowed his actors, they did not indulge in the sort of gratuitous sensationalism that characterized Charles Sturridge's *Seagull* (1985) or Elijah Moshinsky's *Three Sisters* (1987). Alfreds' resistance to such affectations was exemplified by Petherbridge's interpretation of Gayev. Playing down the miming of the billiard shots, his distinctly half-hearted gesture suggested that this is a family joke of which Gayev is now weary. This was consistent with a portrayal of Gayev as much less whimsical than the eulogies to the bookcase and to Nature have traditionally been understood to imply. Petherbridge's performance revealed that it is others, particularly his sister and Firs, who have cast Gayev in the role of silly brother and uncle.

SCENIC ELEMENTS

While his controversial heightening of the acting is extremely plausible, Alfreds is more vulnerable to criticism precisely where he has shifted most conspicuously from Shared Experience's original principles: in his use of scenic effects. In 'A shared experience: the actor as story-teller', Alfreds objects to these elements because they 'impede the freeing of what [makes] theatre theatre', and 'manipulate' the audience.[41] However, having stripped away so much, there was no alternative but to begin to restore those forsaken elements: 'you can get trapped in your own creation'.[42] Although he describes their use as 'selective', these elements have become regular features of his productions since Shared Experience's *commedia dell'arte Merchant of Venice* (1981), which immediately preceded the company's *Seagull*. Alongside *The Seagull*, which used minimal furniture, simple costumes and no lighting effects and which, in London, was set against the bare brick wall of the Almeida Theatre, *Three Sisters* and the National Theatre's *Cherry Orchard* appear grandiose. They seem less extravagant, however, when compared in turn with the National's production of *Wild Honey*.

Unlike *The Seagull*, Alfreds' *Cherry Orchards* and *Three Sisters* featured taped sound effects and a score of incidental, atmospheric music devised by Ilona Sekacz, while the increased emphasis on design in Alfreds' productions has been marked by the collaboration of Paul Dart, who has designed all their sets and lighting since 1982. In spite of the apparent concession to conventionality in actually introducing more elaborate design, Alfreds departs radically from the naturalism with which British Chekhov traditionally complies. Relying only on the costumes to suggest the period of the plays' settings, Dart's designs for both the National's *Cherry Orchard* and Shared Experience's *Three Sisters* were highly stylized and expressive of Alfreds' distinctive visions of the two plays. Because Alfreds interprets Chekhov's description of the colonnade in the settings for Acts 1 and 2 as denoting 'ironic' tragedy,[43] the design for *Three Sisters* included four looming columns which created a sense of monumentality: in the first two acts they were set on diagonal lines; in the third they formed a phalanx behind a cramped bedroom; and in the last act they represented trees, three of them (upstage right) suggesting the avenue of firs. The columns featured expressionist designs of broad, black brush strokes, which were carried over onto a backcloth. Both the backcloth and the columns evoked a bleakness which bold lighting effects accentuated and charged with violence. In Act 3, for example, blood-red lighting suffused the backcloth, symbolizing not only the fire raging in the town but the characters' emotional anguish. The expressionism of this effect was consistent with the general lighting design: the harsh white light of the first act, and for Act 2 the division of the stage into three isolated areas of dim light. Reinforcing the impression of oppressive bleakness, the furnishings and costumes were almost consistently black or dark green. The only contrast was provided by Olga's blue uniform (and it was a drab blue), Irina's stridently white party dress in Act 1, and Natasha's garish wardrobe of clashing pinks and purples. Dart's set for *The Cherry Orchard* created a very different tone: a bright blue and white box hung around and above with diaphanous white curtains, it projected lightness, lyricism, and fragility. Banished was any suggestion of the pseudo-Chekhovian 'misty landscape'.

The chief misgivings that arise from Dart's Chekhov designs stem from contradictions with other tenets of Alfreds' credo. Firstly, they seem to violate the principle that scenic elements should be essentially extensions of the actors. In *Three Sisters* the scenery and the atmospheric lighting, far from being incidental, threatened to overwhelm the actors, and, shortly before *The Cherry Orchard* opened, the National cast expressed serious doubts about the production's design.[44] However, just as for *The Marriage* Alfreds stacked the stage deep and high with furniture to encourage the actors in a thoroughly grotesque performance style appropriate to Gogol, so the settings for Chekhov were intended to serve the acting: in *The Cherry Orchard*, to liberate the actors to explore a style of playing whose 'tone is firmly set in the nursery'.[45]

'IF YOU JUST LET A PLAY SPEAK, IT MAY NOT MAKE
A SOUND'[46]

More contentiously, Dart's designs belie Alfreds' repeated insistence that he does not wish to impose an interpretation on actors or an audience because that restricts their freedom 'to explore, to imagine, to create'.[47] Alfreds insists that it is not his role to tell the audience what to think.[48] Yet the designs for *Three Sisters* and the National *Cherry Orchard* clearly directed the audience's thinking by defining the plays in a way in which the minimal setting of Shared Experience's

Seagull had not. In *Three Sisters* the set became a visual metaphor for defeat and entrapment. This emphasis was highlighted by the failure in Act 3 to heed the stage directions implicit in the text: the intensity of the backlighting did not decrease as the fire died down, nor did the general lighting change to suggest the incipient dawn. This impression of bleakness was reinforced by sound effects: the noise of the wind blowing in the stove-pipe became an 'omen of catastrophe';[49] the portentous ticking of the clock before Acts 1 and 2 signified that Chekhov's characters are oppressed not only by space, but also by time. The tyranny of time was underlined when Holly Wilson's Olga stopped to listen to all twelve chimes of the clock at the beginning of the first act: this gave the full weight of ironic counter-point to her remark that 'a year's gone by and we can talk about it so easily'.

The fallacy of Alfreds' argument that 'the interpretation of texts is not the main business of theatre' is similarly illustrated by his *Cherry Orchard* productions, which presented essentially the *same* reading of the play. He finds in *The Cherry Orchard* the optimism that he fails to acknowledge in *Three Sisters*: in the National Theatre production, not only did the exuberance of the acting create a lighter tone, but the finale admitted no hint of autumnal melancholy. Like Simeonov-Pishchik, Gayev and Ranevskaya were seen as survivors. Only Julie Legrand's Charlotta introduced a distinctly poignant note when she abandoned her ventriloquist trick. However, the pathos was not allowed to deepen for Firs' final scene. The breaking string was metallic and resonating, neither 'distant' nor 'sad'. Meanwhile the lighting brightened sharply, jaunty music began to play, and the curtains were briskly drawn back, the one suspended above the stage released to float down over Firs. Although Firs did not obviously die, the curtain covering him appeared to represent a shroud for the old order to which he subscribes. Alison Fiske, who played Ranevskaya in the Oxford Playhouse production, confirms the adamant note of hope: 'Certainly there's hope. The old order is being swept away: that must be hopeful.'[50]

Whereas in their interpretation of *The Cherry Orchard* Trevor Griffiths and Richard Eyre claim the future primarily for Trofimov, Alfreds' National Theatre production privileged Lopakhin. Indeed, for the first time in the British theatre the casting of the play identified the merchant as the 'central' role. Because he was apparently cast against type, the choice of McKellen caused surprise and was actually described by Michael Meyer as 'perverse';[51] of slender build, McKellen exudes none of the coarseness or oafishness generally ascribed to Lopakhin. Although the character was presented with the same equivocation as the others, through the physical and social gaucheness could be seen the gentleness and sensitivity Chekhov's letters describe.

In spite of allusions to the wider context of social change, which he recognises as fundamental to the meaning of the plays,[52] Alfreds was primarily concerned to illuminate personal experience rather than to engage with the broader social discourse of the plays. In his production notes he gave this account of the theme of *The Cherry Orchard*: 'In a period of social change and crumbling frameworks people have difficulty in defining their identities.' It is with these identities and the possibilities they offer for characterization that Alfreds is primarily concerned. Accordingly, he describes Lopakhin's superobjective as 'wanting to be accepted and loved by Ranevskaya and to shake off his peasant past' and, only parenthetically, to own the cherry orchard. Similarly, although he identifies the passer-by as a 'social victim', Alfreds defines Ranevskaya's 'function' not as a representative of the landowning class but as 'a beloved/mistress/ wife', and Trofimov is not a revolutionary but an 'inspirer/orator'.[53] Alfreds' priorities are exemplified by his use of the original version of Act 2, whose revision by Chekhov he attributes to Stanislavsky's dubious intervention. Consequently, displaced from the end of the act was the scene between Trofimov and Anya which Griffiths and Eyre interpret as endorsing (revolutionary) change. Alfreds substituted the subdued coda in which Charlotta makes her personal testimony (which in Chekhov's revised version occurs at the beginning of the act) to the deaf Firs and not Yepikhodov, Dunyasha, and Yasha, whose presence during this monologue Alfreds believes to be incongruous and distracting.

Unlike Griffiths and Eyre, therefore, Alfreds offers no rationalization of the social change reflected in *The Cherry Orchard*. Indeed, unlike Max Stafford-Clark and Thomas Kilroy in their reading of *The Seagull*, he is not even interested in substantiating the conditions of the world of the plays: 'What I'm trying to do, in fact, is to create a world which actually does not exist ... What I hope we achieve is a created "world" which has the soul and essence of the original play.'[54] His primary concern with the integrity of the individual character is absolutely consistent with an approach which locates the basis of theatre in the actor's performance. In this respect Alfreds is entirely typical of a tradition which, since the 1930s, has looked upon Chekhov's plays primarily as acting vehicles. Inevitably those 'theatrical class sectaries' whom Griffiths refutes have found it easier to accommodate stylistic rather than ideological challenges;[55] therefore, while Griffiths and Bond have remained out on a limb, Alfreds was admitted (at least for a time) closer to the mainstream. Although he may not have succeeded in demythologizing the plays completely, by scrubbing away the half-truths that have accreted round Chekhov Mike Alfreds has provided a significant reappraisal of the conventions of a theatrical tradition. In the process he has generated some of the richest, most penetrating and most exciting performances of Chekhov in Britain.

Notes

1 'Drama Awards for the year 1981', Drama, 143 (Spring 1982), p. 10.
2 Sunday Express, 15 December 1985.
3 The Guardian, 12 December 1985.
4 'Drama Awards 1986', Drama, 163 (1st quarter 1987), p. 27; 'Plays and Players Awards 1986', Plays and Players, 400 (January 1987), p. 9.
5 After touring for a month from late February 1986, Three Sisters opened in London on 1 April at the Bloomsbury Theatre, where it ran until 3 May 1986.
6 Alfreds, in Christopher Edwards, 'Behind the fringe', Plays and Players, 340 (January 1982), p. 16.
7 Mike Alfreds, 'A shared experience: the actor as story-teller', interview with Peter Hulton, Theatre Papers, Third Series, 6 (1979–80), pp. 5, 4.
8 In Kenneth Rea, 'The theatre of Mike Alfreds', Drama, 163 (first quarter 1987), p. 6.
9 Alfreds, 'A shared experience', pp. 4–5.
10 Alfreds, in David Allen, 'Exploring the limitless depths: Mike Alfreds directs Chekhov', New Theatre Quarterly, 2:8 (November 1986), p. 320.
11 Advance publicity for the Oxford Playhouse Cherry Orchard.
12 The references to Alfreds' methods, as well as many of the observations on his understanding of the plays, are based on my attendance at rehearsals for Three Sisters.
13 These were all Shared Experience productions.
14 Alfreds, in Claire Armistead, 'After a bigger share', Ham and Hi, 4 April 1986.
15 Alfreds, 'A shared experience', p. 9.
16 Ibid.
17 Alfreds, production notes (Shared Experience archives).
18 Alfreds, production notes for The Cherry Orchard and Three Sisters (Shared Experience archives).

19 In Allen, 'Exploring the limitless depths', p.325.
20 In Edwards, 'Behind the fringe', p.16.
21 *Jewish Chronicle*, 11 April 1986.
22 *The Daily Telegraph*, 3 April 1986.
23 In Val Hennessy, 'A new role and lasting character', *The Times*, 9 December 1985.
24 Milton Shulman, *London Standard*, 11 December 1985.
25 Letter to Olga Knipper, 14 October 1903, in *The Oxford Chekhov*, 9 vols., ed. Ronald Hingley (London: Oxford University Press, 1964–80), III, p.326.
26 David Nathan, *Jewish Chronicle*, 20 December 1985.
27 Michael Coveney, *Financial Times*, 10 August 1982. Michael Billington described the production as an 'unfeeling romp that might be entitled *Carry on Chopping*' (*The Guardian*, 10 August 1982).
28 Alfreds, production notes for *The Cherry Orchard*.
29 *London Standard*, 10 August 1982.
30 *London Standard*, 11 December 1985.
31 N.S. Butova, 'Iz vospominany' ('From reminiscences'), in *Chekhov i teatr: pisma, felyetony, sovremenniki o Chekhove-dramaturge (Chekhov and the theatre: letters, newspaper articles, and contemporaries on Chekhov the dramatist)* (Moscow: Iskusstvo, 1961), p.346; cited in *The Oxford Chekhov*, III, p.302.
32 In Rea, 'The theatre of Mike Alfreds', p.6.
33 Alfreds, in Allen, 'Exploring the limitless depths', p.324.
34 Helen Rose, *Time Out*, 9 April 1986.
35 Alfreds, in Allen, 'Exploring', p.333.
36 Alfreds, in Malcolm Hay, 'Shared experience', *Plays and Players*, 379 (April 1985), p.8.
37 See Alfreds, 'A shared experience', pp.4, 6.
38 Michael Billington, *The Guardian*, 12 November 1982.
39 Letters to Stanislavsky, 2 January 1901 and 30 October 1903, *The Oxford Chekhov*, III, pp.313, 327.
40 In Allen, 'Exploring', p.324.
41 Alfreds, 'A shared experience', p.5.
42 In Clare Colvin, 'Good experience', *Observer*, 8 August 1982.
43 Alfreds, in Allen, 'Exploring', p.332.
44 Petherbridge, in a memorandum to Alfreds, 3 December 1985 (Shared Experience archives).
45 Julia Pascal, *City Limits*, 20 December 1985.
46 Peter Brook, *The Empty Space* (Harmondsworth: Penguin Books, 1971 (1968), p.43.
47 Alfreds, 'A shared experience', p.5.
48 Alfreds, in Edwards, 'Behind the fringe', p.16.
49 Allen, 'Exploring', p.332.
50 In Ros Franey, 'Loving it', *City Limits*, 6–12 August 1982, p.49.
51 In 'Kaleidoscope', presented by Paul Vaughan, BBC Radio 4, 11 December 1985. In his review Meyer described Ranevskaya as the play's 'chief character'.

52 Alfreds, production notes for *Three Sisters* and *The Cherry Orchard*.
53 Alfreds, production notes for *The Cherry Orchard*.
54 Alfreds, in Allen, 'Exploring', p. 321.
55 Trevor Griffiths, Introduction to *The Cherry Orchard*, a new English version by Trevor Griffiths, from a translation by Helen Rappaport (London: Pluto Press, 1978), p. v. See David Allen's article (ch. 14) in the present volume.

CHAPTER 16

Chekhov and the company problem in the British theatre

Patrick Miles

Being part of 'we'. I think that's what I would care about the most. That is what I shall *miss* the most.

Terry Hands on leaving the Royal Shakespeare Company[1]

As actors learned to act together and directors to orchestrate them, so Chekhov's plays began to succeed in Britain. Several directors – Komisarjevsky, Gielgud, Saint-Denis, Fernald, Olivier – used their Chekhov ensembles as stepping-stones to longer-lasting, general theatre companies. The view became widely held that Chekhov's plays are best performed by 'permanent' companies (which usually meant companies modelled on MKhT). This view, I believe, is based on a misunderstanding of the relationship between the Chekhovian ensemble and the permanent theatre company.

The reason Chekhov's plays require ensemble-acting, and are themselves such powerful ensemble-makers, is that they present an essentially familial theatre space. The characters of each play constitute an extended family interacting (often negatively, of course) on a stage which usually represents one room. Their personal and physical proximity generates the 'continuous mutual communication' by voice, gesture, eyes, and even silence, which Stanislavsky thought proper to all acting.[2] A relatively flat hierarchy is produced among the characters, and this is lived by the actors. Chekhov's plays work particularly well in studio conditions because the total theatre space is sufficiently room-like for the audience themselves to feel co-opted into the onstage family.

Indeed, communication in Chekhov is so rich, so sensitive, and so unfinalized that it is tempting to regard it as influenced by a wider context than the particular extended family. Nemirovich-Danchenko spoke of the 'deepest force of spiritual communication ... uniting the group on stage' in a Chekhov play.[3] Perhaps Chekhov's people partake of that radical communality (*sobornost*) without which Russian Orthodoxy is said to be unthinkable?[4] Or is this simply another way of saying they are Russians? Such speculations are of little practical use to British actors, but, compared with the demands of communication within the Chekhov group, 'much of the teamwork of which the English theatre is so proud' is indeed 'external ensemble playing'.[5] It may be that true psychological sharing on the stage has been Chekhov's, and Russia's, greatest gift to our theatre.

If Chekhov's plays are based on the family, however, this was not true of MKhT, nor is it the case with our own permanent companies. The 'theatrical family' of MKhT's early years and Stanislavsky's experiments in communal living with his Studio at Yevpatoriya are well known, but the origins of MKhT were pedagogical. It grew out of the theatre schools and their end-of-term productions. The relationship of the directors to the actors remained essentially that of paternalistic teachers to pupils. This brought a spirit of restless inquiry to MKhT, but it also presupposed a hierarchy quite alien to the equality of the Chekhov ensemble. As MKhT grew, this hierarchy lengthened. Not only did its directors relate 'horizontally' to the actors in a pedagogical, rather than familial, fashion, they were also 'vertically' more remote from them than any character in a Chekhov play ever is.

In fact Nemirovich doubted whether the closeness of communication that we associate with a Chekhov ensemble was applicable to other playwrights. He felt that Stanislavsky, in his desire to overcome the absence of onstage communication in the 'old' theatre, had gone to the other extreme: 'our young actors have become so absorbed in this technique of onstage communication that their acting has become untheatrical, uninventive, and tedious. Whatever play one is rehearsing, one must keep tearing the performer away, so to speak, from his partner and directing his attention to all the other, more important, things going on inside the character.'[6] By implication, the Chekhovian ensemble could not form the basis of a general theatre company. 'Excessive' communicativeness was even 'foreign' to Chekhov's characters, who were 'largely immersed in themselves and lead a life of their own'.[7]

The author's own attitude towards the family, the group, and socialization is relevant here. It seems to have been fundamentally ambivalent. The prominent social and political actions of Chekhov's life, for example his journey to Sakhalin, his philanthropy, and his conduct in the affair of Gorky's expulsion from the Imperial Academy, are those of an individualist, a self-made man, and a very private person. Yet he wore a medallion on his watch-chain inscribed 'For the Lone[ly] Man the Desert is Everywhere.' On the one hand he could become the acknowledged head of an extended family at the age of twenty, provide for them tirelessly, and live with them for most of his adult life; on the other hand he could write:

nowadays almost every civilized person, even the most healthy, feels more irritated when he is at home amongst his family than anywhere else, because the discord between the present and the past is felt above all in the family. The irritation is chronic ... it's the kind of irritation that guests fail to notice, and it falls most heavily on the people he is closest to – his mother, or his wife. It is an intimate, family irritation, so to speak.[8]

Chekhov could engage in a bewildering range of social activities from *jours fixes*, masked balls, group holidays, mushroom-picking, and theatre-going, to the zemstvo, famine relief, and MKhT; but he always gives the impression of really being on his way to somewhere else. One moment he will complain that he has no-one to talk to, the next that he is plagued by visitors. His 'sociability', particularly as expressed in his enormous correspondence, was one of his most successful disguises.

The creative tension in Chekhov himself between the 'I' and the 'We' is also a fundamental tension in the extended families of his plays. It is implicit in Stanislavsky's emphasis on how communicative Chekhov's characters are, and Nemirovich's emphasis on their being 'immersed in themselves'. The tension can be sustained within the Chekhovian ensemble, but it cannot be sustained in an organization as big as MKhT. The often precarious balance of the family must give way to a more corporate, less personal identity.

We can see this in the response of our own actors in recent years to working in British 'permanent' companies. 'Part of the problem' for Kenneth Branagh, working in the RSC in 1984, was that it was run 'on the premise that we were one big family', but no-one actually felt they were.[9] For Brian Cox in 1986, 'at Stratford, the home base of the company, you have a powerful sense of family which is vital for maintaining the morale of such a group', but elsewhere in 'such a huge and complex company' this was 'dissipated'.[10]

Clearly actors do want a sense of family in a large permanent company, and feel insecure and demoralized when it cannot be provided. They perceive the cause in the sheer size of the organization and its buildings. 'Somehow this big machine wasn't working.'[11] Of the 'impossibly large' National Theatre Simon Callow writes: 'The company, as such, barely exists. The growth of the individual artist is not attended to in the least ... The involvement of the company in decisions is non-existent ... It is in these subsidized theatres that the directocracy is at its most unqualified ... Heads in these situations roll with remarkable regularity.'[12]

It is important to recognize that such criticisms do not necessarily prove permanent companies are unviable. They suggest that the cohesion, involvement, and energy which are almost synonymous with a small founding company (for example the original RSC) cannot be carried through to a larger one by pretending that the original company has not changed. Bad communication, 'lack of vision' (Callow's phrase), alienation, bureaucracy, and a hire-and-fire approach to employment are, in fact, the typical problems of a 'family' business failing to manage the change to a bigger one.

Understandably, however, British artistic directors have resisted the involvement of professional management in their companies. It is not simply a case of vested interest or the so-called conservatism of the theatre. Directors rightly see the putting on of a play as a feat of management in itself. Every successful director owes some of his advancement to the fact that he has proved consistently capable of this feat. He therefore interprets the suggestion that management skills be brought into his company as an attack on his competence and power as a director. Moreover, he has probably never met a professional manager who understood anything about the theatre, so he is deeply sceptical that such people can contribute anything useful.

These attitudes rest on a number of misconceptions. First, putting on a play is not the same as managing a whole organism called a company. The confusion in directors' minds over this matter derives from the fact that the company as a whole must be *led* by the director since it is an artistic enterprise. Those most immediately involved in the end product are artists, they are led in modern rehearsal by the director as an artist, and they most naturally look to him for leadership outside. But to suppose that the director can supply everything necessary to the well-being of the company's members outside rehearsals, production, and artistic direction, is plainly impractical in a large organization, even if he possessed the vast array of talents necessary for both activities.

Further, many directors genuinely do not understand the difference between administration and management. If they are attempting to manage a company single-handed, as well as artistically direct it, they will naturally acquire more and more paperwork and sit on more and more committees. Faced with the classic symptoms of company breakdown, they may perceive the fault in their own administrative workload. In this case they will be happy to 'delegate' to an administrator with no management responsibility, believing that this will solve the crisis. When it does not, they feel it confirms that there cannot be 'two heads to a theatre company'.

No sensitive manager would remotely wish to split a company by pushing himself forward as alternative leader to the artistic director. On the contrary, he would see his task as being to use all the skills of people and business management that he has to restore the wholeness and purpose of such an organization. This may well mean being rather self-effacing. There is no doubt that the artistic director has a management role in the company outside the artistic sphere, but the manager would effectively, and in contact with the artistic director, manage those parts that the latter cannot (and probably should not) reach. Where the people of the company are concerned, for example, the manager would be working more structurally, more 'from the outside', to create conditions in which may flourish the very sense of belonging, involvement, and fulfilment that cannot be sustained instinctively in a group larger than the family or by the personality of one man 'on the inside'. Where the management of the company's material resources is concerned, for example on the vital committees, he would not be self-effacing at all, and his voice would ultimately carry more weight than the artistic director's.

Directors are right about one thing, however: corporate management techniques are useless without a profound knowledge of, and sympathy with, the theatre. Unfortunately, an understanding of theatre at management level is still almost unknown in Britain. Yet theatre – 'the most complex machine in the world' [13] – offers unique challenges to people with the skills that management has developed in recent decades. Sadly, the fate of our big theatre companies seems to be another example of our national inability to capitalize on our own talents and inventions.

In practice these companies have 'survived' by fragmenting. Peter Hall feels that he 'finally got it right at the National by splitting it up into small companies, each with an individual director, asking them to produce and/or direct three or four plays over a period of two years'.[14] Under his successor there are no 'house directors' of this kind, but a longer list of associate directors coming in and out of the theatre. Adrian Noble appears to be creating a similar arrangement for the RSC. There are no permanent directors and no associate directors; star directors are to be invited in to direct their own productions, and star actors to act in them.

The economics of the eighties hastened this process, but the result would have been the same anyway. The RSC and the NT have completely ceased to resemble permanent theatre companies. There is a pool of actors in each company that regularly plays in that company's productions, but each play is cast separately, with visiting virtuosi, and there is none of the continuity of direction, ensemble, and actor development that was the original purpose of a permanent company. In a sense, the RSC ceased to be a permanent company when it decided on a permanent geographical split. At the National Theatre Peter Hall did not attempt to create a permanent company, because he considered the range of dramatists too wide for this purpose.[15] Perhaps, then, the only time there has been a permanent theatre company in Britain in the MKhT or 'European' sense was at Stratford between 1960 and 1965 when the RSC under Hall was based on Shakespeare and essentially working on a united way of doing his text.

In fact the very idea of the permanent theatre company seems to have died in this country. We seem to have forgotten what it stood for. In the public arguments about subsidy hardly anyone defended our national and regional companies in terms of the desirability of permanent companies as such; the concern was more to protect the state that these companies were actually in. There were no impassioned appeals to the ideals of Stanislavsky, Brecht, and the 'European' ensembles. The last major artist in Britain to fight for the permanent company as an ideal was Peggy Ashcroft. Mike Alfreds sees the permanent company as an 'unrealizable dream'.[16] For Peter Hall it is a pure contradiction in terms, 'like saying, "Let us never age, let us never die, let us never develop, let us never change" ... I fervently believe in ensemble, but if you elevate ensemble into the concept of permanent company, then you have dogma, and that's death.'[17] He has recently set up his own 'impermanent' company, the Peter Hall Company.

The way the NT and RSC are now organized hardly affects the kind of director who sees himself as invited in to set the stamp of his interpretation on an *ad hoc* cast. But it cannot appeal much to actors. Whereas in the eighties they felt alienated and frustrated in the director-run theatrical corporations, now they must see little difference between working in the national companies and working on a commercial production. Neither then nor now have they been able to reap the benefits of collaboration in a real company with continuity and consistency.

One way in which they have responded is to form small impermanent companies run by actors for actors. There are impeccable Elizabethan precedents for this,[18] but I believe Chekhov can make a vital contribution here, too.

The problem that we appear to have had with our theatre companies all through this century derives from the fact that there can be no predetermined model of what a theatre company should be. Various other social forms have therefore been adopted. There have been British theatre companies run like cricket teams, like old-fashioned firms, like socialist collectives, like university English Departments, and we have flirted with MKhT and the 'European' models. One of the most potent models for British actors, however, has proved to be the family of the Chekhov play. Real extended families are not a traditional feature of British life – on the contrary, the British view is that you cannot 'remain' in a family – but the Chekhovian family has repeatedly given British actors the sense of uniqueness, equality, freedom, and support that they need to work well.

Putting on Chekhov's plays, then, can knit the actors of the new impermanent companies together so that, however impermanent, they will still feel themselves to be real companies. It can also help establish a different kind of director – actor relationship. 'The rehearsal period was very happy', writes Bill Gaskill, of his 1967 Royal Court production of *Three Sisters*, 'as I imagine it always is with Chekhov'.[19] The latter may not be literally true, but it is impossible to direct Chekhov from above or outside. As Terry Hands has put it, 'with Chekhov ... you don't want big directorial concepts. You want to feel that a group of actors got together and themselves built the play. You want the improvised feel.'[20] To make the discoveries that Chekhov's texts demand, the director has to share in the communicativeness, openness, and mutual respect of Chekhov's actors. On the other hand, the precarious tension (the 'discord') between the individual and the group in Chekhov's families saves such ensembles from complacency. To an impermanent actors' company Chekhov offers a pledge, as it were, of togetherness in impermanence and impermanency in togetherness. It is interesting to note that the semi-permanent Renaissance Theatre Company, founded by actor Kenneth Branagh after leaving the RSC, plans to present 'all five of Chekhov's major plays with a single company of actors'.[21]

The permanent theatre-company movement in Britain, with which Chekhov was unfortunately associated because of MKhT, failed when the organizations it produced could not be managed. However, the experience of the RSC and NT, together with the repertory theatres, the classical tradition, and everything else that has happened to British actors this century, has bequeathed to us a wider permanent company of hundreds of talented, educated, dedicated, and individual actors who work together all the time. These actors are capable of running 'impermanent' companies that are more viable as real companies than the subsidized houses of the past. Chekhov can help them in this. And such actors we wish him.

Notes

1 'Third Ear', BBC Radio 3, 6 November 1990.
2 K. S. Stanislavsky, *Rabota aktyora nad soboy. Chast I. Rabota nad soboy v tvorcheskom protsesse perezhivaniya (An actor's work on himself. Part I. Work on himself in the creative process of experiencing)*, in *Sobraniye sochineny v vosmi tomakh (Collected works in 8 vols.)*, II (Moscow: Iskusstvo, 1954), p. 256.
3 Vl. I. Nemirovich-Danchenko, *Iz proshlogo (From the past)* (Moscow: GIKhL, 1938), p. 164.
4 Cf. Father Aleksandr Men on the philosopher Berdyayev: 'The approach to the problems of faith "from outside" is alien to us. Berdyayev could never say of Christianity "we". His individualism prevented him' (*Moskovsky Komsomolets* 10 January 1990, p. 2).
5 Peter Brook, *The Empty Space* (Harmondsworth: Penguin Books, 1972), p. 126.
6 Letter to M. O. Knebel, April 1942, in Vl. I. Nemirovich-Danchenko, *Izbrannyye pisma (Selected letters)*, II (Moscow: Iskusstvo, 1979), pp. 536–7.
7 *Ibid.*, p. 537.
8 Letter to Meyerhold, October 1899, in A. P. Chekhov, *Polnoye sobraniye sochineny i pisem v tridtsati tomakh (Complete collected works in 30 vols.)*, VIII, *(Pisma) (Letters)* (Moscow: Nauka, 1980), p. 275.
9 Kenneth Branagh, *Beginning* (London: Pan Books, 1989), p. 159.
10 Brian Cox, *Salem to Moscow: an Actor's Odyssey* (London: Methuen, 1991), pp. 38, 37.
11 Branagh, *Beginning*, p. 161.

12 Simon Callow, *Being an Actor* (Harmondsworth: Penguin Books, 1985), p. 131.
13 Mikhail Bulgakov, *Teatralny roman (A theatrical novel)*, in *Izbrannyye proiz-vedeniya v dvukh tomakh (Selected works in 2 vols.)*, II (Kiev: Dnipro, 1989), p. 300.
14 Sir Peter Hall, interview with the author, 7 February 1991.
15 Sir Peter Hall, *ibid.*
16 Mike Alfreds, interview with the author, 16 January 1991.
17 Sir Peter Hall, 7 February 1991.
18 See John Russell Brown, *Free Shakespeare* (London: Heinemann, 1974), pp. 50–5, 83–9.
19 William Gaskill, *A Sense of Direction* (London: Faber and Faber, 1988), p. 93.
20 Terry Hands, 'Final royal flight', an interview with Benedict Nightingale, *The Times*, 6 November 1990.
21 Kenneth Branagh, 'Production Notes', programme for Renaissance Theatre Company's touring production of *Uncle Vanya*, 1991.

CHAPTER 17

Design for Chekhov

Arnold Aronson

It is probably safe to say that most plays in Western theatre history evoke in the minds of the spectators images and memories of characters, themes, and emotions. This is certainly true of Chekhov as well, but the chances are that when one thinks of Chekhov the first image is of a decor, an environment. More than any other playwright, Chekhov has created a world in which the characters, themes, and emotions are inextricably bound up in the physical space of the setting. This identification of the soul of the character with the setting is literally expressed by Mme Ranevsky in Act 3 of *The Cherry Orchard*: 'I love this house', she says. 'Without the cherry orchard my life would lose its meaning, and if it must really be sold then go and sell me with the orchard.'[1]

So important is the totality of the stage space in Chekhov's plays that even the photographic documentation of productions has tended to encompass the entirety of the setting rather than the more usual narrow focus on the performers. The rooms and gardens created by Viktor Simov for the original productions of the Moscow Art Theatre are amply documented and indelibly stamped on our minds.

Chekhov's plays are, in a sense, about space and about textures. The settings, and the spatial relationships within those settings, tell us about the characters; the textures of the objects within those settings are an extension of the personalities and emotions of the characters. In all theatre history, only Shakespeare is so closely linked to the idea of theatrical space. But Shakespeare is most often dealing with the transformation of the stage – rapid shifting of locales that advance the plot or provide dramatic contrasts, while also reflecting characters' states of mind. Chekhov, needless to say, is more static. There is, to be sure, a significant dramatic procession of scenes, as in *The Seagull* which moves from the park on Sorin's estate to a lawn outside the house, to the dining-room, to a drawing-room. But this movement, as in all his plays, is not so much a function of plot as a representation of some psychological – emotional progression. The move from exterior to interior, for instance, can be seen as an intensifying sense of claustrophobia among the characters and an increasingly inward turning. He is creating a physical manifestation – a concretization – of mood, emotion, and state of mind, the so-called *nastroyeniye*. It is not unlike Richard Wagner's concept of 'soul states'.

Traditionally, the Chekhov landscape has been manifested on the stage through a painstaking creation of historically accurate interiors heavy with furniture, or exteriors of trees and shrubs – not unlike Michael Blakemore's 1988 production of *Uncle Vanya* that was described by one critic as 'choc-a-bloc with saplings, samovars and duff furniture'.[2] And it is to the conscious antithesis of such an approach that the critic of the *Guardian* referred in describing Elijah Moshinsky's production of *Ivanov*: 'The curtain does not rise on any traditional Chekhovian garden view of a country estate. The first act setting of Ivanov's terrace at dusk, as meticulously described by Chekhov, has almost disappeared.'[3] Mike Alfreds, founder of the Shared Experience theatre company, notes that 'we have become very settled in our view of the *look* of Chekhov productions. They are always beige, or, with *The Cherry Orchard*, white.'[4] Interestingly, looking back now on Simov's settings, they strike the eye as false and blatantly theatrical. Such approaches made sense in Chekhov's time; the techniques of Naturalism, though no longer new even then (and certainly not universally admired), were accepted and understood. Furthermore, the connotations and implications of particular types of houses, furniture, decor, and household implements carried great weight and would have had significance even to a non-Russian audience. But this is not true today. A samovar is a curiosity to a British or American audience, but it signifies little. The distinctions among classes as manifested through clothing, not to mention language, are only vaguely sensed by audiences. Ironically, the icons we now associate with Chekhov have come not to signify aspects of Russia at the turn of the century, but Chekhov's plays themselves! A samovar evokes Chekhov; the adjective 'Chekhovian' now refers to a style of decor.

Consequently, the conventional 'Chekhovian' set, that once served as a subtle and detailed semiotic road-map to a complex psycho-social world, is now meaningless, except as a self-referent. It may, in fact, be counter-productive since for many audiences the elaborate interiors associated with Chekhov are indistinguishable from those for the Naturalist Hauptmann, whom Chekhov admired, and Ibsen, whom he detested. A Chekhovian set cannot convey the meanings originally inherent in these interiors. A new visual language must be found, and in order to do this the old language – the established images and references – must first be destroyed.

The contemporary stage is one influenced by the spare minimalism of Samuel Beckett, the self-consciously crude and emblematic scenography of Brecht, the overpowering projections and architectonics of Josef Svoboda, and the neo-surrealist 'theatre of images' typified by the work of Robert Wilson. In such an atmosphere, anything resembling orthodox Naturalism, or even the suggestive realism of the New Stagecraft, is old-fashioned and incomprehensible. Historical modernism now exists primarily as a quotation in post-modern design. A post-modern setting is a web of references in which historical and contemporary images and styles co-exist, thus encompassing the entire history of a particular piece of theatre. But Chekhov is neither old-fashioned nor incomprehensible. In fact, in the 1990s his richness and textures are beginning to seem a more appealing way of presenting the themes and ideas championed by the increasingly dated Beckett. In history and art, everything comes around. The question for directors and scenographers has become, then, a matter of how to present this richness and texture without resorting to past techniques.

The answer, not surprisingly, is to be found in Chekhov himself. The opening stage directions of each act in any of the plays describe a spare, minimal, and suggestive set as if influenced by Craig and Appia. Take the second act of *Uncle Vanya*, for example: 'The dining room in Serebryakov's house. Night. The watchman can be heard tapping in the garden. Serebryakov is sitting in an armchair in front of an open window, he is dozing. Yelena Andreyevna is sitting next to him, and she too is dozing.' That is all. No description of furniture, furnishings, or decor. Throughout the act there are references that suggest the need for a table, a window, a door, a sideboard, and a few chairs, but nothing specific.

Chekhov is stylistically close to the Symbolists – he frequently expressed his admiration for the work of Maurice Maeterlinck – and was thus more concerned with inner states of mind than objective reality. Suggestion and mood are more significant than description. In an essay on 'Chekhov and Naturalism' Nicholas Moravcevich, citing *The Cherry Orchard* as a prime example, points out that Chekhov is attempting in his descriptions an Impressionist/Symbolist fusion of interior and exterior states of mind.[5] The setting for Act 1 of *The Cherry Orchard* is described thus: 'A room that still goes by the name of the nursery. One of the doors leads to Anya's room. It is dawn and the sun will soon come up. It is May. The cherry trees are in flower, but in the orchard it is cold, there is morning frost. The windows in the room are closed.' It is as if the visualization of the room is taken for granted – there is virtually no description of it other than to identify it as the locale of the scene. What is important in this description is the *exterior*. There is a continuity between the nursery and the world beyond. And even exterior scenes have a fluidity that takes them beyond the mere confines of the stage. Take, for instance, Act 4 of *The Three Sisters*: 'The old garden attached to the Prozorov house. A long avenue of fir trees at the end of which is seen the river. On the other side of the river – a forest. On the right is the terrace of the house.' The house is almost an afterthought. What is significant is the vista stretching into the distance with its implication of continuity. What lies beyond the forest? Ultimately, Moscow.

Since the 1960s there has been a conscious attempt in productions of Chekhov to rid the stage of nineteenth-century trappings, most notably in stagings by Otomar Krejca, Peter Brook, Andrei Serban, and several Brechtian-influenced productions in East and West Germany. Additionally, productions in Great Britain by Laurence Olivier, Mike Alfreds, and Philip Prowse have also worked in this direction. Though visually and stylistically different from each other, they all tend to have two elements in common. First, they seem to emanate from the concept of inner – outer continuity; and, second, they frequently use dominant images from the Chekhovian iconography, though they do so in fresh and often startling ways. Consciously or not, it seems that many of these directors and designers are following the advice of avant-garde composer and theoretician John Cage who, when asked about how to treat classics, suggested that rather than simply rejecting them, we could 'quote' them in new works. This approach is clearly seen in examples such as Romanian designer Romulus Fenes' 1965 production of *The Cherry Orchard* in which a period bed and armoire sit like islands in the interior of a rough textured, vortex-like cave; or in Robert Taule's more recent design for Ariel Garcia-Valdes' production of *The Three Sisters* in Paris in which a table and curtain sit stage left on an otherwise bare stage, behind which is a projected backdrop.

The first step in modern Chekhov design was to break the realistic, sentimental grip. A move in this direction can be seen in the 1960 *Seagull* designed by Svoboda and directed by Krejca at the Tyl Theatre in Prague. Svoboda encased the stage in black drapes. The sense of nature, as well as a visual unity, was provided by leaf-filled branches hanging over the stage through all four acts. Interiors were suggested by furniture and fragmentary scenic units such as a window with drapes (but no surrounding walls). More importantly, the atmosphere of each scene was created through the use of changing 'light curtains' that created a scrim-like effect. Thus, the entire play occurred in a fluidly changing, but essentially unified, environment. Exteriors and interiors blended, and the external world was always visibly present in the house.[6]

Interestingly, the same year saw similar approaches for the first time in the Soviet Union. N. Shiffrin's decor for *The Seagull* at the Moscow Art Theatre included a surround that showed trees and the horizon as well as the sky in both exterior and interior scenes – the interiors contained no ceilings and only partial walls. At the same time, tall window drapes, taller than the rooms, hung in the exterior as well as interior scene, so that the memory or anticipation of scenes was everpresent. Daniil Lider used overhanging branches – remarkably similar to Svoboda's – as well as a sort of curtain on a clothes line in his design for *The Seagull* at the Tsvilling Theatre in Chelyabinsk the same year. The motif of branches hanging over the stage through exterior and interior scenes proved popular in the USSR, and could be found in M. Kurilko's design for *Uncle Vanya* in 1966 at the Kupal Theatre in Minsk and in E. Stenberg's 1969 production of *The Seagull* at MKhAT.[7]

This internal–external conjunction was truly explored for the first time in Britain in 1962 at the newly opened Chichester Festival Theatre. Sean Kenny's design for Laurence Olivier's production of *Uncle Vanya* consisted of a simple wooden back wall with two windows and a door. With the windows blacked out in the first act it became the garden; with light coming through them the stage was transformed into the interiors of Acts 2–4. The great innovation, however, was the use, perhaps for the first time anywhere, of a thrust stage for Chekhov. Not only were the internal boundaries destroyed, but some of the separation between the stage and the audience seemed to disappear as well. J. C. Trewin noted that '[Chekhov's] people had not been more closely allied to us.'[8]

Some of this spirit could still be found in Elijah Moshinsky's 1987 production of *The Three Sisters* on the thrust stage at the Greenwich Theatre with settings by John Bury. Though traditionally Chekhovian in feel – 'a dowdy provincial sitting-room with drab green paint, lace table cloths, and shawls draped on ugly furniture to hide worn patches'[9] – entrances and exits, as well as bits of action, occurred in the aisles and throughout the theatre.

The atmospheric, yet non-naturalistic, approach was continued in the famous 1967 London production of *The Three Sisters* at the National Theatre directed by Laurence Olivier and designed by Svoboda. Here light curtains were replaced by a surround of stretched cords tied from floor to grid, while window-frames were placed between two layers of cords. Through the use of light, the cords could become, as described by Jarka Burian, 'solid walls, delicate bars, or shimmering depths without precise limit'.[10] Projections were also employed. Although minimal pieces of furniture were employed to create specific locales, this was an essentially abstract setting – Chekhov in a sort of theatrical void. This was the first truly non-naturalistic scenic approach to Chekhov in Britain, and though praised by most critics, it seemed to have little immediate effect.

By eliminating naturalistic approaches to the scenography, we are eliminating the associations that go with it. The stage reasserts itself – it is no longer an *illusion of* reality, but an *allusion to* reality. Walls, doors, and windows become ephemeral, transformable elements in an atmospheric scenography. Svoboda's comments on the London *Three Sisters* are significant. 'Windows are very special things in Chekhov', he notes. 'The thoughts and desires of the characters fly out through the windows, but life and its realities fly in the other way. The windows must be created by means of light, like that of the French Impressionists – light dispersed in air ... The windows lead us to all of Chekhov's atmosphere. The interiors are not bordered or limited, but diffused.'[11]

The question of fluidity and continuity has generally been approached in two ways: eliminating the walls altogether or creating a sense of endlessness through rooms and spaces that continue beyond the spectator's view. The latter approach is, perhaps, the more interesting since it creates a sense of mystery and fascination. Many of the designs that take this approach create a tantalizing maze of offstage spaces that beckon the audience to explore their depths. Needless to say, the implication is already there in Chekhov in such

14   The set for Act 4 of *Three Sisters*, designed by Josef Svoboda for the National
Theatre production, London 1967

plays as *The Three Sisters*, with the ballroom visible through columns
behind the drawing-room, or in *The Cherry Orchard*, where, again,
the ballroom is visible beyond the archway behind the drawing-room.

One of the earliest productions to approach the play in this way
was the 1969 *Cherry Orchard* designed by Karl Ernst Hermann in Berlin.
There was a classic box set, but the two upstage doors that led to
the drawing-room were placed in the back wall in such a way that
it was impossible for any one person in the audience to see the entirety

of the inner room. Furthermore, these doors were echoed in the upstage wall of the inner room. There was an implication of infinity – if these doors were open the spectators would see another room, and another, and so on. The arrangement of the doors in the back wall of the set, and the perspective vistas they provided, suggested the *scaenae frons* of the Teatro Olimpico with its architectural illusions of vistas and alleyways.

A 1970 production of the same play, designed by Jürgen Rose in Hamburg, also played with neo-classical perspective, but in a more blatant and unrelenting fashion. The eye was ineluctably drawn to a single vanishing point through a door in a stark unrelenting box set. However, the neo-classicism was softened by the romanticism of flimsy gauze curtains and the warm tones of the walls.

In 1984, American designer John Conklin created a *Three Sisters* for the Hartford Stage Company. The basic idea remained the same – an upstage space visible beyond the main playing area. But Conklin opted for a colder formality. The upstage openings could be understood as pillars, doors, or windows; the floor of the thrust stage had a polished surface, thus abjuring the warm textures associated with Chekhov; beyond the openings was cold, unknown space – a void that could be anything.

The elements of formality, texture, isolated iconographic pieces, and the implication of a space beyond were epitomized, however, in a 1983 Cologne production of *The Cherry Orchard* designed by Rolf Glittenberg. This was almost a parody of a box set: towering walls seemingly inspired by Gordon Craig, though textured through the use of wood, dwarfed the performers and the few scenic elements which resembled the vestiges of some earlier Chekhovian set. But, while suggesting a type of prison, the space was not impenetrable. The rear wall could split open, admitting bright light into this confined, barren world, and suggesting a paradisical world beyond.

This latter idea was echoed to some extent in Mark Thompson's design for Moshinsky's *Ivanov* production, succinctly described by Nicholas de Jongh:

a bare and almost windowless cell, like some large prison space. The high walls seem to be built of green-white planks, the room, empty save for a park bench and workmen's dustsheets, is lit from the similarly constructed ceiling, with huge high doors that swing mysteriously open to the sides and rear.

The only relief from this stifling uniformity is a square hole, a glass-less

window cut high in the back wall, through which can be seen a passing
vista of blue and white clouds, and where Ivanov's watchful wife appears.
This back wall does slide back to reveal a fledgling silver birch against a
white backcloth or a posted tableau of drunken party guests ... The setting
is constant.[12]

This setting conveys graphically – some might say overly so –
the typical Chekhovian dilemma of a character trapped or imprisoned
in a life, or philosophy that is represented by the concrete elements
of a house. The freshness or freedom of the outside world is tantalizingly
visible yet inaccessible. Chekhov creates an interior by describing
the exterior; these settings, however, create a formidable barrier
between the two worlds.

On the other hand, the alternative approach – the wall-less set
in which interiors and exteriors blend – owes something to Svoboda,
certainly something to the heritage of the Symbolists, and something
to the environmental theatre movement of the late 1960s. The latter
influence was most evident in a 1974 production of *The Seagull* at
New York's Public Theatre directed by André Gregory in which
the set consisted of furniture and shrubs, but no walls, set in a bifurcated
arena space. The audience sat around the outdoor setting for the
first two acts, then moved to the other side of the stage for the indoor
scenes of the last two acts. Though the 'environmental' approach
never gained much favour, the onstage environment that blends
interiors and exteriors is the most dominant in British productions
that veer at all from the 'traditional'. In this it probably expresses
the influence of the Chichester productions and the Olivier – Svoboda
collaboration. The blended scenes also are the dominant approach
to Chekhovian production in the Soviet Union, especially in the
designs of Valery Levental, Sergey Barkhin, David Borovsky,
Mart Kitayev, Daniil Lider, and Eduard Kochergin.

But the most aggressive proponent of this approach in recent times
has been the Romanian-born director Andrei Serban, who has worked
since the early 1970s in the United States. In his 1977 *Cherry Orchard*
at Lincoln Center, designed by Santo Loquasto, symbolic elements
were isolated against a luminous background of barren trees, and
the visual images were echoed by symbolic actions such as a plough
dragged across a field by peasants. The ballroom was depicted as
a structure that could be viewed as either a giant gazebo, or as a
cage. The white-on-white colour scheme suggested a formality and
isolation or barrenness. Despite the decidedly negative response this

15   Model for *The Seagull* by Valery Levental, MKhAT 1980

16   Model for *Ivanov* by David Borovsky, MKhAT 1976

production received from the conservative New York critics, it spawned a host of imitations.

Serban did a *Seagull* in Japan in 1980, designed by Kaoru Kanamori, that took a more romantic turn but none the less carried on the motif of a continuous exterior and interior. The inside was suggested by a repetitive row of window-frames that, while reinforcing Svoboda's remark about the importance of windows in Chekhov, functioned almost as an abstract motif. A wood-planked stage floor unified the entire stage space.

Any hint of coldness gave way totally to the warm wood textures of Serban's 1983 *Uncle Vanya*, also designed by Loquasto. But just as the symmetrical row of windows of the Japan *Seagull* worked in opposition to the romanticism of the wood and trees, the romanticism of this *Vanya* was offset by the geometric pattern of the groundplan. The setting here consisted of platforms and steps with a few pieces of furniture. The idea for the set was generated by a reference in the play to the empty house being like a maze. As described by Loquasto, the space was 'seemingly simple but long, creating an unnatural spatial relationship among people. The characters talk to each other in a normal way, but they may be 30 feet apart.' Rooms and spatial divisions were defined by differing levels rather than actual walls. The effect was 'the sweep of a Beckett landscape, but one where you also had warm wood and familiar Chekhov textures ... But by stretching the space, it took on the ascetic serenity of an Oriental walkway as well.'[13]

Two final productions from the mid-1980s encapsulate tendencies in modern Chekhovian design. One is Peter Brook's *The Cherry Orchard* done at the Majestic Theatre in Brooklyn, New York with an international cast in 1987, the other is by performance artist Stuart Sherman who, in a 1985 piece simply entitled *Chekhov*, reduced or deconstructed the entirety of Chekhov's dramaturgy to a twelve-minute performance of gestures and emblematic set pieces. In Sherman's piece the set consisted of two halves – stage left was a grove of six wooden cut-out trees with fragments of Chekhovian text on them, and stage right consisted of a fragmentary drawing-room tellingly described by almost every critic as 'a typical Chekhovian setting'. Sherman's description reads: 'A realistic Chekhovian drawing-room, with large Persian rug and dining-table (on which can be seen teacups, playing cards, an ashtray containing a half-smoked cigar, and candle sticks) ... an armchair, a samovar, and a cabinet, which holds icons, books,

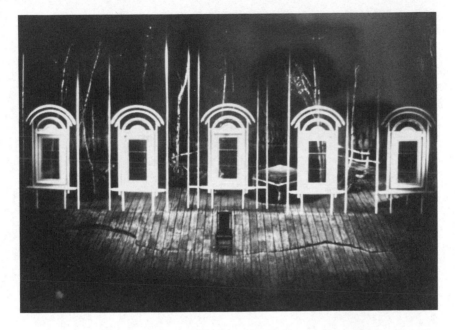

17   Model for *The Seagull* by Kaoru Kanamori, Japan 1980

and family photographs.' As we have seen, Chekhov never described a room in such detail, yet this is a veritable catalogue of the semiotics of Chekhov. The audiences at Sherman's *Chekhov* were instantly familiar and comfortable with the setting; they knew exactly where they were. This was the Chekhovian landscape that inhabits the mind of most late twentieth-century theatre goers. Performers emerged from behind the trees – which fell with a thud to the ground, only to rise again – but never uttered a line other than, at one point, 'chook, chook, chook'. At another point there was a twenty-second recording from a staged version of a play.

But, at least in New York in 1985, this reduction, this essence of Chekhov, seemed appropriate and necessary. The literal Chekhov, the 'real' Chekhov, would have fallen as flat as one of Sherman's cut-out trees. This is not, Sherman points out, intended to replace other productions. 'I'm not attempting to stage his plays', he states. 'I present my reading of the plays – and literally a reading of the texts, going back after you know the endings. There's an automatic telescoping, a personal collage that goes on in time and in memory.'[14]

18 *Chekhov* by performance artist Stuart Sherman at The Kitchen in New York
City, 1986

Brook's production, designed by Chloe Obolensky, in one sense
took the Chichester and Greenwich approaches a step further. Any
production, Chekhov or other, that incorporates or attempts to
incorporate the audience and house into the production runs into the
problem of clashing worlds. The suspension of disbelief can extend
only so far when we are surrounded and confronted with our fellow
patrons and the accoutrements of the theatre. But the Majestic was an
abandoned movie palace and vaudeville house that was only partially
renovated as an annexe for the Brooklyn Academy of Music. Fragments
of plaster remained on exposed brick walls, the once gaudy paint of
this theatre could be seen in faded patches on a decayed ceiling, and
the proscenium arch hinted at its former glory. The theatre became
a perfect metaphor of the Ranevsky estate. In the rather cavernous
space of the stage, made even larger by an extension over the former
orchestra pit, Brook created spaces through the use of a few well-chosen
objects: an armchair, a bookcase, a screen, some Persian rugs, and
a few pillows. The performance extended into the decrepit stage boxes

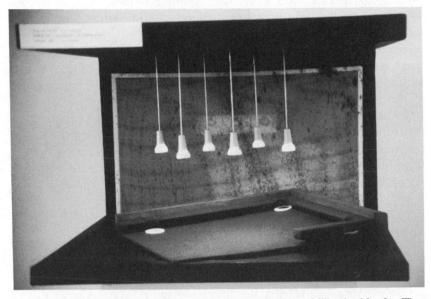

19   Model of Jacques Berwoots' design depicting a large billiard-table, for *The Cherry Orchard*, Belgium 1987

and used the proscenium doors to suggest entrances to other rooms in the house. It ranged from the back wall of the theatre to the very edge of the thrust. Brook and Obolensky had merged the fictional world of the characters with the very theatre itself.

In the last few years there has been a romantic revival of sorts, and something more akin to 'Chekhovian' design has resurfaced, for example in the work of Yannis Kokkos, albeit informed by the deconstructions of the past two decades. And, for all their bizarre reductionism, such sets as Sherman's and Berwoots' are, ultimately, romantic.

It is always the most recent that seems the most old-fashioned – last year's suit, yesterday's music, the art of the fading generation. It is for that reason that it must be rejected by contemporaries. Although it is now more than 100 years since the première of *Ivanov*, the Chekhov world of samovars and drawing rooms, old book cases, and beloved gardens seems still too close. To recreate that world on the stage would be an admission of the playwright's 'old-fashionedness' – it would give the appearance of irrelevance. So, for the time being we invent bare stages, wall-less rooms, projections, reflective surfaces,

mysterious depths, and game-like colour schemes. In this decon-
struction of Chekhov we are not merely illuminating him, rather
we are shaking loose the last vestiges of the nineteenth century,
separating him from Ibsen and Hauptmann, from Belasco and Irving,
from Komisarjevsky and from Stanislavsky. In this way, we can
look at him afresh, with modern eyes; with eyes that have experienced
all the cultural, social, and political changes of the last 90 to 100 years.

In a few more decades, when the late nineteenth century is as
far from us as the early nineteenth century is now, when the socio-
cultural implications of particular details can be understood only
through footnotes, then, perhaps, we can return, unrestricted, un-
encumbered, to a scenography like the one Chekhov knew.

Notes

1 This and all subsequent translations are by Eugene K. Bristow.
2 Steve Grant, 'Uncle Vanya', *Plays and Players*, July 1988, p. 19.
3 Nicholas de Jongh, 'Ivanov', *The Guardian*, 4 April 1989.
4 David Allen, 'Exploring the limitless depths: Mike Alfreds directs
   Chekhov', *New Theatre Quarterly*, 2:8 (November 1986), p. 324.
5 Nicholas Moravcevich, 'Chekhov and Naturalism: from affinity to
   divergence', *Comparative Drama*, Winter 1970–1, pp. 219–40.
6 See Jarka Burian, *The Scenography of Josef Svoboda* (Middletown, CT:
   Wesleyan University Press, 1974), pp. 62–3.
7 See Viktor Berezkin, *Khudozhnik v teatre Chekhova* (The designer in
   Chekhov's theatre) (Moscow: Izobrazitelnoye iskusstvo, 1987), pp. 84–5.
8 *Illustrated London News*, 28 July 1962, p. 154.
9 Felix Barker, 'The Three Sisters', *Plays and Players*, May 1987, pp. 20–1.
10 Burian, *Scenography*, p. 49.
11 Quoted in Burian, *ibid*, pp. 49–50.
12 Nicholas de Jongh, 'Ivanov'.
13 Quoted in Arnold Aronson, *American Set Design* (New York: Theatre
   Communications Group, 1985), pp. 113–14.
14 Quoted in David Spears, 'Tipping the scales', *East Village Eye*, July
   1985.

CHAPTER 18

My search for standards as a translator of Chekhov's plays

Ariadne Nicolaeff

Somewhere between the bias of the ego and the illusion of absolute values, one judges a translation and says it is good or bad. I am going to indulge in some theory by describing my own search for standards as a translator. I propose to divide this complex, obscure, largely subconscious, and automatic process of play translation into three activities: reading the original; doing the English text; and playing one's part in the stage production.

I

In the early sixties I was asked to read the original of *The Seagull* without having to do the English text. The Royal Court Company commissioned Ann Jellicoe to translate the play.[1] She had an idea: she would find the momentum of Chekhov's Russian rhythms in her English dialogue. The theatre was then buzzing with ideas. Nothing was taken for granted, nor was Chekhov. Was he élitist? Did he have to be boring? Did his dialogue have to be slow? What about his pauses? What was Chekhov?

She knew no Russian and she wanted me to read *The Seagull* out loud to her, translate impromptu, and discuss it. She would make her own notes. I would check her rough version before she finalized it.

We tested alternative vocabularies and the tolerance of the English ear for the Russian form of address by name and patronymic; also Russian nicknames and diminutives in all their variety. We concluded that Chekhov's vocabulary on the whole is mainstream modern, in contrast to Ostrovsky's for instance, and should be translated accordingly. If he uses an ordinary or scientific word of Greek or Latin origin, it is a good idea to use the English equivalent in the way he does, if it exists. The Russian form of address should be used because the translated play remains a Russian play; but it should be used sparingly.

It further helps the audience if only one Russian nickname per character is used. The audience is unlikely to grasp the shades of affection and mockery built into Russian nicknames. It starts by being rather stupefied by a foreign play however often the play may be revived.

In the marginal area of English and Russian usage, instant recognition by the audience comes first. For instance, Russians swear by sending people to the devil; the English damn them or send them to hell. Constance Garnett largely avoided the issue, because at the time she was translating it was not done for people of her class in England to swear at all. As translator I use *damn* or *go to hell* because *go to the devil* sounds slightly eccentric. The translator usually faces more complex choices, for instance, with emotive words like imperatives and adjectives.

Obviously our discussions went some way towards the translator's second activity of doing the text. I cannot remember now how much ground we covered and in what detail. I do remember Ann Jellicoe's concern with Chekhov's punctuation. In her search to find the momentum and tempo of his action, she noted his commas, inverted commas, full stops, dots and dashes, exclamation and question marks. She placed the stage-directions, including the pauses, either as part of the dialogue or on a separate line, exactly as they appeared in my Russian 1956 edition published in Moscow. Punctuation and layout are valid clues to the playwright's meaning. The syntax of each language is based on the classical languages, although subordinate clauses may have different values. Two sentences in English may convey more precisely what Russian says in one. The layout of Chekhov's pauses is sacrosanct. Many years later I checked what other translators had done. Constance Garnett's translation (Chatto and Windus, 1923) ignored original punctuation and layout; Elisaveta Fen's (Penguin, 1951 and 1954) and Ronald Hingley's (OUP, 1964) were inconsistent.

Counting the syllables and stresses of Chekhov's Russian dialogue is also helpful as long as the translator does not try to reproduce them. It cannot be done. Russian is a highly inflected language. The endings of nouns, adjectives, and verbs change according to gender, number, and case. As subject, the noun controls the ending of the verb. The verb controls the relationship of subject to object. As object, the noun changes its ending roughly according to who or what belongs to whom, who does what, to whom, how, and where. Adverbial particles, a grammatical trap to translators, may also be used. The verb itself changes its ending according to the duration, frequency or probability of the action in the present, the past or the future.

Inflections or suffixes may lengthen a word by as much as two syllables, shifting the stress. Inflected nouns, adjectives, and verbs often half-rhyme with each other like an echo of the meaning. It is easy to set the words to music.

English nouns and verbs have a few residual inflections, mostly -*s* and apostrophe *s*, and -*ing* and -*ed*. Adverbial particles and the verb *to be* largely perform the other functions of English grammar without altering the stress of grammatically related words or making half-rhymes and echoes. Inevitably, then, the difference between the two languages is rhythm and speed: blank verse or feet of two syllables compared with hexameters or feet of three syllables, if you like.

There was an excellent example of this at the 1987 Anglo-Soviet Chekhov Colloquium in Cambridge and the subsequent television interview of Oleg Yefremov, Principal Director of the Moscow Arts. First, delegates of the Colloquium watched a video of Act 3 of *Uncle Vanya* produced at Chichester in 1962. Laurence Olivier, as Astrov, was showing his ecological map to Yelena. He talked very fast. In English he was able to sustain and build up the passage at speed and then toss it away with a few pauses. When, on television, Yefremov asked a Russian actor to do the same speech in Russian as fast as he could, the effect struck me as very different. I heard an undertow of echoes as though the actor was slowing down inspite of himself; it affected his characterization and his relationship with Yelena. Also relevant to the natural tempo of the two languages are Aleksey Arbuzov's comments on English acting: 'I like English actors in my plays. They act as if they're living their parts. They don't show they're acting. They talk fast. They react quickly. It's slower with us.'[2] In Moscow and, oddly enough, in New York the overall timing of stage dialogue is slower than here but, in spurts, it can be faster at the fast end and slower at the slow end. Russians at an English revival of a Russian classic here may complain that a favourite scene is butchered.

II

In 1966 I translated *Ivanov* for Sir John Gielgud. It was my first English text of a Chekhov play. Gielgud produced a version of his own from mine.[3] He also directed his version and played Ivanov. It was Gielgud's play.

This production was my education in great acting. With different audiences, the play fluctuated night after night. Transferred from London to New York, the play's balance, its light and shade, and tempo changed with the changes of cast and the new audiences. But it stayed in one piece.

Gielgud might have played Chekhov's Ivanov at an earlier stage of his career, when in one of his Hamlets he used Shakespeare's words like a knife to cut through the traps in which Claudius enmeshed him. Now his greatness as an actor lies in his complete control of his audience as he weaves subtle gradations with the greatest of clarity. This control was threatened by *Ivanov*. Its mercurial transitions between tragedy and comedy can turn into melodrama and farce. Both would work. In fact some of Gielgud's casting suggested a grotesque and farcical interpretation of the social scene. But as Ivanov he avoided direct conflict with it by his manner. He gave a meticulous study of discontinuous withdrawal, keeping the pain, but not the anger or the laughter. He tamed his own part. He gave a rational gloss mostly to his own dialogue, paraphrased it, and cut some of Ivanov's obsessive repetitions.

The end of Act 2 is one of those points of stress on which the main action turns. It reveals the relationship between Sasha and Ivanov. The translator has to be especially careful. According to Chekhov, Sasha tells him that as a child she loved him and now urges him to take her away, anywhere, 'even into the grave, only for God's sake hurry, or I'll suffocate'. He roars with happy laughter and says: 'What is this? You mean, to begin life from the start? Yes, Shurochka? My happiness! (*He draws her towards him.*) My young, green girl ...' And before they kiss, Anna overhears him say: 'You mean, live? Yes? To work again?' After the kiss, they turn and see Anna and he says, horrified: 'Sarah!'[4]

In Gielgud's Act 2, Sasha says at the same point: 'die with you if you like ... but let me come to you, soon, before it's too late ... before I'm stifled by my existence here ...' He does not laugh but says: 'You really mean it, Sasha! You believe that I could begin once more? Start a new kind of life – with you to make me young – to make me happy'. And Anna overhears him say: 'Oh! My dear child! Do you really think you could help me to find a way to live again? To get to work again – with you beside me?' He kisses Sasha as if she were a child. The sound of Anna falling down in a faint makes them both turn. The scene ends in the same way with: 'Sarah!'[5]

Here I have to confess that Chekhov's 'My happiness!', an abstract noun which in Russian works in this context, is doubtful in English. The two following abstract nouns, literally 'My youth, my freshness', are impossible in English. On revising my translation, I used Toby Robertson's solution in his two productions of the play (1972, 1978): 'My young, green girl', which could not be bettered. Robertson's version of the play was based on mine. Derek Jacobi took the lead in both productions and he was a lyrical Ivanov with a full emotional range. The 1972 production was called *A Crisis of Conscience*.

III

Basically, the translator is providing actors with new words to act the playwright's meaning, so elusive on the printed page. The translator should either know the actors or imagine an ideal cast. Immersion in the theatre is essential before the translator can give real actors dialogue they can speak, and can find out what they contribute by their stage performance.

For instance, *The Seagull* in Tony Richardson's production of Ann Jellicoe's text fell apart on the stage. But it had a startling and revealing scene in Act 3 between Peggy Ashcroft and Peter Finch. As Arkadina, she communicated with his Trigorin by acting a set scene of theatrical clichés. She did it almost dismissively because they both knew they were clichés. Ann Jellicoe and I had discussed them at some length and they were in her translation. Hearing them on the stage, framed by Nina's two performances of Konstantin's monologue, I realised vividly the power and endurance of the old guard. Konstantin's conflict was indeed deadly, fought as it was on two levels: in the creative life of the imagination and in flesh and blood.

Anton Chekhov's plays in English inevitably underwent change and unconscious censorship. English actors expressed their own national character, morality, and temperament in his dialogue. But it is extraordinarily satisfying when the stage performance of one of his translated plays gives the audience a flash of new insight. That is theatre: live actors in control on the stage conveying unexpected facets of the author's meaning. As wandering players, they crossed national barriers in the past. Konstantin Stanislavsky influenced acting in London and New York, besides creating a theatrical revolution in Moscow. Public funds largely created the theatrical revolution in England and ended the tyranny of the West End in the provinces.

At the Oxford Playhouse, Chekhov was found to be a popular dramatist. Two of the three productions of his plays went on tour with splendid casts. My credo as a play-translator matured as I worked there with Frank Hauser on *Three Sisters*, *Uncle Vanya*, and *The Cherry Orchard*. I shall put it as simply as possible. I want my translation to be a valid theatre experience for an English-speaking audience of the Russian play in English. To that end I need to be part of the first production. I need the director to discuss my translation with me in great detail, suggesting alterations before rehearsals start; but my decision is final. I like being asked about casting, but there the director's decision is final. I need to attend the actors' read-throughs before they start detailed rehearsals; also later run-throughs and any other rehearsals when there are problems with the dialogue. When members of the cast keep asking me: 'But what does it say in the original?', wait for me to look it up, then tell me their own version, I know that the production will not cheat the playwright.

This procedure has worked at the Chichester Festival Theatre, Bristol Old Vic, and Watford, with Toby Robertson, Richard Cottrell, and Leon Rubin. Other procedures are frivolous and destructive. But even when everyone is doing their best, you wake up after the first night, perhaps years later, saying: 'It was a mistake. We were on the wrong track. Why didn't I think of that?'

My search for standards is open-ended. I should like to leave it where it started in 1945.

To boost civilian morale in London towards the end of the Second World War during the doodle-bugs, Laurence Olivier and Ralph Richardson were released from the armed forces and, with John Burrell, they formed the Old Vic Company at the New Theatre, now the Albery. As well as plays by Shakespeare, their repertoire included *Peer Gynt*, *Cyrano de Bergerac*, and *Uncle Vanya*. The latter was directed by John Burrell in Constance Garnett's translation. In a packed theatre I lived through a vividly paced, complex, spellbinding, total experience. Like all experience in the theatre it happened somewhere in the space between the actors and the audience and it took about two-and-a-half hours. I still believe it was authentic Chekhov.

The play made complete sense in wartime London. His characters were extravagantly alive through our awareness of death shared with Chekhov. They were trapped but lived dangerously because the central conflict took them over the edge.

There is no film record of this production and I should like to mention a few interpretations and moments which I remember. All the actors were the right age. Serebryakov as played by Harcourt Williams was used to authority and, inspite of Astrov's diagnosis, probably had angina and rheumatism as well as gout. Margaret Leighton as Yelena looked stunned, but surprised me every time she said anything because what she said made complete sense. She was very still, beautiful, not coy, not a flirt in any way. Olivier as Astrov also had an unpredictable quality, sensuous but controlled, with a touch of the Wood Demon. Richardson was a witty, crisp, bumbling, and eccentric Uncle Vanya.

In Act 3 Richardson held the longest, most dramatic pause I have experienced in the theatre. The Act started like the day after the night before: everyone tired and irritable, wandering in and out of the drawing-room where a blind is pulled up to let in the sunshine and chairs arranged for the formal family meeting. Richardson, returning with his bunch of flowers for Yelena, came in quickly, very light on his feet. On seeing Astrov kissing her, he stopped dead and did absolutely nothing. Even when he spoke, he was not part of what was going on. He held that pause till he began interrupting the Professor. His inner life had crashed down in the pause. His reason for existence came crashing down again when, far too reasonably, he began commenting on the Professor's plan.

The scene in Act 4 with Olivier in Vanya's office, under the map of Africa on the wall, had a finality beyond friendship, as though they were saying something else to each other.

Notes

1 Published as *The Seagull*, trans. Ann Jellicoe, ed. Henry Popkin (New York: Avon, 1975).
2 In conversation.
3 Anton Chekhov, *Ivanov: A Drama in Four Acts*, English Version by John Gielgud based on the translation by Ariadne Nicolaeff (London: Heinemann, 1966).
4 My own translation.
5 Gielgud's version, *Ivanov: A Drama in Four Acts*, pp. 42–4.

CHAPTER 19

Chekhov into English: the case of 'The Seagull'

Richard Peace

Looking back at the achievements of the Moscow Art Theatre from the viewpoint of the 1930s Nemirovich-Danchenko made a significant admission:

There is no denying that our theatre was at fault in failing to grasp the full meaning of Chekhov, his sensitive style and his amazingly delicate outlines ... Chekhov refined his realism to the point where it became symbolic, and it was a long time before we succeeded in conveying the subtle texture of his work; maybe the theatre simply handled him too roughly.[1]

If the theatre of Chekhov's compatriots and contemporaries handled his symbolic realism 'too roughly', what then must be said of his foreign translators working within the constraints of an alien tongue and different cultural concepts? How do they deal with his 'sensitive style and his amazingly delicate outlines'?

Before the staging of any play the primary task is that of literary criticism. Those producing a play must first come to understand what the text actually contains, as well as what it more subtly suggests, and on this basis evolve a coherent overall interpretation. This primary task – that of the literary critic – is, if anything, even more fundamental to the job of the translator. If he is to communicate the reality of the text to the actors and their director, he must first have clearly understood all the devices and subtle workings of the play itself: how the various parts relate to the whole; the function of recurring images; the repetition of key words; and the little ironies set up by idiosyncrasies of emphasis and usage.

Unfortunately there are translators for whom the problems of the text are not essentially literary, but more superficially linguistic. To be fair to them, they are often harassed by publishers' deadlines and editors ignorant of the original, whose one concern is that a translation read like good English. There are also translators of

The Seagull whose critical standpoint is not that of Nemirovich- Danchenko's 'realism refined to the point where it becomes symbolic', but who adhere to the earlier view that Chekhov is merely presenting us with a 'slice of life'. For them the chief goal is to render the author's colloquial Russian into good colloquial English. The result is the smoothing-out of awkward contours, the muting of echo and reverberation, the stylistic avoidance of repetitions on which Chekhov himself insists. In short, in their efforts to preserve the bath-water of 'style', the baby has been left to drown.

If literary criticism provides the aesthetic and conceptual framework, around which the translator must build his replica, there is a critical function which is anterior even to this: the translator must decide what the canonical version of his text really is. This problem is addressed by Michael Frayn in the introduction to his recent translation of *The Seagull*, when he points out that Chekhov was obliged to remove certain passages from his original version of the play because the censor regarded them as showing Konstantin's awareness of his mother's liaison with Trigorin too explicitly.[2] On the authority of the Soviet Academy of Sciences edition of the complete works of Chekhov, Frayn has restored these excised passages. Nevertheless this initial muting of the oedipal relationship at the hands of censors has been further compounded by some translators, as we shall see, through a more bowdlerized choice of quotation from *Hamlet*.

Despite the protestations of the 'slice of life' school of criticism, it is obvious that Chekhov himself is calling attention to the presence of symbolism in his play by his very choice of title. Chekhov's repetition of the symbol, indeed his repetition of the very word *chayka*, 'seagull', seems to cause some of his translators embarrassment. Thus Hingley changes it on one occasion to 'that white bird'.[3] Others, far from blurring this image, wish to make it more specific. With spurious linguistic subtlety Magarshack seeks to persuade us that the only possible translation of Nina's famous statement in Act 4 is 'I am *the* seagull'. He writes: 'Chekhov made her meaning clear in the Russian text by putting a dash after "I am" and before "seagull": *Ya – chayka*. If he had wished Nina to say "I am a seagull" he would not have put the dash.'[4] This appears to be a rule of Russian grammar invented by Mr Magarshack himself. A similar distinction is made in Frayn's introduction to the play. But the 'logic' of the dashes then leads him to make Nina also say: 'I am *the* actress', which seems to pitch her artistic self-confidence at a level that even her most ardent supporters would find hard to defend.[5]

The seagull is not the only symbol in the play. There is also the lake, whose reflecting surface seems to hint at the mirror-like nature of art itself. The play is obviously about artists, but it is even more about the rapacious, destructive, and self-destructive nature of art and artistic activity. The two rivals Konstantin and Trigorin hunt on the lake for their trophies; the one with a gun (and he shoots the seagull), the other with a fishing rod. Thus, when in Act 1 Konstantin is attacking the artistic credo of his mother's generation, it seems important to preserve the fishing image of Chekhov's text: Konstantin accuses them of 'fishing out a moral [*vyudit moral*] from vulgar scenes and phrases'. Koteliansky alone, of the versions I have examined, attempts this: 'They try to fish a moral'.[6] He also seeks to preserve the fish image used by Sorin in Act 2, expressing his wish to escape from 'the gudgeon-like life' (*peskarinaya zhizn*) by the lake side. This he translates as 'minnow-like existence', but Frayn sticks to the original image and sees in it a reference to 'Saltykov-Shchedrin's chilling fable *The Wise Gudgeon*'.[7]

It is significant that in Act 1 Konstantin needs to begin his play when the moon has risen and is reflected in the lake – the only scenery which his play needs. The moon is symbolic of his art which is one of dreams. But in Act 2 the lake reflects, not the moon, but the sun, and in this act it is Trigorin who is dominant, and already cast as the usurper in Konstantin's artistic and emotional life. Konstantin admits defeat in his bitter words to Nina which identify Trigorin as the 'sun' (though not clearly so in all translations): 'This sun [*eto solntse*] has not yet approached you and you are already smiling, your glance has melted in his rays.' Constance Garnett, Elisaveta Fen, and Michael Frayn all flatten the effect by translating *eto solntse* merely as '*the* sun'.[8] Ronald Hingley ties it more precisely to Trigorin, but loses the sharp impact of the image itself by translating it as 'the great luminary'. Koteliansky is again more accurate with 'that sun'.[9] By contrast Frayn appears to reinforce the image by his repeated references in the same act to Trigorin's 'sunlit life', where Chekhov merely has *svetly* ('bright', 'radiant') and again in Act 3 he reinforces Chekhov's imagery by adding the word 'sunny' to Trigorin's attempt to remind Nina of that earlier scene: 'I shall remember you. I shall remember you as you were on that bright and sunny day ...'[10]

In Act 2, presumably under the influence of this sun, Konstantin feels that the lake itself has dried up or that its water has run into the ground (*budto eto ozero vdrug vysokhlo ili uteklo v zemlyu*)[11] and the images of loss, underground, and dryness are taken up in his confession of failure to Nina in Act 4: 'I am lonely, not warmed by anyone's affection. I am cold as though in a cave [*podzemelye*, literally 'underground'] and whatever I write is dry, stale and gloomy'. The direct connotation of 'under ground' tends, perhaps inevitably, to be lost in the various renderings of *podzemelye*. Thus Garnett and Fen have 'a cellar', Hingley 'a vault', Koteliansky 'a cave', and Frayn 'a grave'.[12]

Some translations even blur the sharpness of the artistic challenge proclaimed by Konstantin in his 'new forms'. His rudimentary but symbolic stage in Act I must be seen in contrast to the conventional theatre which he has just decried. Therefore his assertion '*Vot tebe i teatr*' is rendered more accurately by Fen's 'There's a theatre for you', or even by Frayn's 'Now how about this for a theatre', than by the more neutral 'Here is our theatre' (Garnett); 'Here's the theatre' (Koteliansky); or 'Well, this is our theatre' (Hingley).[13] Hingley even tones down the impact of Konstantin's 'new forms' by avoiding repetition of this programmatic phrase, giving instead the gloss 'new kind of theatre' in Act I, and 'new techniques' in Act 4.[14]

Similar terminological inconsistency marks out Hingley's treatment of Chekhov's references to the decadent movement. In Act I '*eto chto-to dekadentskoye*' is rendered as 'this is something terribly modern', and in the same act '*etot dekadentsky bred*' becomes 'experimental rubbish', and when he does translate the term in Act 3 he qualifies it with the epithet 'miserable', so that *dekadent* becomes 'miserable decadent'.[15] Yet Chekhov himself probably had something more specific in mind in characterizing Konstantin's search for new forms as 'decadent' – it was a term he associated with the theatre of Maeterlinck.[16]

There is a certain irony in the fact that Konstantin, who condemns the banality of his mother's concept of theatre, is in turn obliquely accused of philistinism himself; for the designation *meshchanin*, which he has in his passport, carries the same social and aesthetic ambiguity as the word 'bourgeois': he is a 'townsman/philistine' of Kiev – '*kiyevsky meshchanin*'. Garnett renders the phrase, without consistency, as 'artisan of Kiev' (Act I), and 'Kiev shopman' (Act 3), whereas Koteliansky's rendering sounds almost comically culinary to a later ear – 'Kiev burgher'. Fen, more descriptively, has 'member of the lower middle class from Kiev' and 'upstart from Kiev', whereas both Hingley and Frayn decide to give Konstantin a resonance of authorial self-identification by using the term 'shopkeeper'.[17] Admittedly *meshchanin* is a difficult word to translate adequately.

The theme of the destructive nature of art is centred on Trigorin. It is he who turns Konstantin's symbol of self-destruction, the seagull, into a symbol associated with his own destruction of Nina. She becomes the victim of his continual urge to turn the lives of all around him into material for his art. The telling phrase he uses for Nina in identifying her with the seagull is *'syuzhet dlya nebolshogo rasskaza'* and the phrase is also repeated by Nina herself in Act 4.[18] The way this is usually rendered into English as 'the subject [or plot] for a short story' does not bring out the full irony of its meaning. It is not a genre designation, which the English 'short story' suggests, but a 'not very big tale' (*'nebolshoy rasskaz'*), and the ironical nature of such brief fiction is brought out in Act 4 in Konstantin's comment that what has happened to Nina is 'a long story'.[19]

A dominant motif in the play is the recurrent Hamlet theme, and here we come up against a problem which is unique to English translations. There are two direct quotations from *Hamlet* which form an interchange between Konstantin and his mother, and shed light on their relationship. Yet in the original text these quotations are themselves translations, and we are thus faced with all the problems of translation in reverse. The straightforward answer might seem merely to give the original Shakespearian passages, but there is room for doubt when we compare them with the Polevoy versions used by Chekhov.

Thus Arkadina's quotation:

> O Hamlet, speak no more:
> Thou turns't mine eyes into my very soul;
> And there I see such black and grained spots
> As will not leave their tinct

has been rendered into Russian by the usual diluting and levelling hand of the translator as: 'My son, you have turned my eyes inwards to my soul, and I have seen it in such bloody and mortal ulcers – there is no salvation'. The original is obviously to be preferred here, and all translators have adopted it. The second quotation from *Hamlet* is, however, more problematical.

Konstantin answers his mother using Hamlet's speech replying to the first quotation. The original is:

Nay, but to live
In the rank sweat of an enseamed bed,
Stew'd in corruption, honeying and making love
Over the nasty sty!

For this Polevoy has: 'And why did you submit to sin, seek love in an abyss of crime?'[20] The dilution and levelling are here quite glaring, so much so that the actual Shakespearian text seems too strong. Indeed in Constance Garnett's translation a completely different *Hamlet* quotation from earlier in the same scene has been substituted:

And let me wring thy heart; for so I shall,
If it be made of penetrable stuff.[21]

The same passage is used in Elisaveta Fen's translation. The effect of this substitution is to direct attention towards Konstantin's intentions for his play, and away from the more sensitive area of his emotional attitude to his mother. The oedipal overtones of the original Shake-speare, still present even in Polevoy's pale rendering, have gone completely, and thus Garnett and Fen have further executed the wishes of Chekhov's nineteenth-century censors to tone down Konstantin's knowledge of his mother's sexual guilt.

Yet, as with Hamlet, Konstantin's tortured relations with his mother are a potent factor in his tragedy. His very last words are of concern for her; he fears that Nina's visit may distress his *mama* (a word far nearer to 'mummy' than the more neutral *mat'* – 'mother'): '*Nekhorosho, yesli kto-nibud vstretit yeye v sadu i potom skazhet mame. Eto mozhet ogorchit mamu.*'[22] Yet here Hingley weakens the impact, not only by translating *mama* as 'mother' (Fen for example has 'mamma'), but also by refusing to repeat the actual word: 'It might upset *mama*' becomes merely 'It might upset her', and so the very last word, *mama*, uttered by Konstantin before his suicide, is lost and the impact muted.[23]

The hallmark of Chekhov's minor characters is eccentricity, and the translator needs to pay particular attention to the way in which Medvedenko, Shamrayev, Sorin, and Dorn actually express them-selves. At the very beginning of the play Medvedenko complains to Masha of her 'indifference' towards him. The word he actually uses is *indifferentizm*, not the more usual *ravnodushiye*.[24] The introduc-tion of this pompous word is an early indicator of character on the part of Chekhov – it is the comically pedantic expression of the dull schoolmaster. Although the word stands out, scarcely any of

Chekhov's translators have picked it up, and it has been smoothed out into neutral, acceptable English.

Shamrayev's speeches are full of conscious or unconscious irony directed at the pretensions of others. His loudly proclaimed veneration for Arkadina frequently masks an attempt to deflate her. Thus Shamrayev's first words in the play, if the original word order is preserved, form a crescendo of bathos at her expense: 'In 1873 [*i.e.* some twenty years ago] in Poltava [a provincial town] at the fair [not even a proper theatre] she played marvellously'. For reasons of good 'style' most English translators alter this word order, but Michael Frayn's translation has the sense to preserve it.[25]

Shamrayev's words in Act 3 reveal a similar comic ambiguity: 'I have the honour, with profound sorrow, to announce that the horses are ready.' Throughout the play Shamrayev has refused horses to everyone (including Arkadina) and now his 'sorrow' seems to refer as much to the fact that he has had to part with them, as to his grief at Arkadina's departure. Unfortunately Frayn flattens out the first part of the comic formula with his blunt 'I have to inform you', which deprives Shamrayev of his 'honour', whereas Hingley misses out on the second part, when, because of his refusal to repeat key words, he substitutes 'carriage' for 'horses'.[26]

One of the most controversial examples of the smoothing out of language occurs in the case of Dorn, who is perhaps not quite the straightforward character that English translators make him appear. Rather than being the doctor figure, suggestive of Chekhov himself, he has perhaps more in common with such incompetent doctors as Chebutykin in *The Three Sisters* or Ragin in *Ward No. 6*. His refusal throughout the play to give Sorin any medical attention at all is perverse to the point where it verges on the cruel. It is medical attention ('*lechitsya*') which is at issue, not the refusal to 'dose' him, as Hingley suggests: 'What, dose yourself at the age of sixty!'.[27] Indeed his only prescription appears to be Valerian drops – the nineteenth-century equivalent of Valium. In Act 3, when Konstantin needs to have his bandages changed after his first abortive attempt at suicide, we are told that the doctor had promised to come by ten, but that it is now almost midday. In fact Dorn makes no appearance in this act at all. His treatment of Polina, his throwing away of Masha's snuff box, and the constant bursting out into snatches of song, all suggest a quirkiness of character, which needs to be brought out in the translations.

It is against this background that we should probably judge his lone

voice of approval for the talent of both Konstantin and Nina. When
in Act 4 Konstantin gives Dorn his devastating account of Nina's
glaring lack of talent as an actress, Dorn seizes on the one or two
moments which Konstantin says she manages to bring off, and
comments: 'So, all the same, she has talent.'[28]

The figure of Nina, particularly as she appears in Act 4, presents
us with a problem of interpretation: is she completely deranged
and broken, or will she win through? Following Komissarzhevskaya's
original interpretation of the role, most actresses wish to see her
as an ultimate victor. Frayn in his introduction complains about
her final appearance being played as a traditional mad scene, and
it must be said that his own translation tends to soften the image
of madness and failure. Thus Konstantin's assessment: '*lichnaya
zhizn Niny ne udalas sovershenno*' is softened to 'Nina's private life
has not been a total success', instead of the more accurate Fen translation: 'Nina's personal life turned out a complete failure.'[29] When
Nina, with the stage direction '*rasteryanno*' (*i.e.* 'confusedly', 'per-
plexedly'), addresses Konstantin as though he were a third person,
and with a repeated question: '*Nina* (confused): Why is he speaking
like this? Why is he speaking like this?' Frayn makes it sound far
more normal by substituting the stage direction 'dismayed', turning
the question in the third person to one in the second, and eliminating
the obsessive repeat: '*Nina* (dismayed): Why are you talking like
this?'.[30]

Frayn is also embarrassed by the vestiges of traditional soliloquy
remaining in *The Seagull*. He confesses: 'I was tempted to reorganise
the scenes a little to avoid the need for soliloquy.'[31] That he has
resisted this is to his credit. For, although the translator of Chekhov
should begin his task as a literary critic, he should not end it as
his editor. His sole aim must be to reproduce as accurately as possible
what is in the text. There will, of course, have to be concessions to
the canons of English usage, but a translator's own view of style
should not lead him into unnecessary changing of recurrent words,
to omissions and additions, let alone tampering with the structure
of the play itself. The fate of Chekhov's text from then on will be
at the interpretative mercy of a director and the sympathetic skills
of the actors.

Notes

1 Quoted in E. Braun, *The Director and the Stage; from Naturalism to Grotowski* (London: Methuen, 1982), p.73.
2 Anton Chekhov, *The Seagull, A Comedy in Four Acts*, translated and introduced by Michael Frayn (London: Allen and Unwin, 1986), pp. xxii–xxiii.
3 Anton Chekhov, *Five Plays*, translated and with an introduction by Ronald Hingley (Oxford: OUP, 1980), p.93.
4 D. Magarshack, *The Real Chekhov: An Introduction to Chekhov's Last Plays* (London: Allen and Unwin, 1972), p.60.
5 Frayn, *The Seagull*, p.63.
6 Cf. A.P. Chekhov, *Polnoye sobraniye sochineny i pisem v tridtsati tomakh (Complete collected works and letters in 30 vols.)*, XIII (*Sochineniya*) (*Works*) (Moscow: Nauka, 1978), p.8 (hereafter referred to as *PSS*) and Anton Tchekhov, *Plays and Stories*, translated by S.S. Koteliansky (London: Dent, 1937), p.56.
7 Koteliansky, *ibid.*, p.79; Frayn, *The Seagull*, p.37.
8 Anton Tchehov, *The Cherry Orchard and Other Plays*, translated by Constance Garnett (London: Chatto and Windus, 1923), p.184; Anton Chekhov, *Plays*, translated and with an introduction by Elisaveta Fen (Harmondsworth: Penguin Books, 1954), p.146; Frayn, *The Seagull*, p.28.
9 Hingley, *Five Plays*, p.88; Koteliansky, *Plays and Stories*, p.73.
10 Frayn, *ibid.*, pp.29, 36.
11 *PSS*, p.27.
12 Garnett, *The Cherry Orchard and Other Plays*, p.226; Fen, *Plays*, p.180; Hingley, *Five Plays*, p.113; Koteliansky, *Plays and Stories*, p.98; Frayn, *The Seagull*, p.63.
13 Fen, *ibid.*, p.121; Frayn, *ibid.*, p.3; Garnett, *ibid.*, p.156; Koteliansky, *ibid.*, p.55; Hingley, *ibid.*, p.68.
14 Hingley, *ibid.*, pp.70, 111.
15 HIngley, *ibid.*, pp.75, 76, 97.
16 See: R.A. Peace, 'Chekhov's "Modern Classicism"', *The Slavonic and East European Review*, 65:1 1987 January, pp.15–25.
17 Garnett, *The Cherry Orchard*, pp.159, 201; Koteliansky, *Plays and Stories*, pp.57, 82; Fen, *Plays*, pp.124, 159; Hingley, *Five Plays*, pp.70, 97; Frayn, *The Seagull*, pp.6, 41.
18 *PSS*, pp.31, 58.
19 *PSS*, p.49 ('*eto, doktor, dlinnaya istoriya*').
20 *Hamlet*, Act III, sc. iii; *PSS*, p.12.
21 Garnett, *The Cherry Orchard*, p.164; Fen, *Plays*, p.128. I am indebted to Patrick Miles for pointing to the original source of this substitution, as given by George Calderon in a footnote to his translation of the play: 'In the Russian Tréplef answers with a garbled version of Shakespeare's "nasty sty" lines. If we quoted them we should have to be inconveniently exact. For this excellent substitute the translator is indebted to the

ingenuity of Mr Hanray, who played Sorin in Glasgow' (*Two Plays by Tchekhof: 'The Seagull'; 'The Cherry Orchard'*, translated with an introduction and notes by George Calderon (London: Grant Richards, 1912), p. 34).

22 *PSS, p.* 59.

23 Fen, *Plays*, p. 182; Hingley, p. 115.

24 *PSS*, p. 6. George Calderon substitutes '*non possumus*' with the following justification: 'The village pedant emerges. In the Russian Medvedenko says "*indifferentism*" instead of "*ravnodúsczie*" indifference. The words are so much alike in English that a literal rendering would spoil the point' (Calderon, *Two Plays*, p. 26).

25 *PSS*, p. 12; Frayn, *The Seagull*, p. 10.

26 *PSS*, p. 43; Frayn, *ibid.*, p. 45; Hingley, *Five Plays*, p. 100.

27 *PSS*, p. 23; Hingley, *ibid.*, p. 84 (Cf. Frayn, *The Seagull*, p. 23).

28 *PSS*, p. 50.

29 *PSS*, p. 50; Frayn, *ibid.*, p. 54; Fen, *Plays*, p. 171.

30 *PSS*, p. 57; Frayn, *The Seagull*, p. 63. Hingley also manages to turn Nina's very Russian 'ability to endure' – '*umenye terpet*' – into the English virtue of 'stamina' (Hingley, *Five Plays*, p. 114).

31 Frayn, p. xviii. By contrast Calderon, in his introduction, gave a spirited defence of Chekhov's use of soliloquy: 'For his plays, rightly understood, are more than half soliloquy; the characters seem to converse, but in reality sit side by side and think aloud' (Calderon, *Two Plays*, p. 20).

CHAPTER 20

English translations of Chekhov's plays: a Russian view

Valentina Ryapolova

Translation is a form of interpretation; in the wider sense, interpretation of one national culture by another culture. Its problems are many and complex.[1] Obviously the translator has to convey the original faithfully ('versions' and 'adaptations' are a special case which will be examined later), but the question immediately arises as to how he is going to do this. More often than not, a literal reproduction of the original in another language has the reverse effect: the translation becomes incomprehensible and far *removed* from its original. This is one explanation for the 'outlandish' impression created by early productions of Chekhov on the British stage.[2] Thus in Constance Garnett's translations, which are on the whole too literal, Russian set phrases such as *'tsarstvo yey nebesnoye'* are rendered not by the corresponding English idiom ('God rest her soul') but word for word ('The Kingdom of Heaven be hers'). In Trevor Griffiths' version, too, they are usually translated literally. For instance, Varya's words in Act I of *The Cherry Orchard 'gospod' s vami, mamochka'* are a reaction to Ranevskaya 'seeing' her mother walking in the orchard, and mean 'what are you saying, Mother', 'come to your senses', 'it's impossible', 'you're seeing things', and so forth. Griffiths, however, has Varya get down on her knees, kiss the crucifix she is wearing (!), and pronounce 'God is with you, Mama'.[3] British readers and audiences are bound to find people who express themselves in this way 'outlandish'.

On the other hand, if the translator is concerned merely to make the text sound like 'normal English', then the richness, originality, shades of meaning, and stylistic nuances of the source text will be lost, as Richard Peace demonstrates in his article in the present volume.

It seems that, in order adequately to convey the original, at least three factors have to be taken into account: (1) the national specifics of the life and culture of the country in which the work was written; (2) the historical features of the period reflected in it, if as with

Chekhov this period is past; and last but not least, (3) the author's sensibility, since the translator does not 'reproduce' in his own language the life of a country as such, but that life as seen by a particular writer.

Before making a translation it is, of course, necessary to understand the original text well. Stylistically, Constance Garnett's translations are weak. But she makes hardly any errors of straight meaning. This is a considerable merit: after all, even one misunderstood and mistranslated word in a text can seriously distort its sense. Plenty of examples of this could be given, but I shall confine myself to the word '*nedotyopa*' in *The Cherry Orchard*.

Of the alternatives suggested, 'duffer' comes closest to the original in sense. The Russian word means 'someone incapable', 'someone awkward', 'someone clumsy', 'someone dim', 'someone inept', as well as 'someone unlucky', 'someone always failing'. It comes from the dialect verb '*tyopat*' (a variant of '*tyapat*'), meaning 'to chop with an axe or cleaver' (Dal's *Dictionary*, 1880–2). This produces '*dotyapat*', 'to finish hewing or chopping, to complete in some fashion with an axe' (*ibid.*), and '*nedotyap*', 'something not fully chopped, something slashed, something rough-hewn' (*ibid.*). Consequently '*nedotyopa*' (a variant of '*nedotyap*') literally means 'someone not fully completed, someone still rough-hewn'. Chekhov himself used the word in his letter to Lika Mizinova of 13 August 1893, and this is the first written example etymologists have found of it in its figurative sense. Neither there, nor in its present-day usage, is there anything abrasive about '*nedotyopa*', let alone obscene, as there is in some English translations of the word. These translations, therefore, seem to be a case of incomplete understanding leading to manifest distortion of the sense.

There are certain difficulties of translation, however, that are connected not so much with how well the translator understands Chekhov's text, as with the differences between Russian life and British life, and their corresponding vocabularies. I am not referring to such things as 'Titular Counsellor' (grade 9 in the Tsarist Civil Service) or '*altyn*' (a pre-revolutionary 3 kopeck piece), but to words and expressions that have a similar sense in both languages, yet different 'volume'. These present the biggest problem. They appear to be extremely simple words, but judging from the English translations it is not easy to render them precisely into the English language. Examples are the Russian '*roskoshny*', '*chudny*', '*svetlaya lichnost*', '*obshchestvenny chelovek*', '*meshchanin/meshchanka*', and '*blagorodny*'.

'*Roskoshny*', which was a fashionable word of Chekhov's time, is translated as 'glorious', 'marvellous', or 'sumptuous', and '*chudny*' as 'magical', 'wonderful', or 'exquisite'. This is quite right, as both Russian words are very rich in nuances which cannot be conveyed in English with a single word. In each case the translators have made a choice depending on the context, and accentuated one or other of the words' shades of meaning.

The problem with the expressions '*svetlaya lichnost*' and '*obshchestvenny chelovek*' is somewhat different. Kulygin uses them in Act 1 of *Three Sisters* to describe his boss, the headmaster of the local grammar-school.[4] Here Garnett translates the first of the expressions as 'an excellent, noble personality', and Frayn as 'a wonderful person';[5] the adjective '*obshchestvenny*' in the second expression is rendered by both translators as 'sociable'. In *Uncle Vanya* Mariya Vasilyevna seriously calls her son a '*svetlaya lichnost*', but he casts the expression back at her with bitter irony: 'MARIYA VASILYEVNA. *Ty byl chelovekom opredelennykh ubezhdeny, svetloyu lichnostyu* ... VOYNITSKY. *O, da! Ya byl svetloyu lichnostyu, ot kotoroy nikomu ne bylo svetlo* ...'[6] In her fairly free translation of *Uncle Vanya* ('A new version') Pam Gems renders this as: 'MARYA. You used to be a man of such conviction ... principle ... you were a shining example to us all ... full of ideas, inspiration ... VANYA. Oh yes! world influence ... such an inspiring man!'[7] Unlike Garnett and Frayn, Gems has opted for an extended paraphrase here, whereas '*svetlaya lichnost*' is a phrase that sums everything up.

The reason it is so difficult to find succinct English equivalents to these two phrases is that they are not just expressions, but symbols. Behind them lurks a whole era of Russian social thought. In particular they allude to the ideals and ideas of the 1860s, the notion of fighting the dark forces of ignorance and despotism in the name of a bright future (Vanya's mother is still 'looking for the dawn of a new life in her clever books'),[8] of serving society and the people. There is no need for me to discuss here how Chekhov sends up the ideas of the sixties. It is an important theme in his work which has been analysed many times. The problem for the translator is how to convey to the British reader the ideas themselves and Chekhov's ironical attitude to them. Thus 'sociable' and 'wonderful person' are too neutral and flat. What Kulygin and Mariya Vasilyevna say is intended to have a comic effect. '*Obshchestvenny chelovek*' means 'a public-spirited man', but Kulygin is saying it of a narrow-minded, petty school tyrant who makes his teachers' lives a misery even when they are off duty.

Words and expressions, therefore, that look simple but are firmly rooted in Russian rather than any other life, are exceedingly difficult to translate. They include the word '*intelligentsiya*' and its derivatives, which, as we know, have no exact equivalents in English.

Chekhov's heroes, and their manners, exemplify for us Russians what the quality of '*intelligentnost*' is. In a radio interview, talking of *Three Sisters*, Michael Frayn found that Chekhov's characters, and Russians generally, express themselves too bluntly and abrasively for British ears. This is a very interesting observation, as it shows yet again how different a national culture looks from the inside and from out. Indeed, Masha is offhand with her family, her friends, and her old nurse; Irina unceremoniously calls Masha 'Mashka'; and, instead of greeting the newly arrived Vershinin properly, Olga asks him 'Are you from Moscow?' and declares that she doesn't remember him ... None of this accords with the way well-mannered people would talk in Britain. And yet it is the three sisters, not 'suave', 'genteel' Natasha, who are genuinely well-mannered, considerate, and '*intelligentny*'. This is a 'Russian paradox' that has to be conveyed in any English translation.

Although something of a mouthful, Garnett's 'petty, vulgar creature!'[9] for Masha's indignant '*meshchanka!*' in *Three Sisters*[10] is probably closer to the original than Frayn's 'little shopkeeper!'[11] Masha is defining her sister-in-law morally and spiritually here, not socially: there is no snobbery in her use of the word, even though originally '*meshchanin/meshchanka*' referred to a particular social category, the urban lower middle class. As *emotive* descriptives '*meshchanin/ meshchanka*', '*meshchansky*', and so on, are as far from their literal meaning as Russian '*blagorodny*' and English 'noble' are from theirs. Socially, the Prozorovs and Natasha are on a par – a fact that is not always recognized.

Stereotyped ideas about other nations, derived from the exaggeration of certain features of their national character, undoubtedly influence translation. It is often assumed, for instance, that Russians go in for purple and romantic speech, unlike the British, who express their feelings simply. If we are talking of the characters in Chekhov, how-ever, I think we must bear in mind first the difference in period and second the individual style of the author himself.

A lot has changed since the turn of the century in the way people live, behave, and communicate. This is true not only of Russia, but of Britain and other countries. As a result, some of the features of the way Chekhov's characters speak are just as alien to Russians today as they are to the British. For example, *'milaya'* is no longer used as a colloquial form of address between women; it sounds either affected or ironical. But if such things are smoothed out of the translation, or replaced with forms that we use today, there will be no sense of the period, and certain very important overtones of Chekhov's text will be lost.

Lines such as 'my heart is like some priceless grand piano' (*Three Sisters*, Act 4) or 'we shall see the sky sparkling with diamonds' (*Uncle Vanya*, Act 4) are, however, a completely different matter. These do not derive from the everyday life and colloquial speech of the turn of the century. They are Chekhov. If they too are edited out in the urge to produce a 'natural-sounding' English text, Chekhov himself may disappear from the translations of his plays.

At the end of Act I of *The Seagull*, for instance, Masha says to Dorn: *'k vam lezhit moyo serdtse. Pochemu-to ya vseyu dushoy chuvstvuyu, chto vy mne blizki.'* [12] Literally this means 'my heart is disposed to you. For some reason I feel with all my soul that you are near to me.' Jean-Claude van Itallie conveys the emotion of Masha's speech here, but lexically it comes out flat and colourless: 'I feel we have a lot in common ... I feel you're close to me.' [13] The same occurs in Tania Alexander and Charles Sturridge's translation: 'I've always liked you ... I feel somehow much closer to you' (i.e. than to her father). [14] The urge to write 'good' or 'normal-sounding' English can sometimes produce a comic effect where there is none in the original. In Act I of *Uncle Vanya* Sonya, who is in love with Astrov and his ideas, delivers a whole poem in prose on the influence of the forests on people's way of life, culminating in: *'otnosheniya k zhenshchine polny izyashchnogo blagorodstva'* [15] (literally, 'their relations to woman are full of elegant nobility'). This is 'anglicized' by Pam Gems as 'oh, and they're much nicer to women'! [16]

As interpretations, the versions produced by writers who are themselves professional dramatists are particularly interesting. Not only are they of a high literary quality, but they generally bear the stamp of their authors' personality as well. Many of Chekhov's plays have appeared in English over the past 10 to 15 years in translations made by well-known playwrights: *Uncle Vanya* was translated by Christopher Hampton and Nina Froud (1970), Pam Gems (1979), and Michael Frayn (1987); *The Seagull* by Jean-Claude van Itallie (1973), Thomas Kilroy (1981), and Michael Frayn (1986); *Three Sisters* by Michael Frayn (1983);

The Cherry Orchard by Peter Gill and Edward Braun (1978), Trevor Griffiths and Helen Rappaport (1977), van Itallie (1977), and Frayn (1978); in 1984 Frayn adapted Chekhov's 'untitled play' as *Wild Honey*, and so on. Those familiar with these dramatists' own plays will undoubtedly sense their style in their translations, too, especially of course in the freer translations such as Kilroy's *Seagull*, Griffiths' *Cherry Orchard*, or Frayn's *Wild Honey*.

The appearance of these new versions and adaptations of Chekhov is an interesting phenomenon. In the first instance it is presumably a sign of how ensconced Chekhov now is in British culture. As a rule classics undergo fundamental reinterpretation only after they have become 'established' (thus adaptations of Shakespeare and Molière have existed in Britain for a long time). The new free translations of Chekhov are a reaction against a previously unfree attitude towards him and against a certain style of 'British Chekhov' – 'beautiful', 'timeless', and nostalgic – which held sway for a long time and is still with us. The translations of the seventies and eighties are closely associated with stage interpretation (often they have been commissioned for a particular production). If audiences laugh at Chekhov's characters more than they used to, or are made more keenly aware of the contrasts between comedy and drama in his plays, this is as much thanks to the translators as to directors and actors. Finally, there is another tendency in recent translation/versions which is contentious where the tradition is concerned: they focus not on the Russianness of the characters or any universal human substance to their feelings and attitudes, but on aspects of the socio-historical moment captured in Chekhov's plays which are relevant to the current situation in Britain.

This change of emphasis in the British view of Chekhov illustrates how much the interpretation of another country's culture depends on the state of culture in the country that is doing the interpreting. The 'sober', 'abrasive', 'brutal', and 'sociological' Chekhov emerged at a time when both British play-writing and the treatment of the classics on the British stage became overtly sociological and political. Classic texts were freely updated in this way; for instance Shakespeare in Charles Marowitz's 'adaptations and collages' of *Othello*, *The Taming of the Shrew*, and *The Merchant of Venice*, and de Musset in Paul Thompson's *The Lorenzaccio story*. It was natural, then, for translation/ versions like Trevor Griffiths' *Cherry Orchard* or Thomas Kilroy's *Seagull* to appear at this time, and to some extent Pam Gems' *Uncle Vanya* falls into the same category.

It is curious that Chekhov has come to be regarded as a writer with a message. At the beginning of the century, both in Russia and in Britain, he was criticized precisely for not having a message. In this respect, then, the attitude to Chekhov would appear to have moved through 180°. Actually, though, Chekhov's turn-of-the-century critics and some of his ardent admirers today share a common ground: they equate the perspicacity and maturity of an author's social thinking with overt tendentiousness. In the case of translations, this means that, because they rate Chekhov very highly as a social writer, they edit him in that direction.

It was natural that in transposing the action of *The Seagull* to Ireland in the late nineteenth century Thomas Kilroy should alter the *realia* of Chekhov's play. The conflicts in *The Seagull* are exacerbated in his version by the fact that Trigorin (Mr Aston) is an Englishman. The theme of Anglo-Irish relations runs through the whole play. Moreover, the characters are socially identified much more sharply and crudely than in Chekhov. In the opening conversation of the play, for instance, Mary (Masha) talks down to James (Medvedenko) as though he were her inferior. For his part, James comes out with social criticism rather than 'philosophizing' like Medvedenko: 'I can't abide the way the well-off like to pretend they know what it is to be poor. They don't. They can't. And that's an end to it.'[17] In Act 2 Pauline (Polina Andreyevna) tells Dr Hickey (Dorn) that the estate is bankrupt and she is afraid of what is going to happen to her when it is sold up. Put in this context, her desire to leave with the doctor straightaway, to 'go anywhere' with him,[18] looks quite different from Polina Andreyevna imploring him in Chekhov's text 'take me to you'.

In the introduction to his version of *The Cherry Orchard* Trevor Griffiths writes: 'I *edited out* next to nothing, save for some patronymics ... I *added* fewer than fifty words of dialogue.'[19] Nevertheless, a strong 'directorial' hand is visible throughout. As David Allen mentions in his article in the present volume, Griffiths put in new stage-directions even before the text was produced. Thus, to some extent, he was actually 'staging' it as he worked on his translation. The stage-directions and emphases that he introduces serve to underline the class origins of the characters and highlight the social and political themes.

It has been claimed that in many cases Griffiths has conveyed Chekhov more accurately than, for instance, Ronald Hingley and Elisaveta Fen, who have tended to tone him down. There is much truth in this, and no doubt that in Griffiths' version some important themes of the play come across with new bite. But Griffiths' method also has its drawbacks. His text is much drier and more monotonous than the original; individual speech characteristics, and what one might call the musical score of the play, are rather muted. However, in so far as this is not a straight translation but a 'version', the author of the English text ('I wrote this new English version of *The Cherry Orchard*')[20] is, as it were, exempt from having to reproduce the flesh and form of Chekhov's play.

From the point of view of what the English playwright himself set out to do, what matters more is the fact that the bold, vigorous touches he has superimposed on Chekhov's text often do not deepen the 'message' of the play, they merely simplify it. For instance, the master–servant relations are presented far more starkly and crudely than in Chekhov. Varya is made to treat the servants no better than Natasha does in *Three Sisters*. It is doubtful whether the social criticism present in *The Cherry Orchard* is intensified by this, any more than it is by transparent hints (in stage-directions) at goings-on between Ranevskaya and Yasha,[21] or by having Trofimov refer to Varya's 'narrow bourgeois head' ('bourgeois' has been added).[22] The reason the upper class had to leave the stage of history in Russia was nothing to do with landowners being rude or licentious; in fact, the manners and morality of many of them, including characters in Chekhov, left little to be desired. The problem was immeasurably deeper and more complicated, both in life and in Chekhov's plays, and 'doing Chekhov's thinking for him' results in diminishing it. Nevertheless, the versions created by Griffiths and others with a similar approach are a new, interesting, and significant development in the British theatre and the British tradition of translating Chekhov.

Where translation proper is concerned, the task is evidently to produce as far as possible the same effect on the reader or audience as the play has in its original, but how this is achieved depends on the sensitivity and skill of the translator.

This appears to be the approach of Michael Frayn,[23] who has applied it with great success in his work on Chekhov's plays. His translation of *Three Sisters* seems to me in this respect a model. For me the 'sameness effect' is produced on the very first pages, and I have the complete illusion that I am reading Chekhov's text in Russian, not English. The key to this lies not just in a very high order of semantic and stylistic accuracy, but in a fine feel for the rhythm of the text, from its smallest elements to entire speech periods, and an ability to convey the sound texture of Chekhov's original. It is a very difficult and complex task, executed brilliantly.

The opening of the play, Olga's monologue interrupted by Irina's brief *'Zachem vspominat!'*, is a good example. Right from the start – and this is very important for the effect it has on our perception – Frayn imparts Chekhov's light breathing to the English text. In doing this he does not attempt slavishly to reproduce the rhythms of the original. This would be impossible anyway, as English words are generally shorter than Russian. He alters the way the utterance is composed, so that it sounds natural in English. Thus for Chekhov's first five phrases he has seven. However, the English text preserves, or rather *re-creates*, the body and musicality of Chekhov's Russian. One of the characteristic features of Chekhov's speech is the tendency for its parts, its syntagmas, or even entire short sentences, to be fragments of verse. In Olga's opening monologue, within a single sentence, there are amphibrachs: *'i my vspominayem ob etom legko'*, anapaests: *'ty uzhe v belom platye'*, and an iambic trimeter: *'litso tvoyo siyayet'*, whilst Irina's interjection *'Zachem vspominat!'* again contains an amphibrach.[24] Frayn practises the same technique: 'I thought I should never survive it' is amphibrachs, 'You're back in white, your face is shining' is a whole iambic tetrameter.[25] Syntactically and rhythmically the English text does not duplicate the Russian, so it is even more remarkable when within a very small textual space the number of syllables and the metre almost coincide: *'v tvoi imeniny, Irina'*/'it was on your name-day, Irina', and *'Zachem vspominat!'*/ 'Why keep harking back?'.[26]

Numerous examples could be given of how accurately and sensitively Frayn conveys Chekhov's style and the period flavour. He does not cut any of the *'milaya''*s, but renders them as 'dear', 'my dear', 'my love', depending on context. He copes very well with the typically Russian expressions featuring God and the Devil, which the literalists make sound so outlandish. Thus in addition to using 'God rest her soul' for *'tsarstvo yey nebesnoye'*, he properly conveys Vershinin's *'Khochetsya zhit chertovski ...'* in Act 3[27] with the normal-sounding English 'Oh God, but I want to live!',[28] where Constance Garnett has 'I have a fiendish longing for life'[29] – a phrase worthy of Solyony. Finally, Frayn's translation of *'nedotyopa'* as 'sillybilly' strikes me as the best equivalent found so far. It retains the meaning, it is stylistically right, being jocular and not abrasive, and it has the same number of syllables and the same rhythm as the Russian word.

As in Chekhov, each character in Frayn's translation has its own manner of speaking which is achieved without forcing. For instance when Natasha is not confronting someone she says nothing out of the ordinary, but her every phrase grates on the ear as it does in Chekhov's original. The speech of the uneducated characters Anfisa and Ferapont is noticeably different from the rest, but again this is achieved subtly, with a few deft strokes. When Ferapont says of the Fire of Moscow in 1812: '*Frantsuzy udivlyalis*',[30] one needs a very sensitive ear to hear in this apparently neutral phrase the tone successfully conveyed by Frayn's 'weren't the French surprised!'[31] (compare Garnett: 'The French marvelled').[32]

Frayn's translations show what can be achieved by soaking oneself in the play, living oneself into it, and re-embodying it, when the translator is a talented playwright who knows Russian culture well. However, *Wild Honey* demonstrates that Frayn is also capable of a quite different approach to a Chekhov text. He has described this as not a translation but a personal rewriting based on Chekhov's 'untitled play'. It is, indeed, a special case – an attempt at combining Chekhov's dramatic writing with the principles of the 'well-made play'.

The ways in which Chekhov is interpreted in today's English translations are varied and will probably become even more so. They are a proof of the inexhaustibility of his drama and its central place in modern culture.

Notes

I should like to thank Patrick Miles and Stuart Young for enabling me to study a number of recent translations.

1 For a general study of play translation see Patrice Parvis, 'Problems of translation for the stage: interculturism and post-modern theatre', in *The Play Out of Context: Transferring Plays from Culture to Culture*, eds. Hanna Scolnicov and Peter Holland (Cambridge: CUP, 1989), pp. 25–44. An American view of English translations of Chekhov is given by Lauren G. Leighton, 'Chekhov in English', in *A Chekhov Companion*, ed. Toby W. Clyman (Westport and London: Greenwood Press, 1985), pp. 291–309.
2 See the article by Stephen le Fleming (ch. 6) in the present volume.
3 Anton Chekhov, *The Cherry Orchard*, a new English version by Trevor Griffiths, from a translation by Helen Rappaport (London: Pluto Press, 1978), p. 13.

4 A. P. Chekhov, *Polnoye sobraniye sochineny i pisem v tridtsati tomakh (Complete collected works and letters in 30 vols.)*, XIII (*Sochineniya*) (*Works*) (Moscow: Nauka, 1978), pp. 133–4 (hereafter referred to as *PSS*).

5 Anton Tchehov, *Three Sisters and Other Plays*, from the Russian by Constance Garnett (London: Chatto and Windus, 1923), p. 22; Anton Chekhov, *Three Sisters*, translated by Michael Frayn (London: Methuen, 1983), p. 18.

6 *PSS*, p. 70.

7 Anton Chekhov, *Uncle Vanya*, a new version by Pam Gems (London: Eyre Methuen, 1979), p. 7.

8 *PSS*, p. 67.

9 Garnett, *Three Sisters*, p. 48.

10 *PSS*, p. 153.

11 Frayn, *Three Sisters*, p. 43.

12 *PSS*, p. 20.

13 Anton Chekhov, *The Sea Gull*, a new version by Jean-Claude van Itallie (New York: Harper and Row, 1977), p. 30.

14 Anton Chekhov, *The Seagull*, translated by Tania Alexander and Charles Sturridge (Oxford: Amber Lane Press, 1986), p. 25.

15 *PSS*, p. 72.

16 Gems, *Uncle Vanya*, p. 10.

17 Anton Chekhov, *The Seagull*, a new version by Thomas Kilroy (London: Eyre Methuen, 1981), p. 9.

18 *Ibid.*, p. 21.

19 Griffiths, *The Cherry Orchard*, p. vi.

20 *Ibid.*, p. v.

21 *Ibid.*, p. 21.

22 *Ibid.*, p. 29.

23 See, for example, his interview with Heather Neill, 'Bleak comedy of a changing world', *The Times*, 24 October 1989.

24 *PSS*, p. 119.

25 Frayn, *Three Sisters*, p. 1.

26 *Ibid.*

27 *PSS*, p. 163.

28 Frayn, *Three Sisters*, p. 58.

29 Garnett, *Three Sisters*, p. 63.

30 *PSS*, p. 158.

31 Frayn, *Three Sisters*, p. 50.

32 Garnett, *Three Sisters*, p. 55.

A selective chronology of British professional productions of Chekhov's plays 1909–1991

Patrick Miles and Stuart Young

Chronologies of British productions from 1909 to 1987 are given with varying exhaustiveness in Victor Emeljanow, *Chekhov: The Critical Heritage* (London: Routledge and Kegan Paul, 1981); Charles W. Meister, *Chekhov Bibliography. Works in English by and about Anton Chekhov; American, British and Canadian Performances* (Jefferson: McFarland and Company Inc., 1985); Patrick Miles, *Chekhov on the British Stage 1909–1987* (Cambridge: Sam and Sam, 1987); Robert Tracy, 'The flight of a seagull: Chekhov on the English stage' (Ph.D. Thesis, Harvard University, 1959); Nick Worrall, *File on Chekhov* (London: Methuen, 1986); Stuart Young, 'Chekhov on the British stage: reactions to a theatrical tradition' (Ph.D. Thesis, Cambridge University, 1989). The following selection presents all the British professional premières of Chekhov's plays, all the West End productions, and a sample of productions outside London. There is space to give only a selection of roles for each play. Of the one-act plays, roles are given for *The Bear*, *The Proposal*, and *Smoking is Bad For You*. Productions by visiting foreign companies are included (with the name of the director only), but not 'entertainments' about Chekhov or stage adaptations of his stories. The date given is that of the opening night. The theatre is in London unless otherwise stated. Where items of information are missing they were not, unfortunately, available to us. We are indebted to Dr Gordon McVay for verifying a number of facts.

ABBREVIATIONS USED: dir – director; trans – translator; des – designer; *Platonov*: P – Platonov, AP – Anna Petrovna; *Ivanov*: I – Ivanov, A – Anna, S – Sasha; *The Bear*: P – Popova, S – Smirnov; *The Proposal*: N – Natasha, L – Lomov; *The Wood-Demon*: V – Voynitsky, Kh – Khrushchov; *The Seagull*: A – Arkadina, K – Konstantin, N – Nina, T – Trigorin; *Uncle Vanya*: S – Serebryakov, Y – Yelena, So – Sonya, V – Voynitsky, A – Astrov; *Three Sisters*: A – Andrey, N – Natasha, O – Olga, M – Masha, I – Irina, V – Vershinin; *Smoking is Bad For You*:

N – Nyukhin; *The Cherry Orchard*: R – Ranevskaya, A – Anya, V – Varya, G – Gayev, L – Lopakhin, T – Trofimov; an asterisk denotes a British première.

1909
2 November 1909, Royalty Theatre Glasgow, *The Seagull, dir – George Calderon, trans – George Calderon, des – T. F. Dunn, A – Mary Jerrold, K – Milton Rosmer, N – Irene Clarke, T – Campbell Gullan.

1911
13 May 1911, Kingsway Theatre, *The Bear, dir – Lydia Yavorskaya, trans – Arthur A. Sykes, P – Blanche Grand, S – Norman Trevor.

28 May 1911, Aldwych Theatre, **The Cherry Orchard*, dir – Kenelm Foss, trans – Constance Garnett, R – Katharine Pole, A – Vera Coburn, V – Mary Jerrold, G – Franklin Dyall, L – Herbert Bunston, T – Harcourt Williams.

1912
31 March 1912, Little Theatre, *The Seagull*, dir – Maurice Elvey, trans – George Calderon, des – Maurice Elvey, A – Gertrude Kingston, K – Lawrence Anderson, N – Lydia Yavorskaya, T – Maurice Elvey.

1914
10 May 1914, Aldwych Theatre, *Uncle Vanya, dir – Guy Rathbone, trans – R. S. Townsend, S – H. R. Hignett, Y – Ernita Lascelles, So – Gillian Scaife, V – Guy Rathbone, A – Herbert Grimwood.

1916
18 March 1916, Birmingham Repertory Theatre, *The Proposal, dir – John Drinkwater, N – Margaret Chatwin, L – Joseph A. Dodd.

1917
14 May 1917, Grafton Galleries, *The Wedding, trans – Julius West; *Swan Song, dir – Nigel Playfair, trans – Marian Fell, des – Michel Sevier.

1918
3 December 1918, St James' Theatre, *The Proposal*, dir – A. E. Drinkwater, trans – Julius West, N – Lillah McCarthy, L – Michael Sherbrooke.

1919
1 June 1919, Theatre Royal, Haymarket, *The Seagull*, dir – Vera Donnet, trans – Marian Fell, des – Vera Donnet, A – Helen Haye, K – Tom Nesbitt, N – Margery Bryce, T – Nicholas Hannen.

1920

25 January 1920, St Martin's Theatre, *The Bear*, P – Dorothy Massingham, S – Joseph A. Dodd; *On the High Road*; *The Wedding*; dir – Edith Craig.

7 March 1920, Royal Court, *Three Sisters*, dir – Vera Donnet, trans – Harold Bowen, des – Vera Donnet, A – Tom Nesbitt, N – Helen Millais, O – Margery Bryce, M – Irene Rathbone, I – Dorothy Massingham, V – Harcourt Williams.

11 July 1920, St Martin's Theatre, *The Cherry Orchard*, dir – Vera Donnet, trans – Constance Garnett, des – Vera Donnet, R – Ethel Irving, A – Irene Rathbone, V – Margery Bryce, G – Leyton Cancellor, L – Joseph A. Dodd, T – Hesketh Pearson.

1921

27 November 1921, Royal Court, *Uncle Vanya*, dir – Theodore Komisarjevsky, trans – Constance Garnett, des – Theodore Komisarjevsky, S – H. R. Hignett, Y – Cathleen Nesbit, So – Irene Rathbone, V – Leon Quartermaine, A – Franklin Dyall.

1925

25 May 1925, Lyric Theatre Hammersmith, *The Cherry Orchard*, dir – J. B. Fagan, trans – George Calderon, des – Edgar Brickell, R – Mary Grey, A – Gwendolen Evans, V – Virginia Isham, G – Alan Napier, L – Fred O'Donovan, T – John Gielgud.

19 October 1925, Little Theatre, *The Seagull*, dir – A. E. Filmer, trans – Constance Garnett, des – James Whale, A – Miriam Lewes, K – John Gielgud, N – Valerie Taylor, T – Randolph MacLeod.

6 December 1925, Duke of York's Theatre, *Ivanov*, dir – Theodore Komisarjevsky, trans – Marian Fell, des – Theodore Komisarjevsky, I – Robert Farquharson, A – Jeanne de Casalis, S – Eileen Beldon.

1926

16 January 1926, Barnes Theatre, *Uncle Vanya*, dir – Theodore Komisarjevsky, trans – Constance Garnett, des – Theodore Komisarjevsky, S – Boris Ranevsky, Y – Dorothy Massingham, So – Jean Forbes-Robertson, V – Robert Farquharson, A – Henry C. Hewitt.

16 February 1926, Barnes Theatre, *Three Sisters*, dir – Theodore Komisarjevsky, trans – Constance Garnett, des – Theodore Komisarjevsky, A – Douglas Burbidge, N – Dorice Fordred, O – Mary Sheridan, M – Margaret Swallow, I – Beatrix Thomson, V – Ion Swinley.

28 September 1926, Barnes Theatre, *The Cherry Orchard*, dir – Theodore Komisarjevsky, trans – Constance Garnett, des – Theodore Komisarjevsky, R – Dorothy Dix, A – Gabrielle Casartelli, V – Josephine Wilson, G – Lawrence Hanray, L – Douglas Burbidge, T – Wilfred Fletcher.

1927
2 April 1927, Birmingham Repertory Theatre, *Uncle Vanya*, dir – W. G. Fay, des – Hugh Owen, S – William Pringle, Y – Dorothy Turner, So – Jane Welsh, V – Laurence Olivier, A – Stringer Davis.

1928
11 April 1928, Garrick Theatre (Prague Group of MKhT), *The Cherry Orchard*, dir – M. N. Germanova.

30 April 1928, Garrick Theatre (Prague Group of MKhT), *Uncle Vanya*, dir – M. N. Germanova.

1929
16 January 1929, Arts Theatre, *The Seagull*, dir – A. E. Filmer, trans – Constance Garnett, des – James Whale, A – Miriam Lewes, K – John Gielgud, N – Valerie Taylor, T – Henry Hewitt.

23 October 1929, Fortune Theatre, *Three Sisters*, dir – Theodore Komisarjevsky, trans – Constance Garnett, des – Theodore Komisarjevsky, A – Douglas Burbidge, N – Margot Sieveking, O – Prudence Vanbrugh, M – Margaret Swallow, I – Rosalind Fuller, V – Ion Swinley.

1931
7 December 1931, Kingsway Theatre (Prague Group of MKhT), *The Proposal*, *The Anniversary*, dir – P. Pavlov.

21 December 1931, Kingsway Theatre (Prague Group of MKhT), *The Cherry Orchard*, dir – P. Pavlov.

1933
9 October 1933, Old Vic, *The Cherry Orchard*, dir – Tyrone Guthrie, trans – Hubert M. Butler, des – Molly Macarthur, R – Athene Seyler, A – Ursula Jeans, V – Flora Robson, G – Leon Quartermaine, L – Charles Laughton, T – Dennis Arundell.

1935
12 November 1935, Old Vic, *Three Sisters*, dir – Henry Cass, trans – Constance Garnett, des – Bagnall Harris, A – Kenneth Kent, N – Myrtle Richardson, O – Marie Ney, M – Vivienne Bennett, I – Nancy Hornsby, V – Ion Swinley.

1936
20 May 1936, The New Theatre, *The Seagull*, dir – Theodore Komisarjevsky, trans – Theodore Komisarjevsky, des – Theodore Komisarjevsky, A – Edith Evans, K – Stephen Haggard, N – Peggy Ashcroft, T – John Gielgud.

1937
5 February 1937, Westminster Theatre, *Uncle Vanya*, dir – Michael Macowan, trans – Constance Garnett, des – Peter Goffin, S – Mark Dignam, Y – Lydia Sherwood, So – Alexis France, V – Harcourt Williams, A – Cecil Trouncer.

1938
28 January 1938, Queen's Theatre, *Three Sisters*, dir – Michel Saint-Denis, trans – Constance Garnett, des – Motley, A – George Devine, N – Angela Baddeley, O – Gwen Ffrangcon-Davies, M – Carol Goodner, I – Peggy Ashcroft, V – John Gielgud.

1941
28 August 1941, The New Theatre, *The Cherry Orchard*, dir – Tyrone Guthrie, trans – Hubert M. Butler, des – Frederick Crooke, R – Athene Seyler, A – Olive Layton, V – Rosalind Atkinson, G – Nicholas Hannen, L – James Dale, T – Walter Hudd.

1943
2 September 1943, Westminster Theatre, *Uncle Vanya*, dir – Norman Marshall, trans – Constance Garnett, des – Roger Furse, S – Graveley Edwards, Y – Joan Swinstead, So – Vivienne Bennett, V – Harold Scott, A – Frith Banbury.

1945
16 January 1945, New Theatre, *Uncle Vanya*, dir – John Burrell, trans – Constance Garnett, des – Tanya Moiseiwitsch, S – Harcourt Williams, Y – Margaret Leighton, So – Joyce Redman, V – Ralph Richardson, A – Laurence Olivier.

1948
1 June 1948, St James' Theatre, *The Cherry Orchard*, dir – John Fernald, trans – J. P. Davis, des – Paul Mayo, R – Gladys Boot, A – Catherine Bogle, V – Nancie Jackson, G – Cyril Luckham, L – Eric Berry, T – David Phethean.

9 September 1948, Arts Theatre, *The Cherry Orchard*, dir – Peter Powell, trans – George Calderon, des – Fanny Taylor, R – Jean Anderson, A – Daphne Slater, V – Marjorie Stewart, G – Charles Lloyd Pack, L – Elwyn Brook-Jones, T – Marius Goring.

25 November 1948, The New Theatre, *The Cherry Orchard*, dir – Hugh Hunt, trans – Constance Garnett, des – Tanya Moiseiwitsch, R – Edith Evans, A – Josephine Stuart, V – Mary Martlew, G – Cedric Hardwicke, L – Mark Dignam, T. – Robert Eddison.

1949
28 February 1949, Old Vic, *The Proposal*, dir – Laurence Olivier, trans – Constance Garnett, des – Roger Furse, N – Peggy Simpson, L – Peter Cushing.

4 October 1949, Lyric Theatre Hammersmith, *The Seagull*, dir – Irene Hentschl, trans – George Calderon, des – Paul Sheriff, A – Isabel Jeans, K – Paul Scofield, N – Mai Zetterling, T – Ian Hunter.

1950
20 April 1950, Arts Theatre, *Ivanov*, dir – John Fernald, trans – J. P. Davis, I – Michael Hordern, A – Helen Shingler, S – Natalie Jordan.

1951
3 May 1951, Aldwych Theatre, *Three Sisters*, dir – Peter Ashmore, trans – Mary Britnieva and Peter Ashmore, des – Anthony Holland, A – Michael Warre, N – Diana Churchill, O – Celia Johnson, M – Margaret Leighton, I – Renée Asherson, V – Ralph Richardson.

1952
27 March 1952, Arts Theatre, *Uncle Vanya*, dir – John Fernald, trans – J. P. Davis, des – Ronald Brown, S – Noel Iliff, Y – Helen Shingler, So – Jenny Laird, V – Cyril Luckham, A – John Justin.

1953
23 April 1953, Arts Theatre, *The Seagull*, dir – John Fernald, trans – J. P. Davis, des – Disley Jones, A – Catherine Lacey, K – Michael Gwynn, N – Jane Griffiths, T – Alan MacNaughtan.

1954
21 May 1954, Lyric Theatre Hammersmith, *The Cherry Orchard*, dir – John Gielgud, trans – John Gielgud, des – Richard Lake, R – Gwen Ffrangcon-Davies, A – Shirley Roberts, V – Pauline Jameson, G – Esmé Percy, L – Trevor Howard, T – David Markham.

1956
2 August 1956, Saville Theatre, *The Seagull*, dir – Michael Macowan, trans – David Magarshack, des – Motley, A – Diana Wynyard, K – Lyndon Brook, N – Perlita Neilson, T – Hugh Williams.

1958
12 April 1958, Toynbee Theatre, *A Tragic Role*.

15 May 1958, Sadler's Wells (MKhAT), *The Cherry Orchard*, dir – V. Ya. Stanitsyn.

20 May 1958, Sadler's Wells (MKhAT), *Uncle Vanya*, dir – M. M. Kedrov.

16 June 1958, Sadler's Wells (MKhAT), *Three Sisters*, dir – V. I. Nemirovich-Danchenko and I. M. Rayevsky.

1959
6 April 1959, Nottingham Playhouse, *Don Juan (in the Russian Manner)* (*Platonov*), dir – Val May, trans – Basil Ashmore, des – Marsh King, P – Robert Lang, AP – Rhoda Lewis.

1960
1 September 1960, Old Vic, *The Seagull*, dir – John Fernald, trans – J. P. Davis, des – Paul Mayo and Beatrice Dawson, A – Judith Anderson, K – Tom Courtenay, N – Ann Bell, T – Tony Britton.

13 October 1960, Royal Court, *Platonov*, dir – George Devine and John Blatchley, trans – Dmitri Makaroff, des – Richard Negri, P – Rex Harrison, AP – Rachel Roberts.

1961
14 December 1961, Aldwych Theatre, *The Cherry Orchard*, dir – Michel Saint-Denis, trans – John Gielgud, des – Abd'Elkader Farrah, R – Peggy Ashcroft, A – Judi Dench, V – Dorothy Tutin, G – John Gielgud, L – George Murcell, T – Ian Holm.

1962
16 July 1962, Chichester Festival Theatre, *Uncle Vanya*, dir – Laurence Olivier, trans – Constance Garnett, des – Sean Kenny, S – André Morell, Y – Joan Greenwood, So – Joan Plowright, V – Michael Redgrave, A – Laurence Olivier.

1963
19 November 1963, Old Vic (National Theatre), *Uncle Vanya*, dir – Laurence Olivier, trans – Constance Garnett, des – Sean Kenny, S – Max Adrian, Y – Rosemary Harris, So – Joan Plowright, V – Michael Redgrave, A – Laurence Olivier.

1964
12 March 1964, Queen's Theatre, *The Seagull*, dir – Tony Richardson, trans – Ann Jellicoe, des – Jocelyn Herbert, A – Peggy Ashcroft, K – Peter McEnery, N – Vanessa Redgrave, T – Peter Finch.

28 April 1964, The Little Theatre, *Smoking is Bad For You*, dir – Ralph Wilton, N – Peter Miles-Johnson.

29 May 1964, Aldwych Theatre (MKhAT), *The Cherry Orchard*, dir – V.Ya. Stanitsyn.

1965
13 May 1965, Aldwych Theatre (Actors Studio Theatre), *Three Sisters*, dir – Lee Strasberg.

30 September 1965, Phoenix Theatre, *Ivanov*, dir – John Gielgud, trans – Ariadne Nicolaeff and John Gielgud, des – Rouben Ter-Arutunian I – John Gielgud, A – Yvonne Mitchell, S – Claire Bloom.

1966
19 July 1966, Chichester Festival Theatre, *The Cherry Orchard*, dir – Lindsay Anderson, trans – Elisaveta Fen, des – Alan Tagg, R – Celia Johnson, A – Sarah Badel, V – Zena Walker, G – Hugh Williams, L – Ray McAnally, T – Tom Courtenay.

1967
18 April 1967, Royal Court, *Three Sisters*, dir – William Gaskill, trans – Edward Bond, des – Abd'Elkader Farrah, A – George Cole, N – Marjie Lawrence, O – Avril Elgar, M – Glenda Jackson, I – Marianne Faithfull, V – Michael Gwynn.

4 July 1967, Old Vic (National Theatre), *Three Sisters*, dir – Laurence Olivier, trans – Moura Budberg, des – Josef Svoboda, A – Anthony Hopkins, N – Sheila Reid, O – Jeanne Watts, M – Joan Plowright, I – Louise Purnell, V – Robert Stephens.

31 July 1967, Yvonne Arnaud Theatre Guildford, *The Cherry Orchard*, dir – Richard Cottrell, trans – Richard Cottrell, des – Hutchinson Scott, R – Lila Kedrova, A – Marty Cruickshank, V – Stephanie Bidmead, G – James Cairncross, L – Patrick Wymark, T – Terry Scully.

1968
27 November 1968, Nottingham Playhouse, *The Seagull*, dir – Jonathan Miller, trans – Elisaveta Fen, des – Patrick Robertson, A – Fenella Fielding, K – Peter Eyre, N – Kika Markham, T – T.P. McKenna.

1969
28 April 1969, Aldwych Theatre (Otomar Krejca's Theatre Behind the Gate), *Three Sisters*, dir – Otomar Krejca.

29 April 1969, Oxford Playhouse, *Uncle Vanya*, dir – Frank Hauser, trans – Ariadne Nicolaeff, des – Nico Stefanou, S – Laurence Hardy, Y – Nyree Dawn Porter, So – Pamela Moiseiwitsch, V – Robert Eddison, A – William Lucas.

1970
24 February 1970, Royal Court, *Uncle Vanya*, dir – Anthony Page, trans – Christopher Hampton, des – Deirdre Clancy, S – Ralph Michael, Y – Elizabeth Bell, So – Anna Calder-Marshall, V – Paul Scofield, A – Colin Blakely.

25 May 1970, Aldwych Theatre (MKhAT), *The Seagull*, dir – Boris Livanov.

21 July 1970, Arts Theatre Cambridge, *The Seagull*, dir – Richard Cottrell, trans – Richard Cottrell, des – Keith Norman, A – Lila Kedrova, K – James Bolam, N – Susan Fleetwood, T – Derek Godfrey.

1971
20 September 1971, Oxford Playhouse, *The Cherry Orchard*, dir – Frank Hauser, trans – Ariadne Nicolaeff, des – Alix Stone, R – Phyllis Calvert, A – Susan Macready, V – Barbara Laurenson, G – Michael Gwynn, L – Lee Montague, T – David Leland.

5 October 1971, Ashcroft Theatre Croydon, *Three Sisters*, dir – Richard Cottrell, trans – Richard Cottrell, des – Keith Norman, A – Michael Pennington, N – Prunella Scales, O – Stephanie Bidmead, M – Virginia McKenna, I – Patricia Blake, V – Alan MacNaughtan.

1973
23 May 1973, Chichester Festival Theatre, *The Seagull*, dir – Jonathan Miller, trans – Elisaveta Fen, des – Patrick Robertson, A – Irene Worth, K – Peter Eyre, N – Maureen O'Brien, T – Robert Stephens.

24 May 1973, Old Vic, *The Cherry Orchard*, dir – Michael Blakemore, trans – Ronald Hingley, des – Alan Tagg, R – Constance Cummings, A – Anna Carteret, V – Gillian Barge, G – Michael Hordern, L – Denis Quilley, T – David Bradley.

10 September 1973, Arts Theatre Cambridge, *The Wood Demon, dir – David Giles, trans – Ronald Hingley, des – Kenneth Mellor, V – Tenniel Evans, Kh – Ian McKellen.

3 October 1973, Bristol Old Vic, *Uncle Vanya*, dir – Val May, trans – Constance Garnett, des – John Elvery, S – Nigel Stock, Y – Sara Kestelman, So – Penelope Wilton, V – Peter O'Toole, A – Edward Hardwicke.

1974
Summer 1974, Mull Little Theatre, *Tatyana Repina*, dir – Barrie and Marianne Hesketh, trans – Ronald Hingley, des – Barrie Hesketh.

1 October 1974, Theatr y Werin Aberystwyth, *The Seagull*, dir – Geoffrey Reeves, trans – David Magarshack, des – Bernard Culshaw, A – Madge Ryan, K – Hywel Bennett, N – Amanda Knott, T – Trevor Martin.

17 December 1974, The Other Place Stratford-on-Avon (RSC), *Uncle Vanya*, dir – Nicol Williamson, trans – Mike Nichols and Albert Todd, des – Debbie Sharp, S – Michael Aldridge, Y – Jill Townsend, So – Jane Lapotaire, V – Nicol Williamson, A – Patrick Stewart.

1975
28 October 1975, Lyric Theatre, *The Seagull*, dir – Lindsay Andersen, trans – Galina von Meck and Lindsay Anderson, des – Alan Tagg, A – Joan Plowright, K – Frank Grimes, N – Helen Mirren, T – Peter McEnery.

1976
20 April 1976, Yvonne Arnaud Theatre Guildford, *Three Sisters*, dir – Jonathan Miller, trans – Elisaveta Fen, des – Patrick Robertson, A – John Shrapnel, N – June Ritchie, O – Susan Engel, M – Janet Suzman, I – Angela Down, V – Nigel Davenport.

2 September 1976, Aldwych Theatre (RSC), *Ivanov*, dir – David Jones, trans – Kitty Hunter-Blair and Jeremy Brooks, des – William Dudley, I – John Wood, A – Estelle Kohler, S – Mia Farrow.

1977
10 March 1977, Nottingham Playhouse, *The Cherry Orchard*, dir – Richard Eyre, trans – Helen Rappaport and Trevor Griffiths, des – John Gunter, R – Bridget Turner, A – Lynsey Baxter, V – Annie Hayes, G – Ralph Nossek, L – Dave Hill, T – Mick Ford.

26 October 1977, Royal Lyceum Edinburgh, *The Cherry Orchard*, dir – Stephen MacDonald, trans – Ronald Hingley, des – Colin Winslow, R – Moira Shearer, A – Susan Macready, V – Maureen Beattie, G – John Grieve, L – Richard Moore, T – William Lindsay.

1978
13 January 1978, Riverside Studios, *The Cherry Orchard*, dir – Peter Gill, trans – Edward Braun and Peter Gill, des – William Dudley, R – Judy Parfitt, A – Caroline Langrishe, V – Julie Covington, G – Philip Locke, L – Michael Elphick, T – Stephen Rea.

14 February 1978, National Theatre, *The Cherry Orchard*, dir – Peter Hall, trans – Michael Frayn, des – John Bury, R – Dorothy Tutin, A – Judi Bowker, V – Susan Fleetwood, G – Robert Stephens, L – Albert Finney, T – Ben Kingsley.

21 February 1978, Royal Court, *The Bear*, dir – Stuart Burge, des – Pippy Bradshaw, P – Pauline Collins, S – David Suchet.

18 August 1978, Old Vic, *Ivanov*, dir – Toby Robertson, trans – Ariadne Nicolaeff, des – Robin Archer, I – Derek Jacobi, A – Louise Purnell, S – Jane Wymark.

1979
29 September 1979, The Other Place Stratford-upon-Avon (RSC), *Three Sisters*, dir – Trevor Nunn, trans – Richard Cottrell, des – John Napier, A – Timothy Spall, N – Susan Tracy, O – Janet Dale, M – Suzanne Bertish, I – Emily Richard, V – Edward Petherbridge.

22 November 1979, Hampstead Theatre, *Uncle Vanya*, dir – Nancy Meckler, trans – Pam Gems, des – Alison Chitty, S – Maurice Denham, Y – Susan Littler, So – Alison Steadman, V – Nigel Hawthorne, A – Ian Holm.

1981
8 April 1981, Royal Court, *The Seagull*, dir – Max Stafford-Clark, trans – Thomas Kilroy, des – Gemma Jackson, A – Anna Massey, K – Anton Lesser, N – Harriet Walter, T – Alan Rickman.

12 September 1981, Crucible Theatre Sheffield, *The Seagull*, dir – Mike Alfreds, trans – Lilia Sokolov and Mike Alfreds, A – Gillian Barge, K – Philip Osment, N – Lorna Heilbron, T – Jonathan Hackett.

1982
18 May 1982, National Theatre, *Uncle Vanya*, dir – Michael Bogdanov, trans – Pam Gems, des – John Bury, S – Basil Henson, Y – Cherie Lunghi, So – Patti Love, V – Michael Bryant, A – Dinsdale Landen.

5 August 1982, Theatre Royal, Haymarket, *Uncle Vanya*, dir – Christopher Fettes, trans – John Murrell, des – Daphne Dare, S – Harry Andrews,

Y – Sheila Gish, So – Frances de la Tour, V – Donald Sinden, A – Ronald Pickup.

9 August 1982, Round House, *The Cherry Orchard*, dir – Mike Alfreds, trans – Lilia Sokolov and Mike Alfreds, des – Nadine Baylis, R – Alison Fiske, A – Chloe Salaman, V – Maggie Wells, G – Charles McKeown, L – Roger Sloman, T – John Dicks.

1983
18 October 1983, Theatre Royal, Haymarket, *The Cherry Orchard*, dir – Lindsay Anderson, des – Kenneth Mellor, R – Joan Plowright, A – Cora Kinnaird, V – Joanna David, G – Leslie Phillips, L – Frank Finlay, T – Frank Grimes.

1984
19 June 1984, National Theatre, *Wild Honey (Platonov)*, dir – Christopher Morahan, trans – Michael Frayn, des – John Gunter, P – Ian McKellen, AP – Charlotte Cornwell.

1985
2 August 1985, Queen's Theatre, *The Seagull*, dir – Charles Sturridge, trans – Tania Alexander and Charles Sturridge, des – Eileen Diss, A – Vanessa Redgrave, K – John Lynch, N – Natasha Richardson, T – Jonathan Pryce.

16 December 1985, National Theatre, *The Cherry Orchard*, dir – Mike Alfreds, trans – Lilia Sokolov and Mike Alfreds, des – Paul Dart, R – Sheila Hancock, A – Claire Moore, V – Eleanor Bron, G – Edward Petherbridge, L – Ian McKellen, T – Laurance Rudic.

1986
1 April 1986, Bloomsbury Theatre, *Three Sisters*, dir – Mike Alfreds, trans – Nikita Stavisky and Mike Alfreds, des – Paul Dart, A – Jonathan Hackett, N – Maggie Wells, O – Holly Wilson, M – Leslie Udwin, I – Chloe Salaman, V – John Price.

1987
23 March 1987, Greenwich Theatre, *Three Sisters*, dir – Elijah Moshinsky, trans – Michael Frayn, des – John Bury, A – Hywel Bennett, N – Susan Penhaligon, O – Sara Kestelman, M – Francesca Annis, I – Katharine Schlesinger, V – Ian Ogilvy.

12 August 1987, King's Theatre Edinburgh (Gorky Theatre Company, Leningrad), *Uncle Vanya*, dir – Georgy Tovstonogov.

1988

9 February 1988, Donmar Warehouse, *Trinidad Sisters (Three Sisters)*, dir – Nicholas Kent, trans – Mustapha Matura, des – Poppy Mitchell, A – André Peters, N – Suzette Llewellyn, O – Joan-Ann Maynard, M – Pauline Black, I – Joanne Campbell, V – Patrick Drury.

24 May 1988, Vaudeville Theatre, *Uncle Vanya*, dir – Michael Blakemore, trans – Michael Frayn, des – Tanya McCallin, S – Benjamin Whitrow, Y – Greta Scacchi, So – Imelda Staunton, V – Michael Gambon, A – Jonathan Pryce.

4 August 1988, Barbican Theatre (RSC), *Three Sisters*, dir – John Barton, trans – Helen Rappaport and John Barton, des – Timothy O'Brien, A – Bruce Alexander, N – Pippa Guard, O – Deborah Findlay, M – Harriet Walter, I – Stella Gonet, V – Brian Cox.

27 September 1988, Aldwych Theatre, *The Sneeze* (Plays and stories), dir – Ronald Eyre, trans – Michael Frayn, des – Mark Thompson, *The Bear*, P – Cheryl Campbell, S – Timothy West; *Smoking is Bad For You*, N – Rowan Atkinson; *Swan Song*; *The Proposal*, N – Cheryl Campbell, L – Rowan Atkinson.

1989

10 April 1989, Strand Theatre, *Ivanov*, dir – Elijah Moshinsky, trans – Ronald Harwood, des – Mark Thompson, I – Alan Bates, A – Felicity Kendal, S – Karen Ascoe.

13 July 1989, Old Vic (Katona Jozsef Theatre, Budapest), *Three Sisters*, dir – Tomas Ascher.

14 September 1989, National Theatre (MKhAT), *Uncle Vanya*, dir – O.N. Yefremov.

24 October 1989, Aldwych Theatre, *The Cherry Orchard*, dir – Sam Mendes, trans – Michael Frayn, des – Paul Farnsworth, R – Judi Dench, A – Miranda Foster, V – Lesley Manville, G – Ronald Pickup, L – Bernard Hill, T – Nicholas Farrell.

1990

19 July 1990, Royal Court, *Three Sisters*, dir – Adrian Noble, trans – Rose Cullen and Frank Guinness, des – Bob Crowley, A – Mark Lambert, N – Lesley Manville, O – Sorcha Cusack, M – Sinead Cusack, I – Niamh Cusack, V – Nicky Henson.

6 November 1990, Swan Theatre Stratford-upon-Avon (RSC), *The Seagull*, dir – Terry Hands, trans – Michael Frayn, des – Johan Engels, A – Susan Fleetwood, K – Simon Russell Beale, N – Amanda Root, T – Roger Allam.

11 December 1990, Queen's Theatre, *Three Sisters*, dir – Robert Sturua, trans – Helen Molchanoff and Nikolas Simmonds, des – Giorgi Meskhishvili, A – Jeremy Northam, N – Phoebe Nicholls, O – Vanessa Redgrave, M – Lynn Redgrave, I – Jemma Redgrave, V – Stuart Wilson.

1991

19 February 1991, Theatr Gwynedd Bangor, *The Cherry Orchard*, dir – Graham Laker, trans – W. Gareth Jones, des – Martin Morley, R – Maureen Rhys, A – Catherine Aran, V – Morfudd Hughes, G – Trefor Selway, L – John Ogwen, T – Alun Elidyr.

22 April 1991, Lilian Baylis Theatre, *The Seagull*, dir – Mike Alfreds, trans – Mike Alfreds, des – Paul Dart, A – Pam Ferris, K – Michael Mueller, N – Irina Brook, T – Nicholas Clay.

12 August 1991, Lyric Theatre Hammersmith, *Uncle Vanya*, dir – Peter Egan and Kenneth Branagh, trans – Pam Gems, des – Kenny Miller, S – Patrick Godfrey, Y – Sian Thomas, So – Annabel Arden, V – Richard Briers, A – Peter Egan.

Index

Names follow the forms used in the text, normally using the transliteration system detailed on p. xii; there are no cross-references from alternative transliterations. Chekhov's works are placed under their titles; works by other authors normally appear under the author. The appendix and illustrations are not indexed.